The Book of the

CORONATION PACIFICS Mk2

By Allan C. Baker

IRWELL PRESS Ltd.

Copyright IRWELL PRESS LIMITED

ISBN 978-1-906919-17-7

First published in the United Kingdom in 1998
by Irwell Press Limited, 59A High Street,
Clophill, Bedfordshire MK45 4BE
Reprinted 2000, 2003, 2006
This new Mk 2 edition, amended and expanded, published 2010
Printed by Konway Press

CONTENTS

This photograph is the work of a master of his craft, the late and lamented W.J.V. Anderson and while it has appeared in print many times before, I make absolutely no apology for using it again as it is one of my favourites. A Crewe North engine for many a year, 46241CITY OF EDINBURGH has just passed Hilton Junction at Perth at the start of its 296 mile journey to Crewe with the heavy 8.50 pm train in July 1960. The two overnight trains in each direction between Crewe and Perth were the longest regular locomotive/crew diagrams in this country and the sole preserve of Crewe North. I have written before about my train spotting days south of Crewe at Stableford, Whitmore or Madeley, wondering where all these engine were, as I am sure other young spotters

did too. Well, so many of them were quite nocturnal beasts but here we have it. What a magnificent sight, a tight front end, a wisp of steam from the safety valves and a nice fire just starting to burn through with the fireman taking the evening air; he will have deserved it by the time the train arrives at Crewe over six hours later with around eight tons of coal under his belt. This is what these engines were all about and how grateful we should be that Verden Anderson made it his business to catch this one as there were few occasions when it was possible to photograph these trains in daylight. Photograph W.J.V. Anderson, Rail Archive Stephenson.

1. AN INTRODUCTION TO THE CLASS
Big 'Un's Old and New; All Roads Lead to Crewe

In almost 50 years as a railwayman, from humble 15 year old apprentice fitter at Crewe North, through all the former BR Regions, to Engineering Director of a rolling stock leasing company, to private consultant on traction and rolling stock matters both in this country and abroad, as I reflect back in my arm chair, perhaps accompanied by a wee dram, nothing gives me more satisfaction than my early experiences. I have written about these before, in books and magazines, but cannot resist the invitation to do it once again! I worked on steam locomotives at Crewe North, without any doubt the premier locomotive depot on the old Premier Line, albeit in BR days and well towards the end of its life. That the first locomotive I worked on was one of the magnificent Stanier Pacifics, gives me as much satisfaction as any other experience, more than any of my readers can possibly imagine – or perhaps they can!

At Crewe these engines, I soon learnt from my new work-mates, were habitually referred to as either *Big 'Uns* (from their great size, obviously) or *Class Eights* (after the BR power classification); I never heard them discussed in any other terms, and we never used the initial 4 in referring to their numbers, just 6253 or whatever. I have chosen 6253 because that was the very first engine I worked on as I commenced my career, never of course expecting to reach the dizzy heights of Engineering Director, and no less a stint as Chairman of the Railway Division of the Institution of Mechanical Engineers (I Mech E), the successor body of the old Institution of Locomotive Engineers (I Loco E). As I mentioned in my Chairman's address to that body, when I used to pore over the writings of the likes of Cecil J. Allen, O.S. Nock and that firebrand Dr W.A. Tuplin, I would marvel at those letters behind their names and wonder, and sometimes dream, about becoming a member of the Institution of Locomotive Engineers; what exactly did you have to do? Would you need the stature of a Sir William Stanier or the like, or would some lesser position be adequate? When I came to sign the attendance book for my first Council meeting of the Institution of Mechanical Engineers Railway Division, I happened to glance back through the pages. These began, as I recall, some time in the early 1930s. There, unmistakably, was the great man's signature, *W.A. Stanier* and, for page after page, all his contemporaries and other famous and not so famous names both before and after; what a slice of history that book represented. It was with enormous humility that I signed my name on that and subsequent occasions. I have to add that quite soon after my first entries the book was full, and a new one had to be started, so I was extremely pleased to have been able to place my name in the same volume as all those celebrated locomotive engineers. I wager that in 60 years time nobody will look back on my name and see very much significance, if any, such is the very changed world we live in.

The very first volume in the 'Book Of' series could not of course have concerned any subject but our wonderful Coronation Pacifics. It is no accident that it has proved the most enduringly popular of them all, running to several reprints (though several sister volumes are pressing it close). Way back then, in 1998, horizons were not so broad as now and books were more restricted as to size. *The Book of the Coronation Pacifics* was overdue for another reprint but it is, when all is said and done, a book that is more than a decade old. This updated and revivified version, it is hoped, will delight both those who (unaccountably) have managed to miss the original and those whose thirst for these magnificent locomotives can never be fully assuaged. Relative costs/prices mean (that's what they tell me!) that the 20-30 pages of introductory notes from the original volume are more or less free!

Carlisle Kingmoor shed on 7 August 1957 with Polmadie's long-time resident 46222 QUEEN MARY waiting for a job to return north of the border. As the engine no longer has the Fowler/Anderson cylinder by-pass valves which were fitted when new, at some date new cylinders must have been fitted. Photograph A.G. Forsyth, Initial Photographics.

Another of the Polmadie faithful, 46230 DUCHESS OF BUCCLEUCH at the north end of Crewe station in the mid-1950s, before the later BR design of tender emblem was applied. The engine will have just left the North shed and having run back to clear the points it is passing over will be proceeding north to await the arrival of a train from the south. It will then work forward to Glasgow. Photograph J.B. Bucknall.

One of the first batch of non-streamlined engines, 46232 DUCHESS OF MONTROSE in BR green livery with smoke deflectors at Carlisle Kingmoor about 1959. The engine has the later tender emblem and electrification warning notices but has not yet been fitted with AWS – this was installed in December 1959.

London beckons, with 46238 CITY OF CARLISLE heading south in the country at Hunton Bridge just south of Kings Langley on 10 August 1951. The engine was enjoying a very short spell at Camden, a little over two months in fact in the summer of 1951, before returning north to Carlisle Upperby.

When all these further photographs arrived on my doorstep, delivered by one of Lord Irwell's liveried servants, I jumped at the opportunity to sort out and caption them and meld them to the original volume. I have to add I often wonder where they keep turning up from, but turn up they do, and as will be seen, there are some very fine views too, often in unusual locations. There are a number of essential 'repeats' from the first edition but I have endeavoured to select ones that have not seen daylight before, although in the event, there are a few that will be familiar to the faithful – the ones it was impossible to resist. I have also tried to show the engines in most of their non-streamlined guises, livery perhaps being the principal consideration, but others too. It has to be said, nevertheless, that to present such a wide selection is getting more and more difficult, as photographs of the engines before and during the war, that have not appeared in print hitherto, are getting harder and harder to come by with every passing year. But, dear readers, knowing the all-powerful influence of Lord Irwell, one just never knows what he might come up with next!

In putting all this together I came across in my library what is perhaps a not too well known book; one in fact I had all but forgotten about. In 1973 Model & Allied Publications Limited (MAP) published *The LMS Duchesses*, a sort of anthology edited by Douglas

Doherty, comprising a series of dissertations, for want of a better word, by various authors – all unfortunately no longer with us. Included are the works of Eric Langridge, John Powell ('45671' to those familiar with *Trains Illustrated* in the 1950s), Dr WA Tuplin and Crewe Driver Peter Johnson. Bill Tuplin is of course as controversial as one might expect, but it is the paper by Eric Langridge that I want to concentrate on. The writings of Langridge will be familiar to any reader who was a member of the Stephenson Locomotive Society (SLS) in the 1970s, as under his pen were a series of articles in its *Journal* spanning several years titled *Under 10 CMEs*. Starting under Drummond on the South Western Langridge graduated to the locomotive design office at Derby in BR days, and worked successively, as his title says, under no less than ten Chief Mechanical Engineers. The articles are a wonderful history of a whole plethora of locomotive design matters, and I understand (at the time of writing) that they are to be published in book form, along with all the correspondence that accompanied them, by the SLS in its centenary year – 2009. Suffice to say, this will be a book I would recommend to anybody in the least bit interested in exactly how locomotives are conceived, designed, and built.

Langridge describes at some length exactly how the design of the Duchess Pacifics evolved; first the concept of a

locomotive to improve on the Princess Royals, then the development of the design itself. But this is not all, as he goes on to elaborate in some detail the problems encountered; not least in the design work itself but also the question of Crewe's ability to build a boiler bigger than the one on the earlier engines. In a masterly way he goes to great lengths to describe the design (for which he was largely responsible) and construction of the boiler, and how he then had to camp out at Crewe to ensure the Boiler Shop put his design into practice. As a description of the conception, design, and building of a new locomotive type this work is in my view unequalled, and I guess unlikely to be, and at the expense of repeating myself, I would recommend it to anyone remotely interested in such matters, and in particular the Coronation Pacifics.

Langridge dispenses, in passing, with the myth that any *one* man designs a locomotive. In the case of these engines Stanier himself had little influence in the detail design work, and in any event was away in India when the bulk of it was done. He had however, agreed on the principle changes from the Princess Royal design that his team had already formulated. These included higher superheat, following the experience with the boiler for the turbine driven 6202, a different cylinder layout and valve gear, larger driving wheel diameter and a shorter wheelbase. He may well have been unaware, however, of the

The allocation at Crewe North varied enormously over the years but this one stuck it out! 46235 CITY OF BIRMINGHAM was there from May 1944 until withdrawn in September 1964 and is one of three of the class preserved; in this case in... Birmingham. It was one of three named after cities that also carried the individual city armorial crest over the nameplate. The locomotive is at Crewe North on 19 July 1958 in green livery with the later tender emblem. Most but not all the engines that were named after cities were involved in civic ceremonies in the cities in question. These were attended by officials of the LMS, the city fathers and other worthies along with of course, the press. In the case of this engine the event took place at Birmingham New Street Station on 20 March 1945, some time after the engine was built (there was a war on) although it carried its nameplates from new. However it was at the Birmingham event that the city heraldic device was presented and mounted over the nameplates. Photograph B.W.L. Brooksbank, Initial Photographics.

CITY OF BIRMINGHAM, almost at the end of its working life, at Willesden shed on 19 June 1964. Along with the other remaining Coronations it was withdrawn in September, but unlike them it was saved as the official 'preservee'. Because the Birmingham Museum of Science & Industry had offered a home for this particular locomotive and as at the time secure locations for the locomotives BR had elected to save were at a premium, this offer was accepted and this is the reason why this particular locomotives was saved. Prior to handing over it was tidied up in Crewe Works and given a fresh coat of the standard BR green livery. With the closure of the museum some years ago the engine was moved and is presently located at Thinktank, Millennium Point, Curzon Street, in Birmingham.

46237 CITY OF BRISTOL at Camden shed. It retains the semi-circular smokebox but has the larger cab front windows and is painted in the blue livery which was standard for the class at the time, although it fact not all of them received it. The photograph dates from somewhere between August 1950 when the cab windows were enlarged and March 1955 when the smokebox was modified.

Euston station on 24 June 1956 with Upperby's rather grimy 46238 CITY OF CARLISLE on the down 'Royal Scot'. It would appear that the engine has just arrived from Camden shed and having buffered-up and closed the buffers on engine and train to allow the screw-coupling to be tightened, the driver has opened the cylinder drain cocks to enable him to easily move the reversing gear into the forward position. The fireman has yet to place that spare headlamp over the left-hand buffer in position over the right-hand one to indicate a class one express passenger train, while the whole process seems to have attracted a goodly number of spectators – quite so. Fittingly this was a Carlisle engine from May 1952 until it was withdrawn in September 1964. Photograph A.E. Bennett, www.transporttreasury.co.uk

46244 KING GEORGE VI at Carlisle sometime between October 1958 and June 1960. We know this because it has maroon livery with the BR style lining which it received at the former date; AWS was fitted, not in evidence here, at the later date. The engine will have worked north from Euston with the down 'Royal Scot' and, having been replaced for the remainder of the journey to Glasgow by a Polmadie engine, is proceeding light to Upperby shed where it was allocated for the entire period mentioned above. Notice there is no coal showing in the tender! Photograph Paul Chancellor Collection.

larger driving wheel diameter, all within the constraints of the loading gauge, as well as keeping the coupled wheel axle-load within the Civil Engineer's limits, was no mean task…

One vital element was Stanier's confidence that the Boiler Shop at Crewe could rise to the challenge of actually making a boiler that would have stretched the designers' ability to the maximum; he was not to be disappointed. It might not be readily appreciated, but the boiler design amounted to a work of genius. The boiler was the most significant single step forward in improving performance over the earlier Princess Royal class. A magnificent example of the design and boilermaking arts, achieving steaming rates unprecedented within the extremely restricted British loading gauge, it was one of the finest boilers in locomotive engineering anywhere in the world. Though not generally realised, this boiler design (known as the type 1X) had a taper barrel that was a proper cone, unlike the Princess Royals and other Stanier designs which followed Swindon practice, where only the top was tapered, with the bottom horizontal. It was also made of only two rings rather than three as used in the earlier design and this, along with the cone shape, made for easier construction of this part of the boiler, as well as giving the designer more latitude in the tube spacing on the firebox tube plate and in the design of the joint with the firebox throat plate. Even that great French locomotive engineer, a name synonymous with the highest levels of best practice in steam locomotive design, André Chapelon, acknowledged the qualities of this boiler.

movement away from a number of otherwise Great Western detail design practices that he himself had introduced. This emerged as the design work got underway. The final decisions were left to Tom Coleman, then in charge of all LMS locomotive and rolling stock design, along with his team at Derby, including Langridge as a leading player, and they just got on with it. While related many times, it is worth mentioning at this juncture that Coleman, who Stanier trusted implicitly, had that uncanny intuitive knack of getting engineering proportions and relationships right first

time; in the design of these engines this talent reached its zenith.

The boiler was key. Somehow or other, to satisfy the operating department that a six-hour (or thereabouts) schedule was possible day in and day out and through all the seasons, between Euston and Glasgow, and with a measure of capacity to allow for the sort of contingencies that so often beset railway operations, the new engines had to have a greater boiler and ashpan capacity together with a higher steaming rate than their predecessors. To design a bigger firebox along with

The south end of Carlisle Citadel in October 1952 and Camden's 46239 CITY OF CHESTER waits to take the up 'Royal Scot' onwards to London. The train will arrive from the north behind a Polmadie engine, almost certainly another Coronation. Jubilee 45605 CYPRUS of Leeds Holbeck is waiting to take the 10 o'clock ex-Glasgow St Enoch to London St Pancras. This train, reporting number W96, was due to leave the Border City at 11.59 am and take the Settle & Carlisle route to Leeds and London on the old Midland route. Photograph R. Butterfield, Initial Photographics.

Waiting for their next turns on Polmadie shed in Glasgow are two Pacifics and a Jubilee. In the middle, Camden's 46246 CITY OF MANCHESTER which having just had a round put on the fire is probably due to leave the shed very soon. On the right is Polmadie's own 46224 PRINCESS ALEXANDRA, which probably has some time to wait before its next job. The Jubilee is 45717 DAUNTLESS, a Liverpool Bank Hall engine at the time which would be waiting to return home on a Glasgow to Liverpool Exchange train. Note that this engine is in the process of taking water. A lovely atmospheric shot for which unfortunately we have no date, but it must be after April 1960 when 46246 had its smokebox modified. Photograph W.A.C. Smith, www.transporttreasury.co.uk

CITY OF LEEDS at Preston on 12 June 1963 and in the process of shunting some vans. Judging by the headcode the engine was working a class 3 van train and is probably either detaching or adding vehicles. By this date the engine is in maroon livery with BR style lining and fitted with a speedometer and AWS equipment. Photograph A.W. Battson, www.tranporttreasury.co.uk

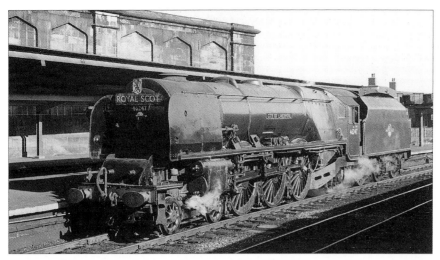

Many readers will have heard how Stanier, when he first visited Crewe Works, donned a pair of overalls and, to the amazement of the Boiler Shop Foremen, E.A. Tizard, climbed into a firebox. As a result of his experience on this and future visits, he got a measure of both the men, their equipment and facilities, such that he gained a higher opinion of Crewe's boiler making

standards than of Swindon's. This was of course an enormous fillip to the management at Crewe, and it is perhaps not fully appreciated what a step change was involved in building these engines and the earlier Princess Royal class at Crewe, over what had been undertaken hitherto. Mention should be made at this point that soon after the formation of the LMS at the 1923 Grouping a

reorganisation within Crewe Works, largely made possible by building a new erecting shop, took place. This was in part originally planned by the LNWR, but delayed due to the First World War, and allowed for the concentration of boiler construction in the otherwise vacated Old Works. This decision was even more far-reaching than that, for it meant that new construction of *all* LMS boilers (other than those on locomotives built by outside contractors) was concentrated at Crewe, thus ending such work at Derby and so on. Montague Beames, the last Chief

Carlisle Citadel and a pretty dirty Crewe North Pacific 46248 CITY OF LEEDS, probably waiting to re-engine an up train and at the same time add an extra coach. Notice the engine and coach are not in a platform road and as the engine is in back gear, it has probably only just set back to attach the coach. This is a late view, some time in 1964 I would say and after Easter. Observe the damage to the front buffer beam and how a wedge shape packing piece has been made to sit behind the buffer so as to maintain its position irrespective of the bent beam. I have a personal recollection of this as I helped to make and fit the wedge after the engine had been involved in a minor collision involving a conflicting move on the North Shed at Crewe. This engine already had a crack in

the right-hand main frame just behind the outside cylinder and starting at the leading axle horn gap. This had been discovered during a X day examination on 20 February and we drilled a hole in the frame plate in an attempt to stop it spreading. This was quite normal practice with cracks in frame plates, to relieve some of the stress and keep engines out of works until they were due a classified repair. I can add however that it was damn hard going with a ¾ inch hand drill! But it worked and we kept a close eye on it to ensure the crack had not extended, at each X day examination. With this in mind the view was that, if the engine had been sent into the Works just for the beam to be straightened, it would not have come back. Photograph Paul Chancellor Collection.

Standing at the north end of Carlisle Citadel 46249 CITY OF SHEFFIELD is doubtless working through from Crewe to Glasgow. The engine has a 5A Crewe North shed plate so this is before its transfer to Polmadie in March 1961; it remained there until withdrawn in November 1963. The AWS was fitted in January 1959, so the photograph was taken between then and March 1961. Looking pretty unkempt for a Crewe North engine it was the first of the four built in 1944 and the first one (except the five built in 1938) not to bear the streamlined casing. This explains the continuation of the running plate between the smoke deflector and the buffer beam. This batch of four locomotives, along with pre-war five non-streamlined ones were the only ones turned out new with this feature. Photograph Paul Chancellor Collection.

The up 'Shamrock' at Kings Langley on 9 April 1955 during a short period, the winter of 1954 to 1955, when 46251 CITY OF NOTTINGHAM was allocated at Edge Hill shed in Liverpool. Normally this shed's Pacific allocation for the London trains was made up of the earlier Princess Royals. Kings Langley signal box can be seen in the left distance. This was one of the wartime batch of five built without streamlining, hence the continuous footplating at the front. With all the hard work behind it the engine is under easy steam on the final stage of the train's journey to the capital.

It is difficult to imagine what is happening in this view of 46252 CITY OF LEICESTER at the north end of Carlisle station on 26 July 1960. The engine is in back gear and running south, but as the tender looks pretty full one would not have expected it to have been detached from a down rain and be heading home to Upperby shed – it was an Upperby engine at the time. This photograph does however illustrate how difficult it was for the cleaners to reach to top of the boiler! As with several other engines with city names this one was given a civic unveiling at its 'home' on 9 October 1944 – some months after it entered service. In this case it necessitated the engine straying away from its usual haunts as engines of this class would not normally visit Leicester. Photograph Paul Chancellor Collection.

This is the very first engine I worked on, 46253 CITY OF ST ALBANS in Crewe Works, just east of the traverser and outside the erecting shop. The date is quoted as 21 April 1963, which I think is correct and the engine is waiting to be pushed down to 'The Melts', or cutting-up shop. This would fit as the engine was stored at Crewe North between January and April 1963 and cut up at Crewe in May. It had a valve and piston examination in July the previous year so had probably run its mileage until due again and may well have been proposed for main works attention due to some problem or other. Presumably it was sufficiently severe to render a further shed valve and piston examination not a viable option hence, as was so often happening at this period in the history of the class, the verdict was withdrawal instead.

A portrait by the master himself, Eric Treacy, of 46255 CITY OF HEREFORD on Crewe North shed on 4 September 1950. The engine is recently out of Crewe Works and painted in the then standard blue adopted for these engines. To the left is Polmadie's 46224 PRINCESS ALEXANDRA while a rather unkempt Caprotti valve gear Class 5 is behind.

Mechanical Engineer of the LNWR, led the team that oversaw these vast improvements at Crewe Works. Despite his obvious disappointment at being passed over for promotion to the top job (not for the first time since the formation of the LMS) his achievements in ensuring that Crewe could rise to the challenge and build locomotives so much larger than any previously attempted, should not go unacknowledged. It was an enormous challenge to confidently lay out, for example, the main-frames of a locomotive almost twice as long as

any built before, never mind the boilers.

Before we leave the boiler it is worth a mention that this was not only the principal reason for the success of these engines, but also what endeared them so much to the men whose daily task was to drive and fire them. Enginemen will take to any engine whose boiler is almost always, barring bad fuel or some other misfortune, master of its work. They will put up with any number of other problems (not that they had to with these engines) in the knowledge that the ability of the boiler to make all

the steam they needed was simply a measure of their ability to shift coal, and theirs alone. There were very few firemen who could 'beat' a Duchess boiler, and even then not for long, as it would almost always be capable of making steam faster than they could shovel coal, even with the driver lending a hand.

Captioning a collection of photographs like the ones in this book involves quite a bit of detective work, but a large collection of working timetables acquired over the years,

I guess for quite a few this might be their favourite in the class, 46256 SIR WILLIAM A STANIER FRS, named after the great man and one of the last two built. At Carlisle in September 1959 it is running light to Upperby shed having been detached from a northbound train; it was a Camden engine at this time. The visible detail differences between the last two engines and the rest are apparent; in particular the revised arrangement of rear end frames, trailing truck, cab side sheets and roller bearing axle boxes on the truck and tender. Note too the position of the battery box for the AWS equipment located under the cab side sheet and the circular reversing shaft rather than the rectangular rod of the other engines. The actual reversing screw was situated under the foot framing adjacent to the quadrant link rather than in the cab as on the earlier engines. This method of mounting the reversing screw and the design of hand-wheel and cut-off indicator was later adopted for the larger engines in the BR Standard range. Photograph Paul Chancellor Collection.

46256 SIR WILLIAM A STANIER FRS at Crewe in June 1961. The engine will have come off the North shed and is running light along platform 4 heading for the engine-slip road ready to take over an up train for Euston; it was a North shed engine by this period. At this time the Manchester and Liverpool routes north of Crewe were electrified so the engine is probably going to work forward on a train from one of those cities. What looks like a small diameter pipe running on the underside of the foot-framing is actually electrical conduit carrying the cable for the AWS equipment to the receiver which was located on the front of the bogie. Where it dips down to clear a circular object above the trailing coupled axle, is the cover over the reversing screw. The principle reason for the redesigned rear end was a larger ashpan than on the earlier engines with better self dumping qualities. Harry Ivatt, the CME at the time the design was being developed, was conscious of the post-war need to burn lower grade coal with a higher ash content and how critical ashpan capacity had already been on through working between London and Glasgow. Photograph Paul Chancellor Collection.

along with runs of journals like *The Railway Observer* of the RCTS and the *SLS Journal*, and to a lesser extent *Trains Illustrated* and *The Railway Magazine*, are extremely useful aids. However, readers will note as they work their way through the pages that follow, that I have failed on occasions, and of course I may have made the odd error. In both cases I am sure the publisher will be glad to hear, and I certainly will, so that a suitable amendment can be made. Having said that, any errors are to my account, and to mine alone. I have to add nevertheless, that while the detective work has been quite stimulating, being surrounded by numerous books and timetables, gradient profiles, sectional appendices and the like, with pages open and book marks all over the place, during and after a writing session, does not exactly help the domestic bliss!

It is fitting in concluding these few remarks to acknowledge the gratitude we owe to all those indefatigable photographers whose work is included here; most are named, but some unfortunately are unknown. But our thanks to them are no less sincere. It

never ceases to amaze me, the places some of these fellows got, along with the excellent results they so often achieved. When one compares the equipment many of them had, heavy plate cameras that could only be used with tripods, slow film and shutter speeds etc, with the digital gear at our command these days – need one say more? The Transport Treasury is a large player in this, and it will not go unnoticed that a considerable part of the photographs in this book come from that stable. The Transport Treasury is doing an excellent job in preserving images like the ones in this book, as well as of course making them available, so I say power to its elbow. Chris Coates of the West Coast Sightings Project (see below) has helped me with some of the locomotive diagrams, and this Project is well worth a mention. A dedicated group of individuals trying to establish as many confirmed sightings of locomotives working identified trains on the West Coast Main Line in the late 1950s and early 1960s, with I have to say, a considerable level of success. My wife Angela is a great tower of support in my writings, as I disappear from

family life for hours on end, so my thanks to her are immeasurable. Last but by no means least, Mr Irwell himself in the form of Chris Hawkins and George Reeve, good friends of mine, for allowing me to just go my own way, albeit this would not have been possible without that inevitable heavy lump deposited by the postman one day on my doorstep. 'Not another load', as my wife would say!

One final comment if I may, before allowing readers to move on to what I am sure they will find more interesting than my ramblings. I have not attempted to change very much in the various statistical notes and tables that appeared in the original book, that are reproduced again here. With Ian Sixsmith's help however, it has been possible to update or correct various items of information where additional data has come to light. For example the later shed allocations have been added and a few other items corrected/amended.

Allan C Baker,
High Halden,
Kent.
April 2010

Camden shed on 7 August 1963 with 46256 SIR WILLIAM STANIER FRS standing on the ash pits, tender full of coal for its next trip north. There was but a month left till the shed closed to steam at the end of the 1963 summer timetable. There is another Pacific to the right (its tender can just be discerned) while through the legs of the ash plant can be seen an English Electric Type 4 diesel. The narrow gauge wagon alongside the engine was part of the ash handling arrangements and that is a fire-bar propped up against it although not from 46256 which had a full rocking grate. Photograph Peter Groom.

A famous name on a famous locomotive. What a great shame this one was not saved for posterity. The photograph illustrates the twin mechanical lubricators and there were two more on the other side of the engine. Between them they provided lubrication to the cylinders and valves, piston and valve rods, slidebars and various other moving parts and (in the case of the earlier engines) the coupled wheel axle-boxes. The siphon feed oil reservoir to the right with its six feed pipes was for lubricating the axle-box horn guides on this side of the engine, while the cut-away part of the boiler lagging was to allow the lubricator lids to be opened. The drive linkage from the expansion link for the lubricators can just be discerned underneath the foot-framing; the sandbox fillers are prominent each side of the lubricators as is the dirt cover for the reversing screw with the AWS electrical cable conduit angled to pass beneath it.

The West Coast Sightings Sheets project has been collating information for over 12 years and has made superb progress in what many considered to be an impossible task. To progress further we urgently need to find enthusiasts who took notes of engines on the LMR in the 1948 to 1968 period. Whilst detailed notes are obviously the most useful, we can still learn and deduce much from just a set of numbers provided a date and location are known. Also shed visits tell us where a particular loco was on a given date. All this info is then entered onto sheets together with train details from the working timetable and, when sufficient data is available, a booklet is created. Understandably there are gaps but, with your help, we may be able to fill some of these.

The booklets that have been produced from the data are quite impressive with a mass of information. All class one passenger and most parcel trains along the West Coast route are shown together with the engine hauling them. To date we have managed ten booklets but, with your help, we could double that figure. If you can help simply contact us and we can discuss the best way of progressing that suits both parties, but please do it urgently, as the project is very time sensitive and is of most interest to enthusiasts who can remember those days.

For further information or to see a sample of our work please contact Chris Coates on 01204 690122 or chris-coates@ukonline.co.uk

Top. One more view of 46256, on this occasion at the north end of Preston station at 8.50 am on 14 December 1963, with an English Electric Type 4 diesel, of a class that did most to supplant these engines. Judging by the headlamp code, 'right and middle' as the enginemen would have described it, the Pacific is working a class 3 van train and just departing on its journey north. The diesel is on 2L81, which was the 8.15 am ex-Preston to Windermere, which if our photographer has recorded the time correctly, was running quite a bit late. Photograph A.W. Battson, www.transporttreasury.co.uk

Left. The last member of the class, 46257 CITY OF SALFORD (hands-up those who knew Salford was a city had it not been for this engine!) outside the repair shop at Perth with unfortunately, no date given. The engine has a 12A Carlisle Kingmoor shed plate and it was allocated there from March 1961 until withdrawn in September 1964. I'd guess the photograph dates from earlier rather than later in that period. Unlike its sister this engine was never painted maroon; in fact it only ever carried two liveries, LMS lined black and BR lined green, albeit in the latter case with the two tender emblems at different times.

46222 QUEEN MARY at Carlisle Kingmoor on 25 March 1962. This locomotive had been a resident of Polmadie shed in Glasgow since November 1939 and remained so until withdrawn in October 1963. By the time this photograph was taken the most prestigious trains on the route between Carlisle and Glasgow were usually diesel hauled although Polmadie still found occasional use for its Pacifics. Photograph R.J. Buckley, Initial Photographics.

2. MILEAGES AND DIAGRAMS

Whenever I see mileage figures quoted for main line steam locomotives, or indeed diesels, I have a little chuckle. One sees for example the final mileage for 46232 as 1,420,948 on withdrawal in December 1962; such precision might have a reassuring feel to it but the figures quoted for passenger steam locomotives in this country are anything up to 20% or more adrift, and always an underestimate. I only have personal experience of how steam locomotive mileages were recorded on the London Midland Region (LMR) but have it on good authority that it is was not much different on the other Regions. Until the Line, Regional and later Divisional Control Offices took over the total responsibility of allocating locomotives to diagrams, it was not much different with the diesels either, and even then the accuracy of the figures could not be guaranteed. Some of the pitfalls and shortcomings of the official figures have of course been noted before in these books while making the point that, nonetheless, the figures in the Engine History Cards are the only figures that we have. To quote from earlier volumes: *they tell a story over time and can at least be compared like for like, that is from engine to engine within a class and from class to class. If figures were high or low or otherwise massaged, it was the same for every engine/class.*

On the LMR at Crewe (it would have been largely the same at other depots) the mileage records were kept by the Mechanical Foreman's clerks. At Crewe North there were three such positions and among other duties the individuals were responsible for programming the allocated locomotives for scheduled maintenance and in so doing, ensure that the correct balance of types of locomotives stopped was achieved. This was important so that on paper at least, the depot could meet its diagrammed requirements against engines stopped for maintenance of one sort or another, as well as those in or awaiting main works attention. Once the diagrams had been agreed for the allocated fleet in accordance with the Working Time Table, each diagram would be given a mileage figure. This figure would be made up of the actual miles to be covered in revenue earning service from leaving the depot to arriving back, plus an allowance for any light engine mileage; to and from the trains they worked for example. This allowance would vary depending on several circumstances, for example how far the starting point was from the shed.

Running Foremen, in conjunction with the Control Offices, were responsible for allocating locomotives to diagrams, endeavouring to ensure the right engines worked the right trains and at the end of each shift, or perhaps on occasions longer periods (such as weekends and Bank Holidays) would submit a list of which engines had worked which diagrams. These lists would be passed to the clerks and these worthies would keep each individual engine mileage record card up to date by adding the figures from the diagram in question. The cumulative total would then be assessed for maintenance programming purposes and towards the end of each week a list would be supplied to the Running Foremen of which engines were to be stopped the following week and for what particular examination. They would endeavour to comply with this but for operational reasons and in consultation with Control, there would frequently be last minute changes on a day-to-day basis. Individual engines and the particular days they would be stopped might be swapped around for example. However, in overall terms every effort would be made to meet the 'plan'.

It should be added at this point that the involvement of the Control Offices

46223 PRINCESS ALICE at Carlisle Kingmoor on the same occasion as in the photograph opposite; in fact this engine can just be seen to the extreme left of QUEEN MARY. Both would have worked in on trains from Glasgow, probably overnight ones and will be waiting turns to take them north again. When the maroon livery was introduced for engines of this class in 1957, the Scottish Region did not join in the fun, and the Polmadie engines remained in green. Photograph R.J. Buckley, Initial Photographics.

This very interesting photograph, dated 2 May 1948, was taken outside the Crewe Weigh House, which at the time was situated in the Old Works. The buildings behind are, to the left the Smiths Shop and to the right, the Drop Hammer Shop, while the distant chimneys serve the Smiths Shop, Power House and Boiler Shop. The leading engine is 46224 PRINCESS ALEXANDRA, which came off a heavy general repair on 3 May 1948 when it received the BR black lined livery as seen here. The one behind is 46232 DUCHESS OF MONTROSE, which was built non-streamlined hence its circular smokebox; it is also recorded off a heavy general repair on 3 May. It too sports the BR lined black livery. This weigh house was later replaced by a new one alongside the Wheel Shop and Vacuum Pits, opposite the Brass Finishing Shop. Notice 46224 has a 27A shed plate which at that time was the code for Polmadie, before the LMS system of shed coding was extended across the whole of BR. The concrete roadway to the right was part of the 1920s reorganisation of the works when the 18 inch gauge railway system for the internal movement of material was replaced by Lister three-wheel diesel engine trucks. Photograph B.W.L. Brooksbank, Initial Photographics.

Aberdeen Ferryhill shed on 24 June 1953 with a blue 46225 DUCHESS OF GLOUCESTER propelling back off the turntable. This Crewe North engine would have arrived at Perth on one of the overnight Crewe-Perth diagrams and rather than laying over on Perth Shed all day until its diagrammed return working, has been used by Perth on an out and back diagram to the Granite City. Whatever the train the engine had worked it would not have been part of its diagrammed working. This was frowned upon by its 'owning' Region, the LMR, which frequently reminded its Scottish counterparts that the Pacifics used on the overnight Crewe to Perth diagrams should not be used on any other duty. This was nonetheless just as frequently ignored and mileage returns would not be submitted, as described in the text. Notice the engine still has the bracket by the trailing coupled axle for the BTH speed recorder, although the actual equipment has been removed. Photograph R. Butterfield, Initial Photographics.

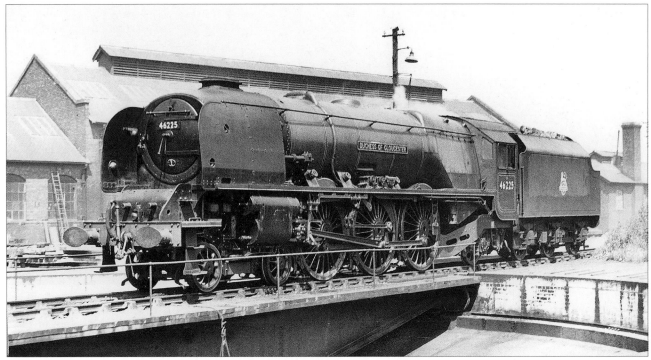

would vary enormously depending on the actual circumstances and type of work the engines were diagrammed to undertake. For example they would have almost no involvement with the allocation of shunting engines, or in many cases local trip working. Control would very likely get involved when there were shortages of power to cover main line diagrams for one reason or another, where special trains had to be arranged at short notice, or with the working of unbalanced engines. These resulted in engines arriving at sheds with no diagrammed return working.

Now while all this might sound pretty clear-cut and foolproof, there were a number of areas where it could and did go wrong. The procedure laid down that if a shed used an engine not on its own allocation on one of its own diagrams, or perhaps on a diagram of a different shed altogether, it was required to send a return to the home depot stating the mileage run. It does not take much imagination to see the pit-falls of ensuring accurate mileage figures once engines got outside their diagrammed working. This would be especially difficult if, for example, shed A used an engine allocated to shed B, on a diagram belonging to shed C and such circumstances were by no means uncommon, particularly during times of service perturbations for one reason or another; for example late running through any number of reasons, diversions due to mishaps, engineering

work, assisting disabled trains and so on. Added to this would be engines 'stopped' at foreign sheds in the course of diagrammed working for unscheduled repairs and thus unable to complete their diagrams. An additional aspect would be any special workings that somehow or other got lost in the system, which in many cases resulted in unbalanced engines having to be sent home, either attached as pilots to other trains, or on occasions light engine. The possibilities for unrecorded mileages being accumulated by main line locomotives, both passenger and freight, were boundless.

Among motive power folk any shed that was not your own was 'foreign' and any engine not allocated to your own shed was a 'foreigner', to be treated with equal suspicion; and there were other perhaps more devious reasons for mileages not being fully recorded. It was quite a common practice for a shed to use foreign engines to fill its own diagrams and in this practice some sheds were worse than others; some very much worse. Take the Crewe North engines that worked the Perth diagrams; they were supposed to lay over on Perth shed from arrival in the morning until departing south again the following evening. This out and home diagram consisted of 592 miles, on top of which there would be a small allowance for light engine mileage as mentioned earlier. Obviously with a diagram like this, the engines laying over at Perth

would in effect be idle for something like 12 hours, which even allowing for servicing would have left them theoretically available for a substantial amount of time. This period of availability nicely coincided with an out and home Perth loco diagram to and from Aberdeen; not infrequently, a Crewe North Pacific was to be found on this job.

Because of the soft coal available in Scotland, a contrast to the harder North Staffordshire and Lancashire coal usually supplied to Crewe North, the LMR authorities had always resisted pressure from their Scottish counterparts for any use to be made of the Pacifics off the Perth jobs during their lay-over in Scotland. This was the result of complaints from the footplate men, who wanted as much North Shed coal as possible left in the tenders of the engines on arrival at Perth, so as to make life easier for them on the return journey. They achieved this by putting anything up to three tons on the fire and then topping the tender up until the coal was literally falling over the sides, prior to leaving the North Shed. I have written about this practice at length in other works, but the aim of the game was to be still drawing on the Crewe coal when the hard work started as they left Carlisle on the return journey.

In the light of the foregoing it takes little imagination to understand why Perth shed was unlikely to send a mileage return to Crewe if it had

This photograph illustrates something of the cyclic diagrams introduced in the summer months during the 1950s, aimed at increasing the utilisation and mileages these engines worked. Polmadie's 46231 DUCHESS OF ATHOLL has brought the down 'Mid-Day Scot' from Euston to Crewe on 4 June 1958 and is about to be replaced by Crewe North's 46225 DUCHESS OF GLOUCESTER. This engine has already been attached to a horsebox and the West of England Plymouth through coach, which will go forward with the train. In the meantime 46231 will be serviced at the North shed before working a train back to Glasgow, probably one of the overnight diagrams. The day before it might have worked the 'Royal Scot' through from Glasgow to Euston, or it might have worked two separate trains with a break at either Carlisle or Crewe, as part of its cyclic diagram, in which case it probably arrived a Euston on an overnight train. Photograph R.J. Buckley, Initial Photographics.

pinched a Pacific to cover an Aberdeen turn, or indeed any other turn and the local Control Office would be party to the deception too. There were of course many other examples of this type of thing, as well as numerous cases where the use of engines was not recorded simply due to forgetfulness, or where returns got lost for one reason or another. On occasions engines might get 'lost' so far as their home sheds were concerned, for days or even weeks on end and this would be especially so with mixed traffic types such as the ubiquitous Class 5s, and even more so if they found themselves on another Region. Clearly this sort of thing would play havoc with maintenance schedules and in particular boiler washout periods, but one could usually be sure errant engines would find their way home when anything much was wrong with them. This would be especially so if they started to prime because of an overdue boiler washout! In many such cases whatever mileage they may have run would be a complete mystery to the owning depot. The terms so familiar to motive power people of 'FHD' and 'LEH' are legendary and I suspect will remain in the memory banks of us old boys for all time: 'For Home Depot' and 'Light Engine Home'. I wish I had a pound for each and every repair card I have seen endorsed with one or other of these abbreviations, and it went on

well in to diesel days. They were just as common in the individual diesel locomotive repair books that eventually replaced the card system.

Engines used on engineering trains – ballast jobs was the ubiquitous term – were allocated a standard mileage irrespective of what the actual mileage run was. Similarly engines working turns within the local 'Shunting Engine & Local Trip Notices' were allocated an average mileage based on some nominal calculation and again, irrespective of how many miles they had actually done. In some cases shunting engines were allotted a pre-determined mileage for every hour they were in service. This might lead one to suspect that in the case of the types of engines used on such jobs the official mileage figures quoted would be even more inaccurate than those of their main line counterparts; I would not argue with that!

There was another form of check on the miles engines ran, although very often it was unlikely to instil any more accuracy into the system than the one already described. Drivers were required at the end of each shift to complete a return of what they had been up to – usually referred to as the *Drivers Ticket*. Part of the information required was the number of any engines they had driven, who the firemen were and details of the journeys. These tickets

found their way to the roster clerks at the men's home shed and were used to compile details of any mileage money due to the men. The roster clerks would also extract the information relating to the engines and mileage accrued and send this to the Mechanical Foreman's clerks. Here then was some sort of check but of course, if the men had been on engines from foreign sheds, the chances of the information finding its way to where it would be of any use was remote to say the least.

The discerning among readers may well be left wondering after this rather sorry tale how maintenance of the engines was affected, for after all, a large part of it was undertaken on a mileage run basis. Well, it really did not matter very much as the periodicity of the mileage based maintenance was born of long experience of the condition of engines, using the system as described. As will have been observed by now, the method of collecting mileage figures was not very scientific to say the least but, in practice, by and large, engines engaged on similar duties tended to accumulate similar mileages against which they would be programmed for maintenance, with the same common level of inaccuracy. Hence the error, whatever it might be, was in effect taken into account in establishing the periodicity in the first place. Over a period of time the mileage between

DUCHESS OF GLOUCESTER again, still a Crewe North engine, in Crewe Works on 6 August 1958. The engine had just completed a heavy general repair and been painted for the first time in maroon livery with BR style lining. The engine is recorded off works the following day, so it is probably being positioned ready to be taken to the South shed having just been moved out of the Paint Shop. Photograph B.W.L. Brooksbank, Initial Photographics.

An unfortunately undated view of two Pacifics at Shrewsbury, 46246 CITY OF MANCHESTER to the left and 46228 DUCHESS OF RUTLAND to the right. Both these engines would have worked to Salop, as Crewe men always called Shrewsbury, on fill-in turns from Crewe and are here waiting to return. In fact 46246 is already attached to its train, 1M89, the Saturdays only 9.12 am Paignton to Manchester due away from Shrewsbury at 3.16 pm which it will work as far as Crewe. Meanwhile 46228 stands in the bay platform taking water and waiting for its train. Both engines are painted maroon with LMS style lining and as the smokebox on 46246 was only modified in April 1960, the photograph was taken sometime after that. However, it was about this time that the Western Region started to use the Warship class diesel-hydraulic locomotives on the West of England trains and they used to work through to Crewe. This saved the Shrewsbury engine change with another one necessary at Crewe after the lines to Manchester and Liverpool were electrified. So this view probably dates from no later than the summer of 1961. Photograph E.A. Elias, www.transporttreasury.co.uk

Another undated view this time with 46229 DUCHESS OF HAMILTON on the up 'Royal Scot' at Hest Bank. This would be one of the summer periods when this train did not run with a limited load, hence its length. I would suggest the engine is painted green, a livery it received in April 1952 and as the smokebox was modified in March 1957, the photograph was taken some time between those dates. It was a Camden engine at this time and as the buffer heads as well as the valve chest and cylinder dirt covers are polished, it may recently have worked a Royal train. Photograph R. Butterfield, Initial Photographics.

The fast London to Glasgow service introduced with the summer 1957 timetable and scheduled at 6 hours 40 minutes in each direction with a two minute stop at Carlisle, was named 'The Caledonian'. This is the inaugural up train on arrival at Platform 3 at Euston on 17 June 1957, with Camden's 46229 DUCHESS OF HAMILTON having worked the train through from Glasgow. Arrival was one and a half minutes early at 3.8½pm, 289½ minutes for the 299 miles. The Euston Station Master Mr Turnell, who greeted the train on its arrival, is flanked by the Camden crew who had worked the train from Carlisle; driver J. Staeker and fireman Thompson, left and right respectively. What a lovely evocative shot; a top link crew could who could not be attired in a more typical fashion and how one would have loved to have been with them that memorable day.

'The Caledonian', the inaugural down working, waiting to depart at 4 pm from Platform 13 at Euston on 17 June 1957. The engine on this occasion very appropriately was 46242 CITY OF GLASGOW, carefully prepared by Camden for this auspicious occasion. Notice the fellow standing by the footplate with a movie camera on his shoulder (I wonder where the film is now?) along with the top-brass observing the proceedings to the left.

Crewe North's long-term resident 46235 CITY OF BIRMINGHAM looking very smart at its home shed in 1958 or 1959. It had received this BR green livery with the later BR emblem in February 1958. AWS was not fitted till June 1959 while the Smith-Stone speedometer on the trailing coupled axle dates from August 1957. This photograph was taken by the late George Wheeler who, though a native of Southampton, was a great enthusiast for these and other big engines. George was a very affable fellow who made it his business to get to know those involved at the various sheds he visited and being so generous with copies of his photographs, managed to negotiate numerous opportunities denied to others. Or alternatively he would be tipped-off when anything special might be happening. Although in this case 46235 is clearly about to leave the shed and head north, notice how clean the engine is and that the tender tank has just been topped up; the fireman can be seen on the tender, doubtless securing the tank filler lid. We can therefore be sure that the shedmaster, Geoff Sands, who George knew well, would have been involved somewhere along the line and that both Geoff and the crew (the driver can be seen alongside the engine) would have be been sent copies of this photograph. While George's work can never be judged against some of the masters, they are generally of good quality; knowing the limitations of his equipment, as he was never a rich man, he never attempted moving shots. I got to know George many years later when I was in charge at Finsbury Park where he was well known from his earlier visits to Kings Cross Top Shed. Later when I was at Eastleigh Depot, where as might be expected he was also well known, I was able to visit his home and delve into his enormous collection of which this photograph is one. Photograph the late George Wheeler.

This photograph was taken on the same occasion showing again how the engine had been specially cleaned for George. Notice how it positively gleams alongside its stablemates! The Jubilee with a straight sided Fowler tender on the right is 45698 MARS, a Liverpool Aintree engine at the time. Photograph the late George Wheeler.

Glasgow Central on 9 June 1956 with 46236 CITY OF BRADFORD setting back onto its train which would be the morning Glasgow-Birmingham. This train followed the up 'Royal Scot' which can be seen waiting to depart at Platform 1 on the extreme right. Although it cannot be positively identified the 'Royal Scot' engine is a Polmadie one as the first four numbers are 4622 and this engine would work the train to Carlisle. The other engine however, 46236, Camden based, would work through to Crewe as part of a cyclic diagram. Contrary to the rules the engine already carries the class one train headcode lamps. Photograph www.transporttreasury.co.uk

CITY OF BRADFORD again, this time arriving at Crewe on 19 June 1957 with the up 'Pines Express' from Manchester to Bournemouth. This would be an unusual working for a Pacific as they were always somewhat rare birds on the line between Crewe and Manchester and as the engine came off a intermediate repair at Crewe a day or two earlier, this was probably a running-in turn for this Camden engine. The Liverpool coaches would be added to the train at Crewe and the Pacific may well have worked it forward to Birmingham. This photograph gives a good view of the North Junction with the main line north in the centre and the Chester line to the left; the Old Works provides a backcloth. The buildings to the extreme top right are part of the Grease Works as it was known; this was where all the old oil and grease from the works as well as other parts of the system was reclaimed for various purposes. The cleaning clothes were cleaned there too, with any oil or grease added to the recovery operation. Photograph B.W.L. Brooksbank, Initial Photographics.

A fifteen coach train (said to be the 6.35 am Workington-Euston) at Hatch End, near the end of its journey on 13 July 1957 behind 46240 CITY OF COVENTRY. Coal is getting low in the tender and though the train started from Workington it picked up additional coaches at several places en-route. One would hardly fill fifteen with passengers wanting to travel from that outpost on the Cumbrian Coast to the capital; the vehicles present quite a variety too. The Pacific would have probably have taken over the train at Preston; Watford DC lines to the left. Photograph B.W.L. Brooksbank, Initial Photographics.

examinations was occasionally refined, in the light of practical experience of the physical condition of the locomotives. In the case of freight and shunting engines much of the maintenance of the moving parts was undertaken as a result of drivers bookings, or local assessment of the mechanical condition by the maintenance staff at the owning depot, rather then on the basis of any recorded mileage. This method of establishing the periodicity of the mileage examinations on the types of locomotives concerned resulted in nobody being very interested in how many miles they had actually run anyway. It really did not matter, was purely academic in fact, but nevertheless figures found their way into statistics that in so many cases have become almost sacrosanct!

The sheds were required on a daily basis to submit various statistical returns to the Control Offices. For example: an analysis of engines stopped for any reason, diagrams covered, including those for which the wrong types of engine had been used, foreign and other unbalanced engines on hand and so on, along with a whole plethora of other information. There were other returns too, but often on a less frequent basis. All this allowed the Control Offices to ensure as smooth an operation of the system as possible and essentially the actual mileages individual engines

accumulated was, by and large, left to the sheds themselves to compile as described above. The Control Offices in their turn compiled statistics which included miles run by engines on different types of trains and these eventually found their way in the annual figures produced by the railway companies and later BR; they can be found in the respective annual reports. I leave readers who consult such documents to form their own views on the accuracy of the information provided.

It is worth saying out at this juncture, and I make the point very strongly, that the X day examinations, when engines were stopped somewhere between seven and 14 days depending on type, were always treated with enormous respect. Concerted efforts were generally made to ensure engines were stopped for the X day work, if not on time, then within a couple of days at most. This was the examination that among other things covered all the safety of the line elements. The maintenance of boilers, along with all their components and fittings were scheduled for attention on a periodicity rather than a mileage basis and in my experience, even in the later run-down days of steam traction in this country, I never saw the slightest deterioration in the level of attention given to boilers that would in anyway have affected their safe operation. In

addition locomotives booked to work passenger trains were checked by an Examining Fitter prior to entering traffic and on every occasion they visited a shed.

****

There are some references in the captions to the low mileages of the Pacifics allocated to the Scottish Region at Polmadie. The allocation of some of the fleet to the Scottish Region was by and large for 'political' reasons and it is perhaps not insignificant that, once the diesels arrived, the West Coast main line diagrams were always covered by locomotives allocated to LMR sheds. This was the case with the English Electric Type 4s (later Class 40), subsequently the Brush-Sulzer Type 4s (later Class 47) and lastly the D400s (later Class 50s). It is worth adding too, that it was not dissimilar when electric traction was introduced north of Crewe, with all the main line locomotives allocated to Willesden.

There were attempts over the years, usually in the summer months when the loads were limited and additional trains were running, to improve the overall mileage of the whole Pacific fleet, with varying degrees of success. This included through engine working between Euston and Glasgow, along with what were referred to as cyclic diagrams, although I do not think this term was universally used at the time. In this type of diagram a Polmadie engine might work a job to Crewe and instead of returning north after servicing, work a train to Euston. This might be followed the next day, or even overnight, by a train to Carlisle and after servicing there it would return to its home shed on a Glasgow bound train.

Through working between the two end terminals, Euston and Glasgow, was never popular with the crews, even though they were always changed en-route. This was because coal got low the tenders, especially in the winter months while the ashpan, on the other hand, might get too full. With a tender full of soft Scottish coal it was sometimes a struggle to get through to Euston without losing time; once again this was especially so in the winter months when adverse weather conditions might add to the delay. This was one of the reasons why 'The Caledonian', after it was introduced, was the only train consistently diagrammed for one locomotive to work through between Euston and Glasgow. Otherwise through engine working was generally confined to the summer timetable periods during a few years in the 1950s, when the trains ran with limited loads, additional capacity being provided by extra trains as appropriate. 'The

Caledonian' always ran with a limited eight-coach load.

It is perhaps worth mentioning that unlike the through workings on the Eastern Region between Kings Cross and Edinburgh, the LMR engines working through between Euston and Glasgow were given no special attention. On the Eastern Region when through working was in operation in the summer months, a small number of the A4s were selected by Kings Cross and Haymarket sheds and exclusively employed on the trains in question. There was one train each way per day; in BR days this was the summer only 'Capitals United', later renamed 'The Elizabethan'. These 'nominated' engines would be low mileage ones not long off repairs at Doncaster and special attention was paid to the middle cylinder big end, in particular the oil flow to the bearing. If this was not 'fine tuned' in terms of the restrictor and felt pad, there was a distinct possibility the reservoir of oil would be insufficient to last for the 398 mile journey. Shortage of oil would of course result in a hot bearing that might eventually lead to failure. During the course of the summer a very close eye would be kept on the engines when they arrived at their destinations to see how much oil had been used, or conversely how much, if any, was left.

There was no similar requirement for the LMR Pacifics; any engine could be and was used irrespective of where it was in any maintenance cycle. They were all maintained in exactly the same way and prepared for each and every duty likewise. There was no need to molly-coddle our engines!

Details of 16 September 1957 illustrate the low mileages of the Scottish winter diagrams. At this date Polmadie had no fewer than nine Pacifics allocated: 46220, 46221, 46222, 46223, 46224, 46227, 46230, 46231 and 46232, to cover but five diagrams; turns 6/1, 6/2, 6/3, 6/4 and 7 each required one locomotive. As this was the start of the winter timetable however, opportunity would have been taken to send any locomotives due main works repairs to Crewe, as well as catching up with any overdue shed mileage examinations. Actually six of the engines received some sort of main works attention during the period of the 1957-1958 winter timetable, with on occasions up to three of them at Crewe at the same time, even if only for a few days. Even so the allocation appears excessive, but this does not mean the engines would not have been used to cover other diagrams, as undoubtedly on occasions they would have been. But all depots had allocations of what were referred to as 'maintenance spares'; that

An unusual location for 46240 CITY OF COVENTRY; Bletchley shed on 11 August 1964. Despite being almost at the and of its life the engine had been selected by its home shed Willesden to act as standby to a Royal train working from Euston to the north. Its external condition is not up to earlier Camden standards but Willesden have made a valiant effort. One asks oneself that if the English Electric Type 4 diesel was good enough to haul the Royal train itself, why was a Duchess used as a standby almost 50 miles into the journey? Photograph C. Stacey, Initial Photographics.

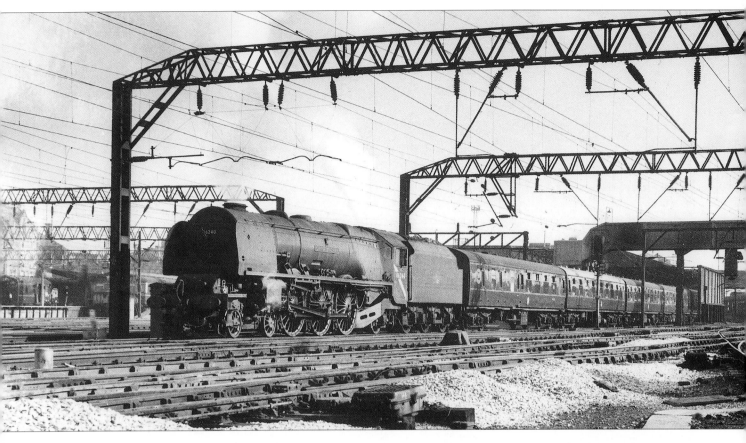

Above. Almost the end. The train here is the daytime down Euston to Perth leaving Crewe on 29 August 1964 with 46240 CITY OF COVENTRY. This engine had recently been transferred from Willesden to Crewe North because of the ban on the class south of Crewe under the overhead line. The yellow diagonal stripe on the cab side was to indicate this restriction, imposed due to height clearance hazards; it had been applied just a few days earlier. This engine was unceremoniously withdrawn from service just fourteen days later and consigned to the scrap heap. Just look at her, hardly a wisp of steam from anywhere except the safety valves, a crisp exhaust I'd say and although we cannot establish how many coaches in the train, it did load well in the summer months. We can be pretty sure thirteen or fourteen would be hanging on the drawbar and the engine would work through to Mossend Yard. There engines would be changed, followed by a run light to Polmadie shed. One can perhaps take solace in that unlike so many of their brethren, these magnificent beasts that had served their masters so well and for so long, did not suffer the indignity of running around bereft of name and number plates with numerals and names crudely painted on. A godsend I say for I could hardly have stomached it. So, better they went when and how they did, while here we have as fine a tribute to those final days as one might find anywhere. Photograph David R. Donkin.

Left. The down 'Royal Scot' waiting to depart Euston on 4 October 1953 behind 46244 KING GEORGE VI. This Camden engine would work the train to Carlisle where a Polmadie one would take it forward. The circular object just behind the headlamp to the left is the anti-vacuum valve for the right-hand inside cylinder. Amazing that at this date such an important London station should have platform extensions made up of rather crudely finished timber planks! Photograph R. Butterfield, Initial Photographics.

KING GEORGE VI again, this time entering Crewe station from the north on 4 June 1958 with the 9 am from Perth-Euston. This train, unlike the overnight ones to and from Perth, was not an English Pacific diagram between Perth and Carlisle, so 46244 would have come on at the Border City and be working through to Euston. Notice another Coronation to the extreme left leaving for the north; this is 46225 on the down 'Mid-Day Scot', as seen in an earlier illustration, complete with the horsebox and Plymouth through coach. Photograph R.J. Buckley, Initial Photographics.

is, additional engines over and above the strict number required each day to allow for scheduled maintenance, main works attention and any other out of course complications that might arise along with a small level of contingency.

The winter 1957-1958 Polmadie diagrams did not involve very high mileages. For example Turn 6/1 consisted of working the up and down 'Royal Scot' to and from Carlisle. The engine was due off Polmadie at 9.30 am with the train away from Glasgow Central at the time honoured 10 o'clock. Due at Carlisle at 11.59 am the engine then repaired to Kingmoor shed for servicing before leaving again at 3 o'clock. The down working was due away from Carlisle at 3.36 pm and in Glasgow at 6.42 pm, for the engine to go light to Polmadie. There was a similar diagram on Sundays, but the timings were longer. Turn 6/3 covered the 9.25 pm overnight train from Glasgow to Euston, but only as far as Carlisle where it was due at midnight. After a sojourn on Kingmoor shed this engine returned north on the 7.15 am train arriving at Glasgow at 9.30, although it was 11 o'clock before it was released to return to Polmadie. The return trip was quite a bit earlier on a Sunday.

Two other diagrams, 6/4 and 7, covered two of the Anglo-Scottish overnight sleeping car trains, the 10.20 and 11.25 pm from Glasgow to Euston. In both cases the engines came off at Carlisle and as neither train was timetabled to stop at Carlisle for commercial reasons, the engines and men were changed alongside Carlisle No.12 signal box. This was adjacent to Upperby shed from where the engine and men diagrammed to go forward would come. The Polmadie engines subsequently ran to Kingmoor shed for servicing. Later in the morning the two Pacifics took northbound overnight trains to Glasgow. The first was the 11.50 pm from Euston, 6.30 am ex-Carlisle, which was routed over the former Glasgow & South Western line via Kilmarnock and into Glasgow St Enoch. Although this train was due at St Enoch at 9.25 am, due to the circuitous journey to Polmadie and empty stock working, the engine was not back on shed there almost until noon. The second train was the 9.10 pm sleeper from Euston, another one not scheduled to stop at Carlisle station; this time the changeover took place alongside Kingmoor shed, departing at 3.32 am to arrive in Glasgow at 6 o'clock

– though it was 8 o'clock before the engine got back to Polmadie. In both cases the LMR engines off the trains went to Upperby for servicing; it has to be remembered that at this period Kingmoor was a Scottish Region shed and Upperby a London Midland Region one; never the twain shall meet, as they say.

Turning now to the Crewe North arrangements, in this case for the summer of 1951; commencing on 18 June when the shed had an allocation of fifteen Pacifics of the Princess Royal and Coronation classes. The individual engines were: 46205, 46207, 46208, 46209, 46210, 46211, 46212, 46225, 46229, 46233, 46234, 46235, 46243, 46246 and 46248. From these fifteen engines the shed had to cover eleven diagrams, giving four maintenance spares. These covered the scheduled shed examinations, including the No.8 valve and piston exam, as well as main works attention. If we look at main works statistics we find that for much of the summer period around three of the Princess Royals and one Coronation had works visits and the dates are such that at least one of them would have been unavailable for almost the entire period. It is interesting to note that four engines,

46207, 46210, 46212 and 46248, all completed works repairs in June, indicating that efforts had been made to ensure maximum availability during the period of the summer timetable. With one of them always undergoing a No.8 exam and at least one more on scheduled maintenance, it is straight clear that the margins were not over generous. These engines, by the way, were on a seven day frequency for X day examinations with a boiler washout every second X day. As a rule however, the X day exam, combined with any 3-5 or 7-9 week examinations would be completed within a 24 hour period at the most. If, on the other hand, one of the lesser mileage examinations was also due, the period stopped could extend to a couple of days, depending on the level of repairs arising.

The Crewe North Pacific workings that summer were divided into five separate turns, as they were then called – the term 'diagram' came later. Turn One covered the 11.15 pm to Perth, which was the 7.30 pm from Euston, due in the Scottish city at 6 o'clock the following morning. The engine from this train returned the same day on the 9.48 pm to London as far as Crewe, which was the 5.15 pm from Inverness, due in Crewe at 4.52 am. The times were slightly different on a Sunday, when the train started from Perth. At Crewe this engine was then diagrammed to work the 10.20 am to Shrewsbury, which was the 9.06 am Liverpool to Plymouth,

returning to Crewe at 4.03 pm on the 8.45 am Plymouth-Liverpool train. This was a fill-in turn before the engine headed north again that same evening and also served conveniently to turn the engine round on the Severn Bridge triangle. Obviously this Turn required two locomotives.

Turn Two, also requiring two locomotives, was the second Perth train, 7.20 pm from Euston for Inverness departing Crewe at 10.29. Incidentally this train, which also carried newspapers, included a through coach to Lairg and was I believe, the longest through working of passenger coaching stock anywhere in the country, a record I think, that has never been broken. As this train did not run on Saturday night/Sunday morning, the engine worked the 1.15 pm ex-Crewe on Sunday morning to Glasgow, which was the 11.15 pm from Birmingham, due in the Scottish city at 6.50am the following morning. The return working was the 5.45 pm from Glasgow to Euston as far as Crewe, where it was due at 12.48, in the early hours of Monday morning. Incidentally Kingmoor men worked this train north of Carlisle and Polmadie men the return trip all the way to Crewe, on a double-home turn.

Turn Three, another one needing two engines, worked a variety of jobs (according to which day of the week it was) including another of the overnight trains north of the border. This was the 11.10 pm from Birmingham to Glasgow,

1.05 am ex-Crewe, except on Sundays when this train was covered by Turn Two. The engine returned on the 5.40 pm Glasgow to Euston as far a Crewe. On Sundays and Mondays the turn covered both the Perth trains, but in this case between Euston and Crewe and in both directions, while for the rest of the week one of the engines worked to Euston and back on a day time train, 7.50 am from Crewe and 7.20 pm return – the Inverness and Lairg train. On Saturdays the other engine worked the 11.25 am ex-Birmingham which left Crewe at 1.15 pm; the engine returned the following day, a Sunday, on the 10.15 am departure from Glasgow to Euston as far as Crewe where it was due at 2.17 pm, the summer relief 'Royal Scot'.

Turn Four required three engines and covered the West Coast Postal between Euston and Crewe in both directions seven days a week, along with the first of the morning Birmingham to Glasgow trains returning on the 9.30 am Glasgow to Euston the following day.

Turn Five utilised two more Pacifics, one covering the West Coast Postal in both directions between Crewe and Glasgow, the other the overnight Inverness train south of Crewe, returning on the 5 20 pm from Euston as far as Crewe – this was a Holyhead train.

Although, nominally at least, the Crewe turns could be covered by any Pacific, either a Coronation or a Princess Royal,

Another Pacific waiting at the north end of Crewe station to take the down 'Mid-Day Scot' forward to Glasgow; once again unfortunately the view is undated. In this case it is 46244 KING GEORGE VI with the Plymouth through coach, albeit on this occasion a London Midland vehicle and not a Great Western one. Although this is a Camden engine on a cyclic diagram this train was almost always worked by Crewe North men on both legs of its journey, that is Euston-Crewe and Crewe-Glasgow and in both directions. The 2P 4-4-0 to the left will almost certainly be either 40659 or 40660, Crewe North residents for a very long time and usually to be found on various duties around the north end of the station and shed. Photograph R.C.Williams, www.transporttreasury.co.uk

in practice the Perth jobs were always covered by a Coronation. These engines had the benefit of a higher coal capacity, coal pushers and were slightly more powerful and certainly more consistent in how they could be handled. If a Princess Royal found its way onto a Perth job, which on rare occasions they did, there were long faces on the men involved!

I will not go through all the 1951 summer Camden diagrams, other than to mention that there were twelve locomotives required on a daily basis and the allocation numbered sixteen, which at the time included the turbine driven 46202. The turbine was diagrammed to work the 8.30 am Euston to Liverpool and the 5.25 pm back on a daily basis. It does not take much imagination however, to work out that to allow for any maintenance this diagram would often have to be covered by another engine and in any event 46202 was out of service for the entire period! In fact it was already in Crewe Works and a decision was soon made to convert it to a conventional locomotive. Generally the Camden engines worked between Euston and Carlisle only, but in the summer of 1951 they were diagrammed to work the 'Royal Scot' right through in both directions; interestingly, Crewe North men worked it in the down direction

from Crewe to Glasgow and south of Crewe in the up direction. Another point of interest is that 46256 and 46257 had a Turn for which they were specifically allocated, although it only needed one of them at a time. This covered the down Mid-Day Scot between Euston and Carlisle returning with an overnight train at 1.06 am, the 10.25 pm from Glasgow, with the engine changed alongside Carlisle No.12 signal box as the train had no commercial reason to stop at the station – it was due in Euston at 7.35 am. While North Shed men worked the down train north of Crewe, the return working was a Carlisle double-home turn right through to Euston.

In view of the miles accumulated there would almost always be two of the combined London Midland allocation of the Coronation and Princess Royal engines undergoing the No.8 mileage exam at Crewe North. With at least another two in main works from the combined allocation it will be seen that of the forty engines of the fleet on the London Midland Region, only 36 would be available, minus those undergoing normal shed maintenance and/or stopped for any other out of course reason. At the very least this would amount to another three, reducing the potential number available to 33, before any other contingencies

are considered. Another point worth noting in connection with the 1951 situation is how slow the timings of the trains were. Remember however, that the railway system was still recovering from wartime neglect of the signalling, structures and track not to mention the locos and a return to anything like the pre-war standards of train timing was still some way off.

For any readers wanting a better understanding of the science of locomotive diagramming, if it can be described thus, I would recommend a paper read before the Institution of Locomotive Engineers by L.C. Welborn, AMI Loco E titled *Locomotive Diagramming & Utilisation with Reference to British Railways*. At the time Welborn was Shedmaster at Polmadie and he first read his paper before the Institution in London on 21 April 1954. Together with details of the ensuing discussion, which is in fact as interesting as the paper itself, a copy can be found in the *Journal* of the Institution Vol. 44 Part 3 of 1954. Copies of the Journal can be seen in the library of the Institution of Mechanical Engineers, 1 Birdcage Walk, Westminster. Although for members use, a phone call to the Librarian is usually all that is necessary to arrange a visit.

46245 CITY OF LONDON, leaving Carlisle on 18 April 1955 with the up 'Royal Scot'. A Camden engine at the time, it would have come on the train here and be working through to London with a Camden crew on a double-home lodging turn; they would have come north the previous day on the down train. At this time I think the job was shared on alternate days by Camden and Carlisle Upperby men with their own engines. The early railcar on the left is one of the 'Derby Lightweights' which in all probability would have arrived at Carlisle from the Cumbrian coast, probably Workington. Photograph J. Robertson, www.transporttreasury.co.uk

Another of George Wheeler's portraits, at Camden shed with 46245 CITY OF LONDON, probably brought outside specially for George's camera as it does not appear to be in steam. The date will be some time between December 1957 when this engine received the maroon livery with LMS style lining along with the Smith-Stone speedometer and March 1959 when AWS was fitted. The engine in the background just emerging from the shed is Holyhead Britannia 70049, complete with 'The Irish Mail' headboard so the photograph was probably taken in the early evening. The Holyhead train left Euston around 9 pm – it varied slightly over the years – to connect with the overnight boat to the Emerald Isle. Photograph the late George Wheeler.

Crewe North's 46248 CITY OF LEEDS at Polmadie shed on 14 August 1958. This was one of the first to be painted by BR in maroon, in this case in June 1958 and unlike some of its contemporaries, it was only ever in this livery with the LMS style lining. It had probably come north on a overnight train and may well be laying over to return on a night train too. It was soon after this that the maroon engines were concentrated at sheds which predominantly worked day time trains. Because most of those worked by Crewe North were night diagrams, the allocation there was made up largely of engines that remained painted green. Why go to the extra expense of painting them red if they were sitting around in shed yards during most of the daylight hours, hidden from an admiring public, or so the argument went! Photograph A.G. Forsyth, Initial Photographics.

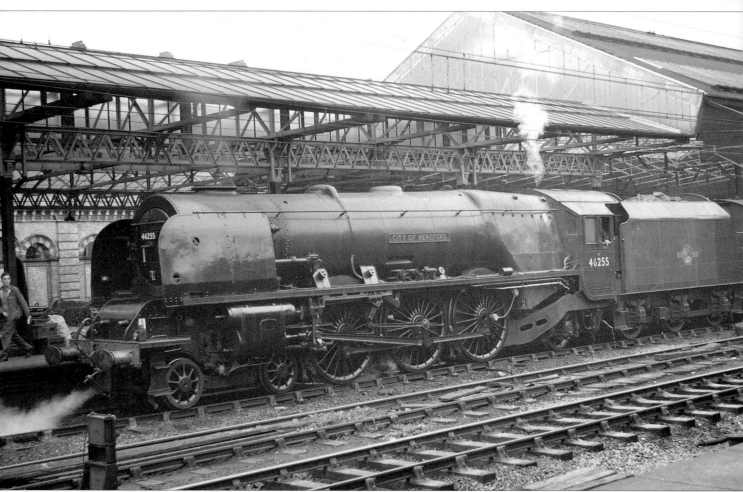

Left. The down 'Royal Scot' snaking its way out of Preston station loaded to 14 or 15 coaches plus a van behind 46254 CITY OF STOKE-ON-TRENT, possibly about 1954. It is so dirty that it is impossible to even hazard a guess as to what livery it carries but despite the poor external condition, the load and the gradient (1 in 101 just here) the engine appears to be making light of its work. The fireman is taking a breather but with no sight of any coal in the tender, he will already have shifted quite a bit since leaving London as the engine would be working through from Euston to Carlisle. That is an unusual looking van behind the engine and not a type one would normally see on this train. Photograph R. Butterfield, Initial Photographics.

Bottom left. Platform 4 at the south end of Crewe station on 20 August 1960 with 46255 CITY OF HEREFORD attaching extra vehicles before departing with an up train; notice the engine is in back gear, die-block at the top of the link with reversing arm raised. This was a Carlisle engine at this date although judging by the amount of coal in the tender it may only have come on to the train here. It had only come off an intermediate repair at Crewe on 17 August, or so the records say. In fact it may have been a day or two later as Works Managers were extremely adapt of massaging the statistics when engines were late off works for one reason or another. Notice the patch painting of the tender, a sure indication of an intermediate repair and in fact the last main works repair recorded for this engine. This photograph illustrates well one of the later engines of the class that were never streamlined and in its final condition with a speedometer, AWS equipment and electrification warning notices. Photograph Paul Chancellor Collection.

Below. The down 'Royal Scot' approaching Kings Langley on 9 April 1955 with Camden's 46256 Sir WILLIAM STANIER FRS probably working through to Carlisle.

Quintessential 'Semi', Crewe North July 1949, with 45543 HOME GUARD. With its curious 'block' cab numbers (it has BR correct Gill San smokebox number, but still 7P on the cab) it would be in the post-war LMS lined black, though grime covers any trace of lining. The smokebox has had a good going over but the tender is filthy, suggesting 46221 is ex-works after some untoward or Intermediate repair. Under a glass the original print reveals the 4 of the cab number to be a feebler, undersized numeral compared to the original 6221. QUEEN ELIZABETH had lost her streamlined case in the period ending 13 July 1946 and was renumbered 46221 week ending 23 October 1948. Note small cab window, soon to be enlarged—this can be compared to conventional and other 'de-streamlined' engines. Photograph W. Hermiston, www.transporttreasury.co.uk

3. SOME BACKGROUND

Notes by Ian Sixsmith from the original edition, with a number of original photographs and some new ones

Stanier's range of standard locomotives has come to personify the LMS, and the thinking and practice that suffused it carried over into the Standard locomotives of British Railways. The BR Standards, though they incorporated much advantageous detail work from the other companies' traditions, owed their lineage above all to the LMS, and the rebirth of its locomotive engineering under Stanier.

It all would have been very different but for the chance vagaries of history. George Hughes had succeeded to the office of CME on the conjoining of the L&Y and the LNWR to form a 'super-company' in 1922, anticipating the Grouping of a year later. Schooled in the principles of standardisation, Hughes announced a scheme of six classes for the combined company and after Grouping this was expanded to twelve. E.S. Cox outlined these in 1924 but, as is recorded abundantly elsewhere, only the 5ft 6in 'Crab' (there was also a planned 5ft 1in 2-6-0) appeared, in May 1926. Hughes had retired in the autumn of 1925 and 'the Horwich Mogul' was the only design sufficiently advanced so

that it could not be cancelled or 'Midlandised' out of existence by the Derby camp, the coming force in the LMS mechanical landscape, and set to remain so for the rest of the 1920s.

Stanier was appointed from 1 January 1932 and a charming account of his 'head hunting' (as it would be termed today) is given by H.A.V. Bulleid in his book *Master Builders of Steam* (Ian Allan, 1963). 'Cloak and daggerish' invitations to London clubs were (very properly) reported by Stanier to his boss Collett, who gave his blessing. (Stanier at 55 was only five years younger than Collett, and thus poorly placed to make a mark if the expected succession occurred and nothing untoward took place.) Sir Harold Hartley of the LMS spoke with Stanier, together with Sir Ernest Lemon, who was briefly a 'caretaker' CME after Fowler, before moving on to be Vice President. Hartley is quoted as deciding that *'Stanier was the man to get our locomotive programme straightened out. The number of different types we had inherited was appalling...'*

And this nearly a decade after the company's foundation! Without doubt,

these sentiments would have been put to Stanier, though he would hardly have entered the discussions at the Athenaeum and the Traveller's Club without having a fairly shrewd idea of how locomotive matters were going on the Great Western's huge rival. From the desperation expressed by Hartley, it is not hard to see the origins of the clout Stanier wielded on the LMS. He would have declared to Lemon and Hartley that he needed to carry though something of a revolution, and would never have left Swindon without assurances that there was full backing for such a campaign. Stanier duly made his way to the LMS and began the great task; 'Augean' would be to make far too much of it, though Bulleid's odd but attractive phrase, 'mighty re-stocking' captures it precisely.

Cox's scheme of 1924 had included a Pacific and Fowler, too, had come up with plans for a sort of 'super-Compound' 4-6-2. Stanier's first locomotive (what he thought of the 0-4-4Ts, already underway and coming out in 1932, his first full year of office, would be a treasure) was a 2-6-0, in

The streamliners were a PR man's dream—the Great Western lined up Kings at Swindon and the LNER lined up A4s for *Picture Post*-type spreads but few locomotives had such dramatic, PR-friendly outlines as the new Stanier Pacifics. This was the traditional place for the LMS publicity shot, outside the Paint Shop at Crewe; indeed the LM became so attached to the practice that it even lined up new Ivatt 2-6-0s, hardly the visual equivalents of the streamliners—see *British Railways Illustrated* Vol.1 No.2, December 1991. The glittering trio is made up of the three new engines of June 1937: 6220 CORONATION, 6221 QUEEN ELIZABETH and 6222 QUEEN MARY.

This photograph illustrates the design of bogie used on the engines, in this case in the erecting shop at Crewe waiting to be fitted to 6220 CORONATION. The design was the result of successive developments by Churchward of the Great Western and then Stanier, embracing both American practice and the French de Glehn design. The principles are a combination of the American influence prevalent on the Great Western Railway in Churchward's time, along with experience of the three French de Glehn compound Atlantic locomotives that were imported by the Great Western Railway in 1903 and 1905. With this design the bar side-frames carry no vertical load as the entire weight transfer of the locomotive is via the bolster. This is achieved by semi-spherical brackets mounted on the main frame of the locomotive, sometimes referred to as hemispheres, resting in the two spittoons, as they were referred to, or cups, mounted on extended wings of the bolster. These cups are not fixed to the bolster and are thus allowed to move around on a bronze bearing surface on the bolster wings. The bolster sits on the buckles of two upturned leaf springs, one each side, themselves attached to equalising beams which rest on the top of the axle boxes. By these means the weight of the locomotive is transferred via the springing to the wheelsets. Side control is via the vertical bogie retaining pin (which takes no vertical load) sitting in the centre of the bolster and a series of coil springs. The bar frames serve to retain the axle boxes and therefore the axles in their relative positions and of course, are subject to transverse flange forces transmitted through the axle boxes. Later engines, from 6235 onwards, had some cross bracing added to the bar frames to increase rigidity and the earlier engines had their bogies altered to match. The engine, the front of which can just be seen, along with the bogie stand at the extreme eastern end of No.6 belt in the erecting shop, while the Super D to the left – notice the four LNWR style wheels – is on No.5 belt. At the time the photograph was taken No.6 was the new work belt.

which he wrestled the big, 'partly-Midland', parallel boiler 'Crab' into the taper boiler world of The Way Ahead. The Crab had been very successful, for it was a modern and forward-looking piece of work; it shone, moreover, against some of the designs going into service around it, such as the 'Midland' design 0-6-0 and the 0-8-0.

Stanier's aim in producing this 2-6-0, it seems, was to stamp the principle of the new order straight away, and a request from the Operating people for 'more Crabs' was a convenient way of doing it. Taper boilers were the most marked departure from time-honoured practice and Stanier was thereafter set to establish his rite of passage. This, as for any new CME, was always the same – the newest and latest express passenger locomotive for the line. As an 'import', with the implicit criticism of former policy that that entailed, he must have been particularly aware of the need to 'get it right' from the off. A year and half from taking office the first such engine, a Pacific, emerged. It had four cylinders ('because he was used to it', says Bulleid) and was in many ways the logical progression, in dimension and form, from a 4-6-0. Three of the new Pacifics had been ordered under the 1933 Building Programme; these were the Princess Royal class and thirteen were built in all, in two batches, between the 1933 and 1935 Building Programmes, from 6200 appearing in July 1933 to 6212 in October 1935.

Onward and Upward

More of these elegant Princess Royal Pacifics might have been built but despite the paralysing Slump (though ended in 1933, it still spread its shadow over much of Britain) this had become the decade of speed and sophistication. Something bigger and better was on the stocks but the process of change, from the Princess Royals to the Coronation Pacifics, goes curiously unheralded in the LMS Minutes. The 1937 Building Programme listed 4F 0-6-0s, 3P 2-6-2Ts and diesel shunters, and was agreed on 26 July 1936. Normally such proposals

A bit of fun in the wind tunnel.

6229 (wrongly presumed to be 6220 in the original book) is wheeled into the light for one of those comparisons beloved of the Publicity Department. On the left of course is the Liverpool & Manchester loco LION.

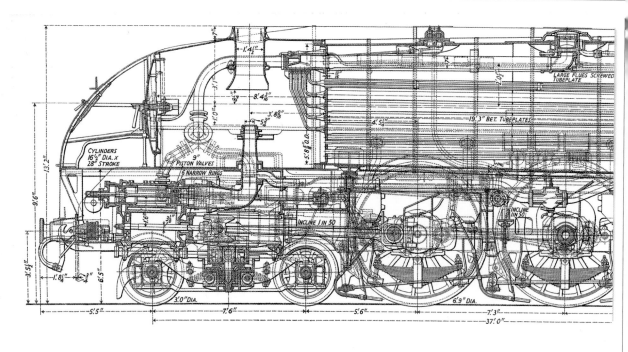

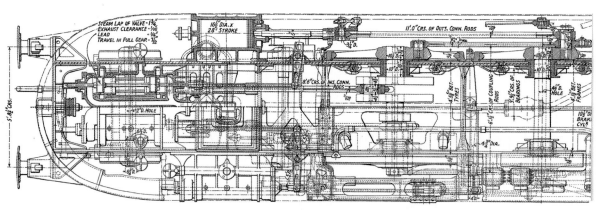

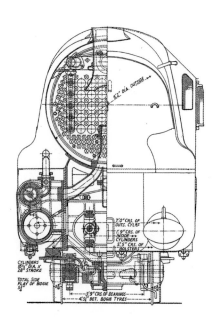

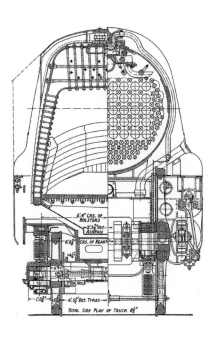

General Arrangement drawings of 6220 CORONATION, with cross sections as they appeared in the technical press at the time the locomotives were first introduced.

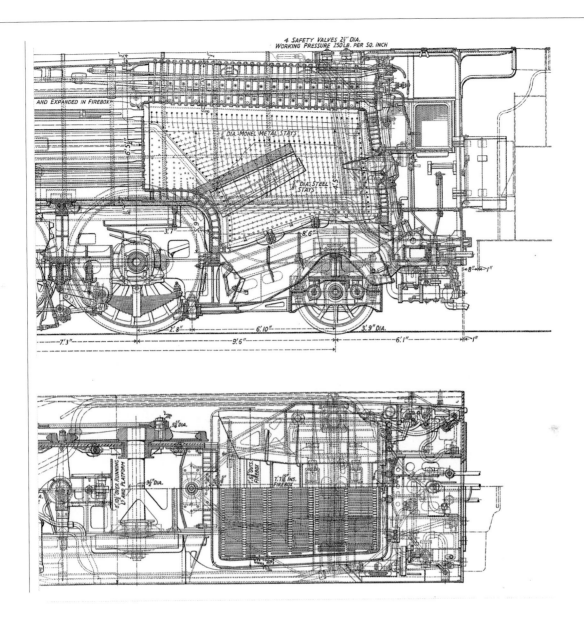

4 SAFETY VALVES 2⅝" DIA.
WORKING PRESSURE 250 LB. PER SQ. INCH

AND EXPANDED IN FIREBOX

DIA. MONEL METAL STAYS

⅞" DIA. STEEL
STAYS

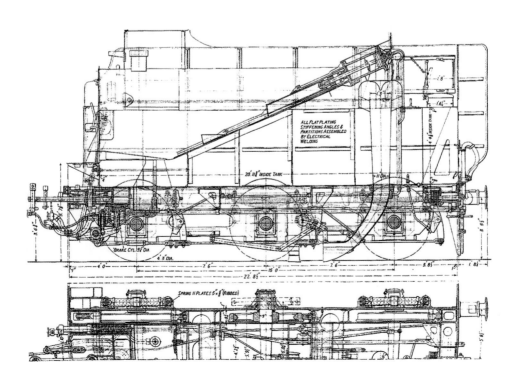

ALL FLAT PLATING
STIFFENING ANGLES &
PARTITIONS ASSEMBLED
BY ELECTRICAL
WELDING

20' 11⅝" INSIDE TANK

BRAKE CYL 9¾" DIA.

SPRING II PLATES 5" × ⅝" (RIBBED)

In its quest for publicity as well as the usual conventional photographs, the LMS arranged for a film to be made of the new locomotive and the 'Coronation Scot' train. Part of the film involved the amazing sight illustrated here with the new engine and train running alongside the former LNWR 1911 built George V class 25348, which was also named CORONATION, although this name was soon removed in deference to the new locomotive. On the extreme left is the Liverpool & Manchester Railway locomotive LION hauling the replica period train that had been built some years earlier. LION had been restored to working order and the replica train vehicles constructed for the 1930 centenary celebrations of the Liverpool & Manchester Railway. Obviously operating constraints made staging this sort of event difficult and it was not possible on any part of the four-track sections of the west coast main line, but on a Sunday morning between Llandudno Junction and Colwyn Bay it could just about be squeezed in. Here we see the filming crew at work on 13 June 1937 with their equipment mounted on a flat wagon in a train hauled by class 2P 4-4-0 number 695; pity the sun did not shine.

went forward to the Board for 'rubber-stamping'. Now, the first five Coronation Pacifics, 6220-6224, were built in 1937 but authority only seems to have been given at a late stage, *after* the 1937 Programme got to the Board. Five more *Princesses* had been envisaged, but memories of West Coast-East Coast speed rivalry were being thoroughly stirred and a series of high speed tests conducted during 1936 proved that better timings on the West Coast were perfectly possible. A degree of secrecy, or at least discretion, was obviously thought prudent. Gresley's three week-old SILVER LINK had reached 112½ mph (twice within ten minutes!) in September 1935, and SILVER FOX 113mph in 1936. The LMS effort was now only a matter of time, and the means to do it would be a class of 'improved Princesses'.

1937: 6220-6224
The first of the new engines, more precisely (and awkwardly - it didn't catch on) called the 'Princess (Coronation) class', came out of Crewe with a 'date

built' of 1 June 1937. This was 6220 CORONATION. The first batch, of five, in 1937, was as follows:

6220 CORONATION
6221 QUEEN ELIZABETH
6222 QUEEN MARY
6223 PRINCESS ALICE
6224 PRINCESS ALEXANDRA

The new Pacifics were very different indeed from the earlier Princesses and something of the way in which they came into being is revealed in the name. An almost covert period of design and construction hid from general view the way the existing Princess design was expanded beyond recognition. Hence the first (amended) official title, which certainly *looked* like an afterthought. A surprising aspect is that Stanier was away for much of the design period; he served in India on the Pacific Locomotive Investigation Committee, leaving it in the hands of assistants, principally Coleman, Riddles and Bond. The boiler was bigger and better, with more superheat, greatly increased firebox and

total heating surface, increased driving wheel diameter (from 6ft 6in to 6ft 9in) and a greater diameter boiler at the firebox end. There were four cylinders again, but an arrangement of rocking levers (the work of Coleman) drove the inside valves from the outside motion. This gave the Coronations two sets of valve gear instead of four. Through this arrangement the outside cylinders could be positioned in a more conventional and satisfying way, between the bogie wheels. (On the preceding Princess Royals they were sited over the trailing bogie wheel.) The disposition had an added advantage, in that the leading flange of the outside cylinders overlapped the rear flange of the inside cylinder casting, imparting great rigidity where such multi-cylinder locomotives had traditionally been prone to weakness. As well as saving weight, getting rid of some of the inside gear saved a constant labour of oiling and maintenance, while the general imperative was to lose weight even as the design expanded to the very limits of loading and gauge. Yet it was, above all, *reliability* that Stanier was after and there was no radical departure from current practice, so far as the materials of construction were concerned. The engine embodied all that was best in modern practice, allied to whatever advantages that modern metallurgical developments offered.

6220 ran a special for the gentlemen of the press on 29 June 1937 to demonstrate what was possible between Euston and Crewe. This led to the celebrated braking incident just south of Crewe. 6220 touched 114mph (some made it 113mph, only the equal of the LNER record) and but for the limited distance available for braking it would have been more conclusive. Rowledge mentions the unfortunate effect on the crockery and Bulleid refers to Lemon bracing his feet on the opposite seat in anticipation of the inevitable derailment.

From this time on, though they were overshadowed by the speedier activities to the east, the Coronation Pacifics established (in the eyes of many) their station as the most powerful and impressive of all the British Pacifics. There are many technical arguments as to which class brought engineering innovation, combined with subtlety of thought and brilliance of design, together with success on the road to a pinnacle of achievement in this country, but that in a sense is a redundant art. Few now even have the rudiments of steam locomotive design and the men responsible for the Pacifics of the 1930s and those who honed such machines through to the 1950s were towering figures in their field. Stanier, after all, was made a Fellow of the Royal Society.

As one raised from the first on East Coast Pacifics, I can attest to the sheer eye-popping majesty of these vast things (all were 'Duchesses' to us) when first visited upon the impressionable mind. Somehow, no other locomotives in Britain contrived to expand and flow outwards to so completely fill the loading gauge, and somehow dwarf anything around them. Thus the Crewe term the 'Big 'Uns' was justly earned.

That Streamlining

It was the engineering which made the 'Improved Princesses' such a success, not the streamlining, which we can now see to have had little more efficacy that the 'go-faster' airfoil on a family car. The LMS streamlining suffered aesthetically too (at least it seems that way to us now), though this might have a deal to do with having 'come second' in the speed stakes. The LNER had got there first of course, in all senses and while to many the streamlining sits well on the A4, the Stanier version has a rather unfortunate 'bulbosity'. The fact is, far fewer people actually remember that LMS streamlining, though the NRM has now brought it into focus once more – perfectly pointlessly in my humble opinion.

It is generally agreed that the LMS streamlining was for publicity reasons and nothing else, whatever technical arguments might have been advanced. Without the PR people 'inquiring as to what might be done' Stanier would hardly have given it a thought. The new engines would power a new high speed train, the Coronation Scot from Euston to Glasgow and streamlining, for the locomotive at least, was *de rigueur*. The fact of streamlining mattered hardly a jot, but it would just have to be used, in keeping with the current public mood. Bulleid in his *Master Builders of Steam* describes a scene in which Coleman ('one of us' in the new order, and highly effective Chief Draughtsman; a Stoke man in charge of both Derby and Crewe!) comes up with a suitable form of casing and the drawings duly go off to Crewe. Vice President Hartley, anxious to be thoroughly up to date, urges Stanier to conduct wind tunnel tests to determine the best shape. This is carried out and Coleman's shape (already 'done and dusted' and being proceeded with at Crewe) inevitably turns out to be the best. The famous Lady Godiva story dates from this time; doubts about the suitability of the streamlining filtered down from the Board and Coleman drew a conventional version, duly named Lady Godiva. The streamlining went ahead.

1938: 6225-6234

New 'Princess (Coronation)' engines were soon on the way and it was not long before the more sensible term 'Coronation' was in use. This is a Mechanical and Electrical Engineering Committee Minute of 27 October 1937:

'Locomotive Programme 1938. Construction of ten additional Passenger Engines and retention in service of engines previously authorised for displacement.

Submitted memorandum (October 1937) from the Chief Operating Manager and Chief Mechanical Engineer, recommending that to meet increased demands in engine power due to the increase in volume of traffic, ten additional Class 7 4-6-2 express passenger tender locomotives (Coronation type) be provided at a total approximate outlay of £138,000, the expenditure to be dealt with in conjunction with the 1938 Rolling Stock Building Programme and reported on completion of that Programme. It was also recommended that certain locomotives

LION and 6229 DUCHESS OF HAMILTON (that's what the nameplate says) in primer at Crewe Works in 1938.

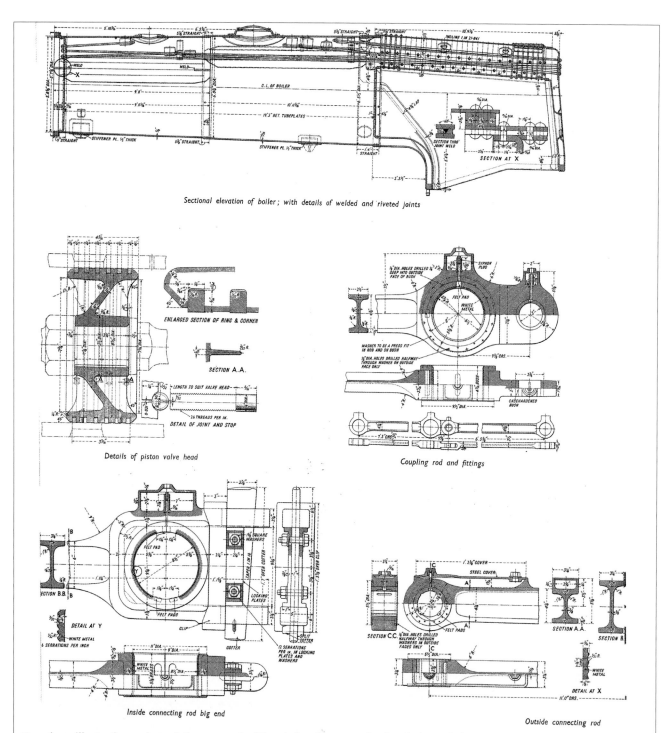

Sectional elevation of boiler; with details of welded and riveted joints

Details of piston valve head

Coupling rod and fittings

Inside connecting rod big end

Outside connecting rod

Drawings illustrating a few of the more significant developments in the design of these locomotives from the earlier Princess Royal class. They accompanied the General Arrangement drawing on pages 38-39 in the contemporary technical press and were doubtless specially prepared by the LMS for that purpose.

already approved for breaking up should be retained, where retention would be possible without the necessity of building new boilers, the actual retentions being reported in due course and reviewed periodically.

'The Executive Committee had approved the proposal and with the Chairman's authority arrangements had been made, in anticipation of the approval of the Directors, for the necessary material for the proposed ten new engines to be ordered.

'To permit of the Class 7 engines running between Crewe and Manchester, and Holyhead, it was proposed to reconstruct Bridge No.90 between Handford and Cheadle Hulme, over which there was at present a

speed restriction, and a separate recommendation would be made in due course to the Works Committee. The bridges at Llanfairfechan and Queensferry on the line between Chester and Holyhead, which were also restricted, were now being reconstructed.

'Approved, so far as the Mechanical and Electrical Engineering Committee was concerned.'

The ten the LMS got for its £138,000 were the 'Duchesses' (by which name most of us habitually called all of them in the 1950s and 1960s), as follows:

6225 DUCHESS OF GLOUCESTER
6226 DUCHESS OF NORFOLK
6227 DUCHESS OF DEVONSHIRE
6228 DUCHESS OF RUTLAND
6229 DUCHESS OF HAMILTON
All Streamlined

6230 DUCHESS OF BUCCLEUCH
6231 DUCHESS OF ATHOLL
6232 DUCHESS OF MONTROSE
6233 DUCHESS OF SUTHERLAND
6234 DUCHESS OF ABERCORN
All Non-streamlined

They appeared between May and September and the crucial change was that some, 6230-6234, were built without

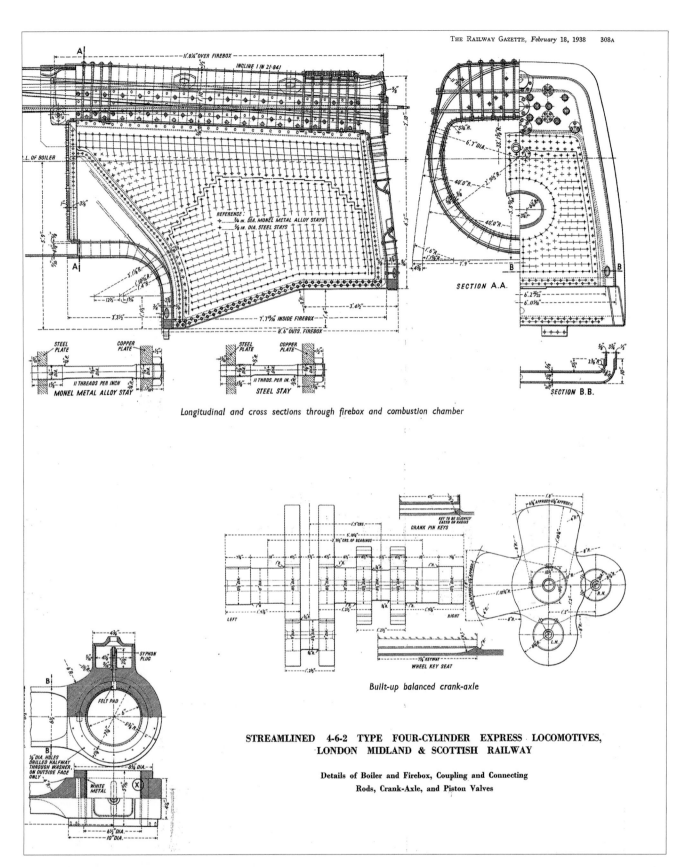

Longitudinal and cross sections through firebox and combustion chamber

Built-up balanced crank-axle

STREAMLINED 4-6-2 TYPE FOUR-CYLINDER EXPRESS LOCOMOTIVES, LONDON MIDLAND & SCOTTISH RAILWAY

Details of Boiler and Firebox, Coupling and Connecting
Rods, Crank-Axle, and Piston Valves

the streamlined casing, but without smoke deflectors. The problem of smoke blowing down and obscuring drivers' vision was yet to manifest itself. Double chimneys, as and when they were fitted were probably also a factor, as with the Gresley A3s. Essery and Jenkinson (*An Illustrated History of LMS Locomotives*, Silver Link, 1989) recount a story of Riddles' at the time; Stanier apparently made little secret of his scepticism regarding streamlining and

simply determined to build 'five proper ones too'.

'...a little over 2%'
Now that there were engines in both streamlined and conventional form, comparisons were inevitably there to be made. Did it make any difference for a start? The Engineering Section of the Research Department at Derby issued a *Memorandum* on 25 October 1938, detailing coal consumption between the

streamlined and non-streamlined 1938 engines, 6225-6228 and 6230-6334 respectively. (6229 was still under construction while the comparisons were being made.) All the engines were put on Camden jobs, including the Coronation Scot, for the sake of the comparison. Coal consumption figures for the eight week period had not showed the streamlined engines in a particularly favourable light; Derby nevertheless provided wind tunnel

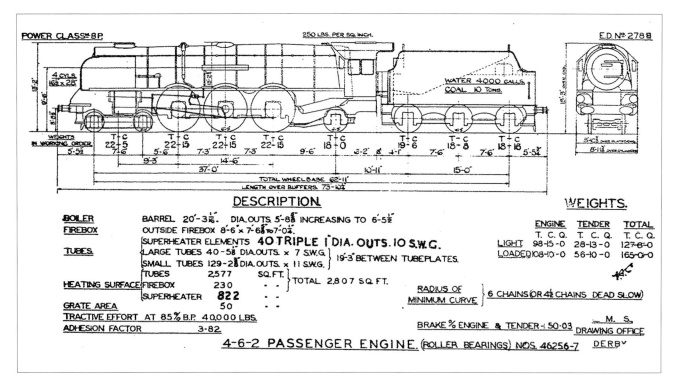

POWER CLASS 8P · 250 LBS. PER SQ. INCH. · E.D. No. 2788

DESCRIPTION.

			WEIGHTS.
BOILER	BARREL 20'-3½. DIA. OUTS. 5'-8⅝ INCREASING TO 6'-5½		
FIREBOX	OUTSIDE FIREBOX 8'-6" x 7'-6⅝ to 7'-0⅞.		
	SUPERHEATER ELEMENTS 40 TRIPLE 1" DIA. OUTS. 10 S.W.G.		
TUBES	LARGE TUBES 40-5⅞ DIA. OUTS. x 7 S.W.G.	19'-3 BETWEEN TUBEPLATES.	
	SMALL TUBES 129-2⅛ DIA. OUTS. x 11 S.W.G.		
	TUBES 2,577 SQ. FT.	TOTAL 2,807 SQ. FT.	
HEATING SURFACE	FIREBOX 230 " "		
	SUPERHEATER 822 " "		
GRATE AREA	50 " "		
TRACTIVE EFFORT AT 85% B.P. 40,000 LBS.			
ADHESION FACTOR	3·82		

WEIGHTS.

	ENGINE	TENDER	TOTAL
	T. C. Q.	T. C. Q.	T. C. Q.
LIGHT	98-15-0	28-13-0	127-8-0
LOADED	108-10-0	56-10-0	165-0-0

RADIUS OF MINIMUM CURVE } 6 CHAINS (OR 4½ CHAINS DEAD SLOW)

BRAKE % ENGINE & TENDER = 50·03

M. S. DRAWING OFFICE DERBY

4-6-2 PASSENGER ENGINE. (ROLLER BEARINGS) NOS. 46256-7

results that showed it did. These 'proved', on computation of 'still air' conditions, a given coal consumption figure, mileages and average speeds, that a 'predicted saving' in coal was inevitable. For the more everyday Camden jobs, this saving varied from 7.72 to 12.79 tons per four week period, and for the Coronation Scot, 11.82 tons every four weeks; near-enough 150 tons a year over a non-streamlined engine.

Results obtained the traditional way had indicated the *opposite*, but Derby had

the answers. The coaling plant records were notoriously inaccurate, it was declared, while the error due to spillage was compounded in the case of the streamlined engines by the shape of the tenders: *'The error due to spillage during the coaling operation is more serious with streamlined locomotives than with others, leading to an apparent coal consumption greater than the actual. The cover over the front end of the tender of the streamlined locomotives directly spills any coal which accidentally falls on it, and such spillage*

may be appreciable since the engine crew try to fill the tender as far forward as possible. At best some empty space under the cover remains, and in the endeavour to compensate for it, coal is piled as high as permissible over the rest of the tender bunker which leads, it is said, to a proportion of spillage that is especially marked with streamlined engines.'

Derby protested that consumption figures used to show that there was in fact *no* difference between conventional and streamlined engines were not

6223 PRINCESS ALICE leaving Euston with the Coronation Scot. The name CORONATION (and the train of course) celebrated King George VI's Coronation of 1937 and the other four of that 1937 batch continued the theme, as it were. They were all named after the immediate Royal Family—the Queen, the Queen Mother—and two Princesses who had not had a Princess Royal Pacific named after them.

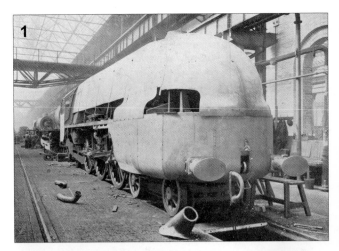

1. CORONATION under erection in the erecting shop at Crewe with other engines of the class behind.

2. The left-hand side driving wheels and motion of 6220 under construction. The speedometer equipment is already in position driven from the trailing crankpin and the lower sections of the streamline casing are in the process of being fitted. With the first engine of the class I wager there was some very strong language among the fitters, along with bruised knuckles, as they struggled with all those angles and curves, painfully gaining experience in fitting all the casing parts.

3. Looking east in the erecting shop at Crewe with the main frames of 6220 complete with smokebox. The smokebox would be in place as part of the 'fitting' process although it would later be removed and mounted on the boiler for the complete assembly to be placed in position on the frames. Being the first engine of the class erection would take longer as it would be inevitable that some design matters would crop up and as experience was gained, gradually eliminated in later construction. Notice the engine has a conventional foot framing which indicates that somebody had in mind that one day the streamlining might be removed. This of course enabled the de-streamlining process to be relatively simple. I was told many years ago, by one who would have known, that when consideration was given to de-frocking the LNER A4 Pacifics after the war, it was the design of the casing, with no thought at the design stage of it ever being removed, that made the costs such that it was decided to continue to suffer the drawbacks of difficult access.

4. The main frames of 6220 CORONATION complete with cylinders in the erecting shop at Crewe. This view illustrates well the main frame extension at the rear cantilevered from the main section. Notice the axle boxes are in place; this would be part of the 'fitting' process as they would later be removed and mounted on the axles. After this the engine would be 'wheeled', as the terminology went. Engines were always wheeled with the axle boxes on the axle journals and not already in position in the horn guides. That is the exhaust injector under the frame to the extreme left.

5

6

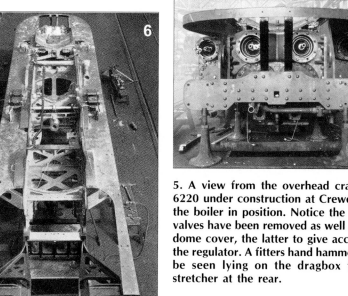

7

5. A view from the overhead crane of 6220 under construction at Crewe with the boiler in position. Notice the safety valves have been removed as well as the dome cover, the latter to give access to the regulator. A fitters hand hammer can be seen lying on the dragbox frame stretcher at the rear.

6. The main frames of 6220, a photograph taken from one of the overhead cranes in the No.10 erecting shop at Crewe. In this view the frame stretchers are well illustrated along with the rear end frame extension, designed like this to take the large firebox and trailing truck.

8

7. Front end view of 6220 under construction at Crewe. The four cylinders are clearly visible with the piston valve tail rods showing as well as the pipe work for the Fowler-Anderson cylinder by-pass valves for the inside cylinders seen underneath the buffer beam. It is a complete mystery why these valves were fitted to the first five engines of the class and one can only assume somebody with an axe to grind and not yet converted to the new design principles introduced by Stanier, got their hands on this part of the design. I bet Stanier and no less Tom Coleman, were not amused when they found out, by which time it was perhaps too late to do anything about it except to ensure they were not fitted to subsequent examples!

8. The boiler for 6220 complete with smokebox and most of the lagging ready to be mounted on the frames. Most of the backhead fittings are in place as the boiler would have been steam tested in the boiler shop. The practice of slinging large items like this was an art in itself. While the draughtsman might indicate the best place to lift in the weight calculations on the drawings, it would be left to the men on the spot to fine tune it by trial and error. With just a single crane, an enormously heavy item like a boiler would be perfectly balanced.

9   10

9. Front view of 6220 CORONATION posed in its special coat of paint for photographic purposes.

10. This view shows well the method of access to the smokebox on the first engine of the class, 6220 CORONATION. One wonders if there was ever a case of these doors when open, being damaged by movements of locomotives on adjacent shed roads. I would be very surprised if this didn't happen somewhere or other!

12. The coal space in the tender of 6220 CORONATION, illustrating clearly the coal pusher mechanism. A piston in the cylinder in the rear centre moved the four rams; that is, the two large ones in the centre and the two small ones, one each side the cylinder to the rear, along the slides mounted on the floor of the bunker. The practice was to move the piston backwards and forwards several times which had the effect of shaking the coal forwards rather that strictly pushing it. To operate the pusher it was first necessary to open a steam valve on the boiler backhead and then operate a regulator mounted on the tender front plate. Movement of the regulator backwards and forwards fairly rapidly would shake the coal down the bunker. Occasionally the rams would get stuck in the slides; we would delight in watching the shed labourers empting the tender before we could get in to see what the problem was!

11. Rear view of the tender of 6220 CORONATION. The sides extended back beyond the end of the tender as part of the streamlining. This resulted in the need for a ladder to gain access. When the tenders were de-streamlined this method of access was retained, differentiating these tenders from those that were never streamlined. The piston valve for the coal pusher is behind the small cover to the top centre.

13. Almost complete, 6220 CORONATION in the erecting shop at Crewe with the second engine of the class, 6221 QUEEN ELIZABETH, just visible behind. Notice by the front of the engine the streamline shroud for the buffer, also that the straps holding the streamline casing over the boiler are already in position.

properly obtained, in that they were not comparing like with like. The streamlined engines covered less miles and the coal consumption figures were given for five non-streamlined engines, while only four (6229 was missing remember) were on trial. Consumption varied (questions had been asked in high places and they didn't come much higher than the Chief Operating Manager and the Chief Accountant) with the same locomotive on different jobs, and between different locomotives of the same group on the same job far beyond that attributable to streamlining, for any number of reasons. The steam locomotive was just *like* that, and 6227 and 6228 for instance, showed a difference of over 14% on some jobs and nearly 23% on others, depending on driver, weather, steaming and any number of other foibles. The interesting figure, that Derby was convinced of, was that, with all these factors stripped

away, streamlining gave a coal consumption advantage of 'a little over 2%'. At this, Stanier probably smiled a bit.

No.6225, new on 11 May 1938, ran a special train between Euston and Glasgow on 8 June, in connection with a meeting of the Institution of Locomotive Engineers held in Glasgow. It was proposed to put on something of a show for visiting officials of the German State Railways (Germany had earlier loomed large in the speed contests, with 124½ mph (200.4 kph) in 1935, with Borsig 4-6-4 05.001) and the special left Euston with these guests and the members of the Institution. The dynamometer car was attached 'in order that observations could be made by the party en route, and that a complete dynamometer car test could be made.' DUCHESS OF GLOUCESTER had run 3,502 miles since new and steamed throughout 'very satisfactorily'. A

schedule of 6 hours 55 minutes gave an average speed of 58.5mph while the actual average was 59.2mph. Steaming was very free, with full boiler pressure maintained 'without difficulty'. Maximum drawbar horsepower registered between Tebay and Shap was 830, and between Beattock and Beattock Summit 1,153. Maximum speed was 88mph approaching Euxton Junction, south of Preston. Train weight was only 232 tons but the outing made the show it was meant to. The LMS Report concluded *'In consideration of the total weight of the engine and train, and the high average speed, the results obtained, both on the Drawbar Horse Power basis and in general, indicate exceptional economy'*. The truly spectacular feats of haulage were to come the following year, heralding what was to come in the War; whatever, there certainly wouldn't be any more German passengers for a while...

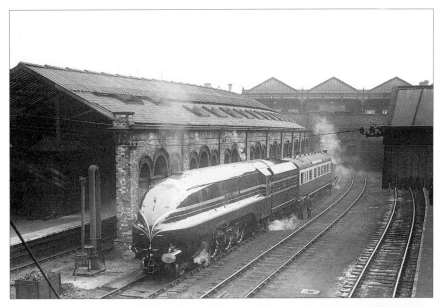

Top. Exquisitely shining 6227 DUCHESS OF DEVONSHIRE at Crewe about 1938; an unusual view, the engine has charge of a single coach, with a 3F 0-6-0T at the other end. The explanation is that the coach is a GWR through vehicle to Scotland, collected by the South pilot and propelled onto 6227 waiting to take over a Euston-Scotland train. The coach would be on the front going north and on the rear coming back, ready for despatch to that strange country ruled by the GWR, while the Euston express hurried south.

Left. Born into dull black for 6248, to traffic in October 1943 and bearing the name first carried by 6244. An excellent view of the hollowed out axles. In the midst of darkness, this was nonetheless the *eleventh* streamlined Pacific of the War—*Kreigslokomotiv* it wasn't.

Below. 6235 CITY OF BIRMINGHAM, the first of the City series, after 'de-streamlining'; an official record presumably taken in 1946, when the casing was removed. 6235 was one of three with crests, or rather coats of arms, placed above the nameplate. 6240 and 6254 were the others, and CORONATION itself had a crown. The curious notch in the boiler cladding had no other purpose than to provide room for the mechanical lubricator lids to be lifted clear, as described earlier.

6221 QUEEN ELIZABETH in its blue livery at Edinburgh Princes Street in 1937. Pre-war, the LMS competed with the LNER for the Edinburgh-Glasgow business, even though its route via Shotts was more difficult. By 1939 there was one train, the 1.30pm Glasgow Central to Edinburgh Princes Street, that did the run in 61 minutes non-stop. The trains had Restaurant Cars and the most powerful locomotives were employed—for the Coronations these were daytime fill in turns, and this practice continued after the War's end. The 'streamlined' lamps are worth a chuckle; the curious 'flag' on the top lamp bracket is a purely Scottish device dating from Caledonian days—the correct Caley term was 'semaphore route indicator'. It indicated the route to be followed, which in the context of Edinburgh would denote Glasgow or Carlisle. They could even be seen on Britannia and Clan Pacifics, well into the 1950s. Photograph P. Ransome Wallis.

6234 and double chimneys

Nevertheless, in the inauspicious year of 1939 a truly awe-inspiring feat demonstrated just what a Coronation could do. Whether in any way it anticipated the sort of work the locos would indeed be called upon to do in the Second World War is not known – probably not, because a number were removed to 'store' in safer climes on the outbreak of hostilities, only to be brought back after a few weeks when someone realised how daft it was. Rowledge in *The LMS Pacifics* and Allen before him, in *British Pacific Locomotives*, describes how 6234 DUCHESS OF ABERCORN, newly modified with double blastpipe and chimney, took twenty coaches (a little over 600 tons) from Crewe to Glasgow on 26 February 1939, returning to Crewe after a couple of hours, with no special attention at Polmadie in the meantime. It was designed to emulate a run in normal service, and the train began the return from Glasgow after just two hours. The trip was full of superlatives, particularly 6234's effort in taking the train, more than twice the load of the Coronation Scot, from Glasgow to Carlisle in only 90 seconds over the schedule of that prestigious train. It was glory-and-trumpets stuff, with an unprecedented

maximum drawbar horsepower of 2,511 southbound from Carlisle (with Crewe men).

DUCHESS OF ABERCORN had been tested only a fortnight before in its single chimney state, with the same load, and the performance had been lack-lustre by comparison. It had proved impossible to keep time or full steam pressure; the contrast was so dramatic that double blastpipes were immediately seen as a most desirable modification. The 1939 engines (and all subsequently) accordingly emerged new with the double chimney. All the existing single chimney engines were converted as soon as maybe - all were done before the end of the War.

1939: 6235-6239

This conventional batch of 1938, 6230-6234, was doubtless the way Stanier would have liked the rest to appear, but once streamlining had taken such a hold it was difficult to shake it off - the 2% figure seems to have 'stuck'. Bulleid in his *Master Builders of Steam* does not mention the streamlining business discussed above but does give a short account of the Research Department and Stanier's relations with it. The Research people were 'inclined to become theoretical' he says, and Stanier found

it 'distant and ponderous'. They had a shorter, easier, line of access to the Vice President and Stanier 'got slightly cross...'

The 1939 Building Programme was approved on 27 July 1938 and gave authority for twenty further Coronations, described as '7P Pacifics' at a cost of £243,000. The earlier batch of ten, 6225-6234, as we've seen above, was still under construction but, it was noted, there was still plenty of work for such engines, 'having regard to the weight of the express passenger trains on which it is proposed to use them, and the speeds at which they are timed'.

The twenty approved in July 1938 were the 'City' ones; as long ago as 1928 Fowler had reported that building new locomotives in the same year in which they were authorised had become impossible and by 1939 other factors were beginning to bear. The country had already avoided what seemed like certain war in 1938 but in the summer of 1939 it was finally apparent to all who could see that it would, indeed, come. Plans were made even back in 1938 (as touched upon above) to put big express locomotives into store when war came, in the belief that no 'ordinary' passenger trains would be run. These plans were dusted off in the summer of 1939, so it was hardly surprising that production of Coronations at Crewe should falter somewhat. In the event only five, all streamlined, came out in 1939:

6235 CITY OF BIRMINGHAM
6236 CITY OF BRADFORD
6237 CITY OF BRISTOL
6238 CITY OF CARLISLE
6239 CITY OF CHESTER

1940: 6240-6244

The Building Programme for 1940, promulgated on 28 June 1939, foresaw no Pacifics. The programme of twenty streamlined engines approved in 1938 was well behind and only five more came out in 1940, all streamlined. These appeared between March and July and it is perhaps surprising that streamlining was retained. The magic figure of 2% saving in coal, perhaps, still held sway over increased awkwardness of servicing and repair. The LNER, remember, took the A4s' sideskirts off pretty quick, and they never returned. Indeed, few engines could look more sorry for themselves than a streamlined Coronation at the War's end, unkempt and tired. It was the same with the A4s, for streamlining suffered disproportionately in the face of neglect.

The five streamlined Coronations produced in 1940 were:

6240 CITY OF COVENTRY
6241 CITY OF EDINBURGH
6242 CITY OF GLASGOW
6243 CITY OF LANCASTER
6244 CITY OF LEEDS (renamed KING GEORGE VI April 1941)

The LMS *War Report* (published after the War but still labelled 'secret') made these comments: *'The succession of air raid warnings during the autumn - winter months of 1940, coupled with the restrictive effect of black-out conditions, had increased the difficulties of the engine power position,*

and in a review prepared for submission to the Minister of War Transport on the locomotive position on the railways during 1940, reference was made to the serious over-taxing of freight engines. On account of the shortage of materials, the locomotive building programmes had not come up to expectations; the actual building completed during the year was described as "trifling". The LMS deliveries of new engines had not exceeded 24, making a total output from the Company's shops of 40 engines since the beginning of the war.'

1943: 6245-6248

The Second World War thoroughly interrupted and upset the Pacific programme on the LMS and came close to choking it off altogether. Had not War broken out doubtless more would have been built and there would not have been such a curiously low total of Pacifics on the West Coast. Assuredly, too, the planned bigger versions would have come to fruition. A Minute of the Mechanical and Electrical Engineering Committee of 24 April 1941 describes the position: *'The locomotives authorised under the 1939 and 1940 Locomotive Renewal Programmes and the Special Programme authorised by Board Minute had not yet been constructed and ... the Chief Mechanical Engineer anticipated 208 locomotives would be completed prior to 31st December 1942 leaving 108 locomotives to be built in 1943 to complete existing authorised programmes. To be built prior to 31st December 1942:*

Class 8 2-8-0 freight tender	*93*
Class 5 4-6-0 mixed traffic tender	*35*
0-6-0 diesel electric shunting	*59*
Class 4 2-6-4 passenger tank	*13*
Class 7 4-6-2 passenger tender	*8*

To be built during 1943:

0-6-0 diesel electrical shunting	*61*
Class 4 2-6-4 passenger tank	*45*
Class 7 4-6-2 passenger tender	*2*

These last two were to have 'experimental features' which included a boiler pressure of 300lb/sq.in., more superheat and other improvements. This was not really feasible in wartime but would at last see completion of the batch of twenty approved way back in 1938 - but no. The report continues: *'Having regard to the necessity for continuity of production, entailing the ordering of material well in advance, it was considered inadvisable to cancel the authority already obtained for building engines which would be delivered by the end of 1942, nor would it be advisable to cancel the authority for the 0-6-0 diesel electric shunting engines in view of the fact that the chassis only were being built in the company's workshop and the diesel engines and electrical equipment were obtained from outside contractors.*

'It was however recommended that the authority for building the 45 class 4 2-6-4 passenger tank engines and the 2 class 7 4-6-2 passenger tender engines be cancelled and a new programme be put forward for 1943 when the position could be reconsidered in the light of the circumstances then prevailing.'

As it turned out, no new Pacifics would come until 1943, and then only four, and streamlined to boot! One, 6248, would keep its casing barely *three* years:

6245 CITY OF LONDON
6246 CITY OF MANCHESTER
6247 CITY OF LIVERPOOL
6248 CITY OF LEEDS

'The position for locomotives had become much more favourable during 1943, and reached a higher level than at any time since the outbreak of the war' declares the LMS *War Report*. The improvement was due to the loan of American and WD engines and the fact that no more engines had to be released for Government use. The four streamlined Pacifics built in 1943,

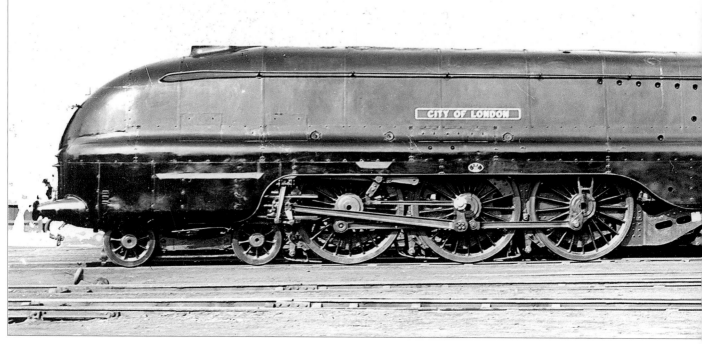

as we have seen, were long overdue from the 1939 Programme, approved in 1938. Along with twenty Class Fives and a pair of 2-6-4Ts from the same programme and a hundred or more 8Fs from the 1940 and 1943 Programmes, these were described as 'Supplementations to the Locomotive Stock'.

1944: 6249-6252

Four more Coronations in 1944 saw the 1939 Programme of twenty nearly complete:

6249 CITY OF SHEFFIELD
6250 CITY OF LICHFIELD
6251 CITY OF NOTTINGHAM
6252 CITY OF LEICESTER

Light was dawning; these were *not* streamlined, and brought to eighteen the engines approved way back in 1938. Two thus remained to be built of that 1939 Programme but these got lost somehow - presumably the two that were to have 'experimental features' were regarded separately. So, by the end of 1944 thirty-three had been built, albeit at an agonisingly slow pace. Few other major classes could have been built in so many batches, of so few locos each. This was all due to the War of course but there was to be no surge of building after 1945. In 1944 five more Coronations were recommended and these would be the last. They were detailed to the Mechanical and Electrical Engineering Committee on 23 November 1944 and it is an indication of how far adrift construction had got that it referred to requirements two years' hence, in 1946:
Locomotive Renewal Programme 1946 Recommend 105 new engines, £905,600; includes five Class 7 4-6-2 passenger tender (non streamlined) £75,850. Total includes ten each of new design of 2-6-2 Passenger Tank and 2-6-0 Freight Tender.

1946-48: 6253-6257

The last five engines (all non-streamlined of course) were:

6253 CITY OF ST ALBANS
6254 CITY OF STOKE-ON-TRENT
6255 CITY OF HEREFORD
6256 SIR WILLIAM A. STANIER, F.R.S.
6257 CITY OF SALFORD

The point could be made that, post-war, there was not all that much suitable work available for many more Pacifics, especially with the rebuilt Royal Scots proving such a success. The first three of this last batch came out in September and October 1946 but there was a pause for the last two. These were different in a way rather beyond the endless detail differences which had appeared so far in the class. These were 'deliberate' and were meant to bring together all the various improvements which more than ten years of experience had thrown up, as well as latest ideas of design, materials and construction. In a sort of carry over from the two which were to have 'experimental features', the last two Coronations were built at the same time as the LMS main line diesels; Ivatt was now in charge but he announced his belief that the *'conventional reciprocating steam locomotive is still capable of considerable advance and that the ceiling of operating availability and maintenance cost per mile had not yet been reached'*.

***

The last two came out in 1947 and 1948 respectively. The intention was to incorporate all the detail improvements to rectify the problems thrown up during the long, hard and drastically changed conditions that had been seen since the first engine had been introduced in 1937, more than ten years to bring a class of 38 into service! Roller bearings throughout and manganese steel linings to the axleboxes and hornguides were fitted, to raise the

mileages between shoppings to an annual magic figure (never realised) of 100,000. The visual differences were fairly marked, and principally concerned the cast steel Delta trailing truck, redesigned to make room for better ashpan capacity, for longer runs with poorer coal. 46257, the last, was always a notorious rough rider, and remained so throughout its career. The trailing truck was closely based on the American S160 2-8-0s which had worked in Britain during the War. The truck did not perform as expected and much time was taken up during this period with modifications and alterations. Another alteration consequent upon these rear end changes was the different cab sheets found in 46256 and 46257. This is said to have imparted a passing resemblance to the WD 2-8-0s(!), and in some quarters (definitely *not* Crewe North) this was said to have made for the nickname 'Austerity 4-6-2s'.

6245 CITY OF LONDON, new in its wartime black, June 1943. The building of streamliners was resumed in 1939 despite the international situation and the acknowledged difficulties of the streamlined case when it came to routine maintenance. And despite the fact that, in any event, it was planned that the big express engines would be promptly mothballed on the outbreak of hostilities anyway! Construction, apparently, proceeded on the orders of Lord Stamp, the LMS President; in the event such engines (on the LNER too) proved invaluable in the War in heaving packed trains of almost unimaginable length between London and Scotland.

51

Left-hand cab side of 46245 CITY OF LONDON almost at the end of its operational life. The yellow stripe was applied in August 1964 signifying that from 1 September the engine was prohibited from operating under the overhead line equipment south of Crewe. To reduce the cost of the electrification works on the line south of Rugby to Euston the clearance allowed between the live equipment and both stationary structures and moving vehicles was reduced. This resulted in a number of bridges and other lineside structures no longer needing alteration or replacement, giving a significant saving in both cost and time. However, as a result the overall height dimension of several classes of locomotive was such that they would infringe the new clearances and therefore, it was essential they did not operate under the new equipment. The Pacifics fell into this category and as it was considered so important, to be absolutely sure there was no transgression a clearly visible reminder was agreed – the yellow stripe. The reduced clearances were actually implemented at Rugby station and south thereof but in view of the way the diagrams operated it was decided to make the ban effective from Crewe. This photograph was taken in London on the day the ban came into force! However, the engine is at Old Oak Common shed on the Western Region prior to working an Ian Allan Locospotters Special which was not routed over the west coast main line. The view shows clearly the live steam injector just below the cab and the arrangement of the main frames which were extended, cantilever fashion, with the trailing truck allowed movement about its pivot between them. The various steam and water pipes between engine and tender can also be seen. The square brass plate on the frames to the left recorded any modifications or experiments applicable to the engine. The small bracket to the right of the 8P power class at the top of the cab side was part of an early 1950s abortive scheme for drivers to insert their own plate with their name on it for all to see. Heaven knows whose idea that was! Notice no cab steps on the engine, only on the tender. Photograph Alec Swain, www.transporttreasury.co.uk

4. SOME CHANGES AND DIFFERENCES; ATLANTIC CROSSING, THE 1948 EXCHANGES

'Engine Picking': Notes mainly from the original, with additions and amendments

There are probably few classes which provide more fertile ground for the 'engine picker'—that devotee of detail—than the Coronation Pacifics. This account attempts to chart some of these, as well as drawing attention to many in the relevant captions. Most such features are well known but others less so, and one or two aspects are shown, it is felt, that do not seem to have got much attention previously. At the same time, a prudent man shrinks from any claim to a wholly definitive guide to detail differences among the Coronations. One of the pleasures of 'engine picking' is that such a complete condition, in which the pen can be put down and the pronouncement made, *'that is the tale complete'*, almost certainly does not exist. Always, one more photograph will turn up, revealing some unsuspected trifle…

The class could not have enjoyed any difference more fundamental than that—uniquely in British practice—it was divided into streamlined and non-streamlined forms, if you ignore half-hearted experiments with odd members of otherwise conventional classes. The extraordinarily long time taken to complete the (relatively small) class, along with the decision to 'de-streamline', exaggerated the range of detail variation. Some engines were losing the streamlined casing before some of the later examples appeared new from Crewe! There was a period when some ran without smoke deflectors, while the 'de-streamlined' examples went about for a further time with that 'shaved off' smokebox, an oddity which came to so typify 'the semi'.

Clothed and Unclothed; Streamlining, Smokeboxes and Front Framing

Streamlining added three tons to the weight of a Coronation. That, really, was it, and little good can be said of it. So far as aesthetics went it is, really, a hard one to call, for inevitably it would be a case of applying the mores and tastes of today. It is, however, useful to make one point; to the modern eye (something already mentioned in the previous section), the appearance of the Gresley A4s benefits no end from the removal of the 'skirts'. It does this, if you think about it, by revealing *the wheels*, and all their sense of power and speed. In the Coronations, on the other hand, although the overall form was probably less rakish, the wheels were boldly revealed from the start. Even so, however 'bulbous' and rather matronly the design might look to us now, certainly the Coronations were regarded as striking at the time. The Coronation Scot train, brought into service between Euston and Glasgow on 5 July 1937, was not itself streamlined and was but standard stock given new interiors and

6224 PRINCESS ALEXANDRA, leaving Crewe for the north with ordinary stock, with through GW coaches at the front. The brilliant blue livery had to be cleaned according to a rigorous regime and just the ordinary stains of starting away could spoil the overall effect—witness the dirty water streaks down the side of the casing. The horizontal stripes rapidly lost their 'speed' effect when marred like this. Out on the road, there was little that could be done about it but the job must have caused staffing problems at Camden, where all the streamliners first went. Photograph P. Ransome Wallis.

A Coronation, whether 6225 DUCHESS OF GLOUCESTER or not but in that guise at least, when brand new, posing for official photographs at Crewe Works in May 1938. This was the first engine of the second batch, 6225-6229 and the first one to enter traffic in maroon livery rather than the blue of the first five – 6220-6224.

Obvious visible differences from the earlier engines are the twin brake blocks and, because there were no Fowler-Anderson cylinder by-pass valves, the streamlined casing curve under the cylinders rather than there being a short vertical section. Although this engine was afterwards painted maroon, it is presently in a special matt grey with white stripes with the motion and tyres white-washed, all part of a technique to ensure clear photographs with all the details well delineated. After posing the engine would return to the paint shop when this livery would be easily removed using large quantities of water, after which it would be finish painted. It was important to ensure the weather was fine on the occasion of official photograph sessions like this one!

Left. Tender 9745 which was not, so far as we know, attached to 6225 leading to the suspicion that the LMS photographers might be up to their old tricks. A good illustration of how the sides were extended back towards the leading coach in an attempt to reduce air turbulence; hence the separate access ladder rather than individual steps. When the tenders were 'de-streamlined' this ladder arrangement was retained helping to distinguish them from conventional examples. The cover and steam pipes to the coal pusher are well illustrated along with the oil reservoir for the controlling valve and piston. The flexible pipe below the buffer beam is the steam heat supply to the train, while the one higher up is the vacuum brake pipe. Note too the lining on the bottom of the buffer beam.

Footplate view; even the cab fittings have been specially painted to ensure the maximum effect. Below the rear of the frames from left to right can be seen: live steam injector overflow pipe; water feed connection from the tender for live steam injector; steam heat pipe; steam feed to coal-pusher piston; steam feed to the tender brake; vacuum brake pipe; water feed connection from the tender for the exhaust injector; exhaust injector overflow pipe. The gauges on the left-hand, driver's side, are the speedometer on the left and the vacuum brake pipe on the right; the extra mounting is for the steam chest pressure gauge which for some reason is not fitted. On the right-hand, fireman's side, the top gauge is for the boiler pressure and the one below the train steam heat pressure. Immediately below the regulator handle is the blower, or the 'jet' as it was called and below that the sand-gun. This enabled the crew to direct a stream of steam propelled sand towards to tube bank in a effort to keep the tubes clean; it was soon removed as it was found to scour the internal surfaces of the tubes. Just above and to the right of the reversing screw is the drivers brake valve and above it the large and small ejector steam supply valves. To the right of the brake valve is the steam sander control. The continuous blowdown valve is below and to the left of the fireman's side gauges; the injector steam valves are between the water gauges.

The front of 6225; there was a step below the drawhook to give access to the lamp brackets, along with the operating handles to open up the casing and gain access to the smokebox. Even along with the small steps higher up and the handrails, I do not think this would have been particularly popular with the crews, or for that matter the disposal and maintenance staff. On the streamlined engines it was not normal practice to carry a screw coupling on the engine drawhook.

The last of 6225 DUCHESS OF GLOUCESTER.

'redecorated' in blue with white stripes; the schedule was nothing dramatic, given the powers of the new engines, but the necessary PR 'splash' was duly made. The accelerated schedules to Glasgow, with one stop at Carlisle, covered the 401½ miles in 6½ hours, an average speed of 62.6mph. In something akin to what we might now call 'electric blue' the first five, 6220-6224, made a very fine show of it, with horizontal white lines sweeping round the casing from that tremendous V at the front.

The streamlining case was borne by a framework of light steel (less weighty materials were sought for every facet of the locos) while at the front it was supported on a forward extension of what would have been the footplate. The casing of course could only be a hindrance to those who had to maintain the engines but shed staff simply 'got on with it' when it came to the inconveniences of the streamlining. The War, however, brought a small revolution in attitudes to maintenance, encouraged by a number of factors. First of all, there was a war on - things *should* be less labour intensive; secondly

American locomotives had shown that labour saving features were perfectly feasible and thirdly (there were other, social factors at work) there were less and less staff prepared to do these jobs. With wartime neglect, moreover (and the prospects of a return to 1930s standards ever more bleak) the streamliners looked absolutely terrible. On 24 October 1945 the Mechanical and Electrical Engineering Committee heard from the 'Acting CME' (this was Ivatt): *'the streamlined casing in the Coronation class 4-6-2 passenger locomotives was a disadvantage both from the point of view of its maintenance and of the inaccessibility of the engine generally resulting in increased maintenance expenditure, and with the concurrence of the Chief Operating Manager, recommended that the casing be removed from the 24 [6220-6229 and 6235-6248] engines and that side deflector plates be provided at an estimated cost of £5,527'.*

Allen (*British Pacific Locomotives*, Ian Allan, 1962) gives a similar technical justification, noting at the same time that *'from the publicity point of view a coal-begrimed streamline casing is worse than none at all'.* The reduction in atmospheric

resistance, if it really existed, only began to make itself felt at speeds in excess of 80mph and as the speed limit generally was down to 75mph, the streamlining was looking sillier and sillier.

6235 CITY OF BIRMINGHAM was the first streamliner to metamorphose, in April 1946, emerging from Crewe with a set of detail differences setting it apart from those Coronations built non-streamlined from the first. The most peculiar manifestation of course was the sloping smokebox top. The wartime air of economy was a long way from the heady PR exercises of the late 1930s but in terms of styling the LMS seems to have gone into reverse. Saving the cost of alteration, the sloping top was retained, imparting a most unsettling effect. By 1952 some were getting new/altered smokeboxes to the conventional pattern but the last was not done until 1960 – there was no particular hurry.

The other altered detail consequent on the 'unfrocking' was the more utilitarian front end. The curved plating in front of the cylinders was removed. This became a feature of the engines that were de-streamlined, and was

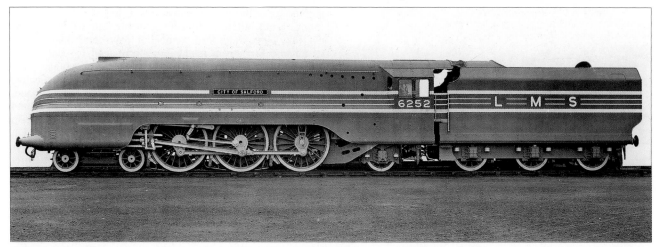

Fake! A streamliner of the 'City' series, 6252 CITY OF SALFORD never existed and this photographic 'record' became nonsensical. 6252, when eventually built, was non-streamlined CITY OF LEICESTER, and CITY OF SALFORD, in the end, turned out to be the very last Coronation, appearing in BR times and incorporating all the Ivatt modifications—it could hardly have been more different from the fake one shown here. Note the early Stone-Deuta speed recorder (later removed) on a bracket by the rear driving wheel.

Pre-war glories, a blaze of red and blue, at Camden shed about 1938, arranged no doubt for the Publicity Department. The streamliner on the right cannot be identified but it is not one of the first five of 1937, for they did not have the little ventilating louvre in front of the left-hand cylinder (denoted by the rectangular pattern of rivets between the buffer and the cylinder casing). One of the original streamliners, 6224 PRINCESS ALEXANDRA, stands in the middle and is seen to lack this little 'extra', which seems to have been restricted to the left side only. The single chimney non-streamliner is 6230 DUCHESS OF BUCCLEUCH and the Jubilee on the far right, closest to the main line is 5559 BRITISH COLUMBIA. Next to it is 6100 ROYAL SCOT, complete with its smokebox nameplate and bell.

A blue DUCHESS OF GLOUCESTER, newly painted, about 1950. A remnant detail is the bracket of the old Stone-Deuta speed indicator. The story is well known of the prodigious output recorded with 46225 on the Rugby Test Plant in the 1950s, and the general conclusion was that the locomotives were really working within the capabilities of the single Fireman, rather than the boiler... Photograph J. Robertson, www.transporttreasury.co.uk

Rain-streaked 46226 DUCHESS OF NORFOLK, in conditions in which few cameramen would even think of risking their precious film back then around 1950. The blue livery (the lining is the giveaway even in such unpropitious circumstances as these) was a poor thing and we are generally well rid of it. Nice 'big' cab window. The scene is the modern open roundhouse at Carlisle Upperby about 1950 where famously a Coronation once slowly ran through the thin brick screening to the outside, regally indifferent to the world of men. Photograph J. Robertson, www.transporttreasury.co.uk

6222 QUEEN MARY uncovered; to many, the very acme of the steam locomotive, unparalleled in its combination of power and grace, swelling and flowing almost to fill every available inch of the loading gauge. The unfortunate slope of the smokebox was eventually rectified in all the engines of course, though it did provide us with the typically opaque nickname, 'semi'. They weren't of course, 'semi' anything by now but a number of us still employ the term for engines that were never streamlined in the first place. To all who came late to the class, when most had a conventional smokebox, 'that slope' always appeared as a sort of deficiency. Note small cab window. A small space to match the handholds in the smoke deflectors was soon cut at the base, to give more room for a cleaner's toe cap. Though it is not readily apparent, the footplate tapered to almost nothing at this point, which was obviously the cause of the problem—the cleaner ran out of room! The engine is at Camden, ready to back down to Euston; hence the heroically over-full tender. Photograph P. Ransome Wallis.

CORONATIONS - SOME DETAIL CHANGES					
Loco	To traffic	S/C	DC	SD added	SB restored
46220	6/37	S	12/44	9/46	3/57
46221	6/37	S	11/40	5/46	4/54
46222	6/37	S	8/43	5/46	8/53
46223	7/37	S	11/41	8/46	8/55
46224	7/37	S	5/40	5/46	10/54
46225	5/38	S	6/43	2/47	1/55
46226	5/38	S	7/42	6/47	10/52
46227	6/38	S	12/40	2/47	5/53
46228	6/38	S	9/40	7/47	12/53
46229	9/38	S	4/43	11/47	2/57
46230	6/38	C	10/40	9/46	-
46231	6/38	C	6/40	9/46	-
46232	7/38	C	1/43	2/45	-
46233	7/38	C	3/41	9/46	-
46234	8/38	C	2/39	3/46	-
46235	7/39	S	New	4/46	9/56
46236	7/39	S	New	12/47	11/53
46237	8/39	S	New	1/47	3/53
46238	9/39	S	New	11/46	10/53
46239	9/39	S	New	6/47	5/53
46240	3/40	S	New	6/47	7/53
46241	4/40	S	New	1/47	2/58
46242	5/40	S	New	3/47	11/53
46243	6/40	S	New	5/49	11/58
46244	7/40	S	New	8/47	7/53
46245	6/43	S	New	8/47	11/56
46246	8/43	S	New	9/46	5/60
46247	9/43	S	New	5/47	9/56
46248	10/43	S	New	12/46	3/57
46249	4/44	C	New	11/46	-
46250	5/44	C	New	3/46	-
46251	6/44	C	New	8/46	-
46252	6/44	C	New	3/45	-
46253	9/46	C	New	New	-
46254	9/46	C	New	New	-
46255	10/46	C	New	New	-
46256	12/47	C	New	New	-
46257	5/48	C	New	New	-

S = Streamliner
C = Conventional
SD = Smoke Deflector
SB = Smokebox
DC = Double Chimney

incorporated on new engines from 6253 to 6257. The other engines built in conventional form from the first, 6230-6234 and 6249-6252 kept the footplate draped in front of the cylinders. 46242

was unusual; 'de-streamlined' in March 1947, it had been near-destroyed in the Harrow disaster of 1952. Emerging after reconstruction it was seen to have the old-style footplating, curving down in front of its cylinders. It was a case of Crewe doing what it felt should be done, rather than what Derby drawings said should be done!

The first smoke deflectors appeared on 6232 and 6252 in 1945 and the rest of the non-streamliners got them the following year. The streamlined engines were equipped with smoke deflectors when the casings were removed. The Record Cards often lack continuity of detail, which is part both of their fascination and their capacity to frustrate the Seekers After Truth. The fitting of 'Smoke Deflector Plates' is noted only on some Cards, to various Order Nos.; 6231 for instance got its plates in the period ending 7 September 1946, at a cost of £45.

Speed Indicators

'Speedometers' were a thorny subject. Instruments with a prominent horizontal rod were fitted to 6220-6224 and 6225 through to 6252 got the BTH speedometer – see photograph below for instance. On 27 October 1937 the

Mechanical and Electrical Engineering Committee had approved the fitting of 998 express locomotives with speed indicators. The outlook seemed good then: *'In view of additional restrictions imposed by the Chief Civil Engineer in relation to the maximum permissible speeds due to the introduction and increase of the accelerated express passenger services, consideration had been given to the desirability of fitting an instrument which would both indicate and make a continuous record of a speed of a locomotive and 20 express engines had been fitted with such a device under the authority of Traffic Committee Minute 5016 and Mechanical and Electrical Engineering Committee Minute 1098 but it was not proposed to recommend the fitting of speed recorders generally owing to possible margins of error and the difficulty and cost of checking such records. It was however recommended that an electrical type of speed indicator be fitted to 998 locomotives working express passenger trains at an approximate estimated outlay of £23,000'.*

Under wartime conditions it proved impossible to maintain and service the instruments. The fitting of 'electrical speed indicators' (as they were termed) on all the 998 engines projected in 1937 had been discontinued owing to shortage of materials and staff and the indicators (fitted to approximately 400 locos) had been taken off and the material placed in store. The Mechanical and Electrical Engineering Committee heard on 29 January 1947 that *'since the cessation of hostilities the question of refitting the speed recorders and indicators had been reconsidered and it was recommended that the speed recorders should not be replaced*

6233 DUCHESS OF SUTHERLAND of the original 1938 non-streamlined, single chimney batch, at Shrewsbury before the War.

Red single chimney non-streamliner 6231 DUCHESS OF ATHOLL, looking new and doubtless on a running in turn with a streamliner behind, at Shrewsbury.

46224 PRINCESS ALEXANDRA in blue, at Polmadie on 13 June 1948. The chalked inscription on the smokebox door reads *DOOR TIGHT 12/6/48*. A number of interpretations might be possible, but probably it was the Fireman, who *had* fully tightened the door, telling the preparing fireman not to bother. Photograph James Stevenson.

6238 CITY OF CARLISLE at Camden. The former streamlined tender is marked by that ladder for access and the lack of a conventional step bracket at the rear running plate, and also the two tender filler caps, just visible with their handles. They had to be positioned like this on the streamlined tenders of course, for the hose was only got in (with some awkwardness and long years of swearing) through those sliding hatches which can be seen at the rear of the streamlined tenders as originally fashioned. Tenders built for conventional engines had the usual central filler and side steps by the rear axle box. The vestigial rearward extension of the sides was also a feature of the former streamlined tenders—indicated by the four angle brackets. On such tenders the downward curve at the front was higher up than on their 'conventional' brethren. The box with its two pipes leading up is of course, the coal pusher and its exhaust, while the little box with two pipes high up on the right-hand side was its siphon lubricator, both for the valves and the main ram piston.

61

6234 DUCHESS OF ABERCORN heads north past Camden shed in its single chimney days. It was the prodigious feats of this engine, newly fitted with double chimney in February 1939, which prompted the rapid conversion of the others to the double arrangement.

and the speed indicators should be fitted to 366 locos of the following classes: class 7 4-6-2, class 6 4-6-0 ('Royal Scot'), class 6 4-6-0 (5X converted), 5X 4-6-0. During the time the speed indicators were fitted certain defects developed which were under consideration with Messrs. British Thomson Houston with a view to their elimination before refitting commenced and immediately these defects had been removed a report setting out the modified proposals, together with the cost of the work already carried out would be submitted'.

This report is unfortunately lost to us, but the prominent 'speedos', driven off the left hand trailing crank pin, were not generally fitted (46256 and 46257 apparently were equipped from new) until 1957, under Order No.R7461. A typical entry on the Record Cards in that year reads *'28.12.57 Prov. of Speed Indicators £151.12.0'.*

Cab Windows

The 'de-streamlined' engines required larger cab windows and these were fitted between 1948 and 1952. The work is hardly noted at all in the Record Cards, though one diligent scribe recorded the job on 6239's Card: *'Fitting of Larger Cab Windows'* is noted for 23 June 1951, though no costs or Order No. are given. The work refers to the front window, and those on streamlined and newly 'de-streamlined' engines are noticeably narrower than on other engines.

Tenders

The LMS built a ten ton tender, No.9359, with coal pusher in 1936, attaching it to

Princess Royal 4-6-2 No.6206. It remained the only one so fitted among the Princess Royal Pacifics and it could only be operated with 6206 (due to the additional steam pipe between engine and tender). However, the principle was borne in mind and ten ton tenders with steam operated coal pushers were provided for the Coronations from the first. On the streamlined locos the side sheets were extended back to close off the gap (so disruptive to airflow) between the rear of the tender and the front of the first coach. Sliding doors in the top of this faring allowed access for the water column hoses. The tenders were welded rather than riveted, which reduced weight by about a ton. Welding was continuous where water tightness was necessary but elsewhere intermittent welding was adopted. By proceeding like this distortion was minimised, though according to *The Railway Gazette* (*The Metallurgy of a High-Speed Locomotive,* 18 and 25 February 1938): '*...there was an inherent distortion in the side plates, where the gussets were welded on, causing small ridges to form on the outside of the plate. These ridges were ground off by portable hand-operated grinding tools when the tank was completed'.* Welding (it was dearer) went out of fashion and the last five, the post-War engines, had distinctive riveted tenders.

The streamlined tenders had a cowl at the front, matching the outline of the cab roof, though at first the 1937 batch, 6220-6224, did not have this. Tenders for the non-streamlined engines (naturally enough) did not have the cowl

though the non-streamlined 6249-6252 went into traffic with 'partially streamlined' tenders, which had already been built in anticipation of more streamlined locomotives. Streamlining duly went and the tenders were similarly 'de-frocked'. The rear sheets began to disappear in the War years for reasons of access but with 'de-streamlining' more or less all trace went, so that all tenders appeared much the same. The only really noticeable difference lay in the shape at the front, where it met the cab. On most the tender front was cut away high up, matching the inward curve of the tender tops. This was the case with all the streamlined engines and the later conventional ones but the first conventional batch, 6230-6234, had a lower 'sweep', and so did the last two, 6256 and 46257. Former streamlined tenders were recognisable by the vestigial sheeting at the rear, extending back by an inch or two, and the access ladder.

More Tenders

The late, estimable John Wright of Glasgow studied the LMS/LMR engine histories and knew them, and their foibles, well. These are his observations on the original Tender notes: 'I had not realised that the last three tenders were riveted, but the story is not as simple as that. No.10622, fitted to 6255, had the streamline-type front, whereas 10623 and 10624 had the non-streamline version. In *Engines of the LMS built 1923-1951* (OPC, 1975). Rowledge claims all three were welded, but your

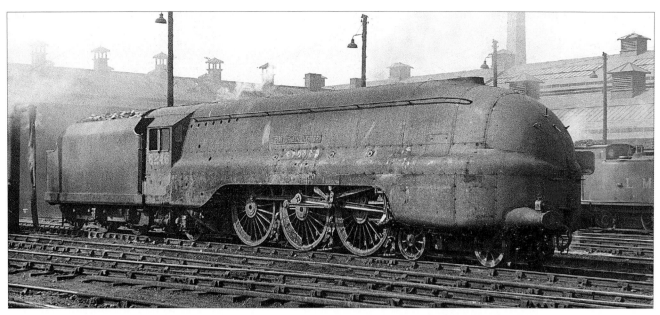

Faded glory hardly begins to describe poor, tired and well, faded 6246 CITY OF MANCHESTER, at Polmadie on 8 June 1946. Its case was removed in the autumn of that year. A relief, you might say. Photograph James Stevenson.

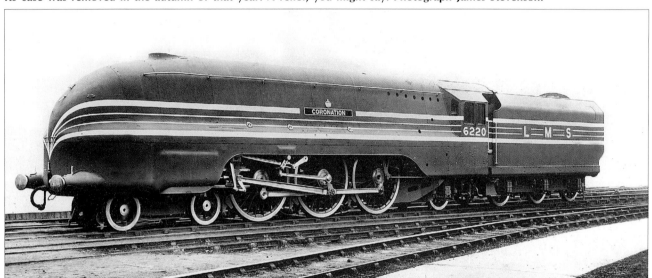

6220 CORONATION in as built condition alongside the paint shop in Crewe Works. Although the background of the photograph has been masked out on the negative, the track layout and roadway in the foreground give the game away and this was a location often used by the official photographer. The metalled road was part of the extensive 1920s reorganisation of the works when the narrow gauge railway was abandoned and Lister three-wheel diesel engine driven trucks introduced for much of the works internal material movements. It is surprising that whoever was responsible for posing the engine did not ensure it was in mid-gear before the photographer set to work. Worth a note is that the plate recording that the engine had been built by the LMS at Crewe in 1937 has yet to be fitted. On the streamlined engines it was placed directly under the middle of the nameplate and just above the intermediate coupled wheel.

photographs clearly show this to be wrong. In *Stanier Locomotive Classes* (Ian Allan, 1991) A.J. Powell states "the tenders for Nos.6253-55 were no longer all-welded; the internal baffle plates were attached by riveting. The front cutaway at the cab remained high, as on the streamline tenders, while the back was similar to those on Nos.6230-34. The 'D' shaped frame lightening holes were left open." He goes on to say external sieve

one—BR lined green, from August 1955 to December 1957—to be applied to the whole class at the same time! Summarised, liveries were blue, then red, for the streamlined and non-streamlined engines until 1943, when wartime black was brought in. Most got this plain black in 1944, one or two not until early 1945. 6245-6252, new from 1943 onwards, were plain 'wartime' black from new.

amended with the revelations of years. An oddity was 46239 CITY OF CHESTER. It must have presented a peculiar sight in July 1950 when, 'owing to the incidence of Works Holidays' it was sent into traffic for four days 'unpainted'.

The Last Two: Rocking Grates, Roller Bearings and 100,000 Miles a Year

The major departure in appearance, after the streamlining/de-streamlining process, came with the last two Coronations of 1947-48, built at least in part as a means of comparison with Ivatt's new diesels, 10000 and 10001 and described earlier.

Engine No.	Engine Order No. *	Boiler Order No.	Boiler Serial No.	Remarks
6220-4	E402	B402	9937-41	Used as intended
6225-8	E408	B408	10297-10300	Used as intended
6230-4	E408	B408	10301-5	
6229	E408	B408	10306	
6235-44	E414	B414	10287-10296	Used as intended
6245-51	E415	B415	10637-43	6245/7/8 received repaired boilers 7 boilers used on engines during repair
6252	E415	B415	10644	Used on 6249 when new
2 cancelled	E415	B415	10645/6	Boilers used on 6246/50
-	-	BS1/39**	10693/4	Used on 6251/2 when new
6253-7	E464	B464**	12470-4	Used as intended
-	-	BS1/76**	13043/4	First used on 46242/56

*Ref 'Stanier Locomotive Classes' by A J Powell, Ian Allan, 1991
**My own researches at NRM
Kindly tabulated by John Wright

boxes were fitted. From your data these tenders would appear to be Nos.9816, 9817 and 10622, and No.9817 is only recorded with 46254. The tender in your photograph of 46254 in the 'Book Of' is not very clear, but there are two or three shots in *LM Pacifics – A Pictorial Tribute* (Roundhouse Books, 1967) which show the rivets clearly. However, your photograph in the original 'Book Of' of 46253 clearly shows rivets. The question is whether this was before tender 9816 was exchanged for 9704 at some unrecorded date; since 9704 was definitely all-welded, I think we must assume the tender in the photograph to be 9816. That being the case it looks as if Powell is incomplete in stating that three tenders were riveted – it looks as if five were, in fact.'

Ashpans, various

Have a look at CITY OF GLASGOW on page 146 and the accompanying caption. 46229 and 46234-46255 had ashpan doors, a form of hopper ashpan which was operated using a long handle stowed on the footplate

Liveries

In nothing so much as livery did the Coronations exhibit change and differences, in abandon; Rowledge makes the eyebrow-raising comment that, of the *eleven* liveries used among this class of 38 locomotives, the constantly changing swirl of colour stood still sufficiently long for only

Apart from an experimental grey on 6234 in 1946 the next general livery was LMS lined black, then the BR black with LNWR lining. All were in one form of black, wartime, LMS or BR, when BR introduced the famous blue (in different shades) which most had got by 1950-51. All got the succeeding BR green in the early 1950s and there then came the celebrated reversion to red, when sixteen Coronations received LMS-style crimson lake—BR's 'maroon'. (There were two different lining styles with the maroon livery, the older LMS-type later being exclusive.) The table below originated with Peter Rowledge's *The LMS Pacifics* (D&C, 1987) and has been altered and

It was hoped to push mileages through to 100,000 per year with the last two Coronations, 6256 and 46257, extending the shopping period at the same time from about eight months to twelve months. The rocking grate, self cleaning smokebox and hopper ashpans, now becoming the standard across the LMS/LMR/BR, would increase availability and manganese steel axlebox and horncheek liners and grease roller bearings on all axles, engine and tender would, it was hoped, be the means of extending the annual mileage. (They weren't.)

The trailing truck on the last two was very different, and the main reason for the visual differences. The whole rear end was redesigned, with the old framing replaced by a sort of bar frame extension; the new Delta truck looked very different and meant that the cab sides could be reduced, losing the attractive curved bottom to the cab.

The three Coronations built in 1946, 6253-6255, had got rocking grates, following the revelations of American practice and on 29 January 1947 the

LIVERY CHANGES, amended and expanded since the original version of 1998 in the light of additional information that has become available.

	LMS BLUE	LMS MAROON	PLAIN BLACK	LMS LINED BLACK	BR LINED BLACK	BR EXP. BLUE	BR BLUE	BR EARLY GREEN 1st CREST	BR LATER GREEN 2nd CREST	BR LINED MAROON	LMS LINED MAROON
6220	NEW		3/44	11/46			1/50	2/52	6/58		
6221	NEW	11/40	6/46				3/50	12/52	11/57		
6222	NEW		8/44	5/46			10/50	8/53	1/59		
6223	NEW		1/44	8/46			4/50	10/52	11/58		
6224	NEW		8/44	6/46		8/48	8/50	2/52	9/57		
6225		NEW	8/44	3/47			3/50	1/55		8/58	1/60
6226		NEW	5/44		9/48		1/51	5/54		11/58	6/60
6227		NEW	12/43	8/46		6/48	8/50	4/53	2/58		
6228		NEW	5/44	10/47			8/50	6/55			6/58
6229		NEW	11/44	1/48			2/50	4/52		9/58	10/59
6230		NEW		9/46		5/48		5/52	9/58		
6231		NEW	9/45	8/46		5/48	1/51	12/53	5/58		
6232		NEW		5/48		5/48		11/51	3/59		
6233		NEW		10/47			5/50	11/52	4/58		
6234		NEW			10/48	3/46*		3/52	7/57		
6235		NEW	7/44	1/47			12/50	5/53	2/58		
6236		NEW	4/44	2/48				11/54		7/58	11/59#
6237		NEW	8/44	3/47			9/49	3/55	10/57		
6238		NEW	7/44	1/47	3/49			2/52			6/58
6239		NEW	7/44	9/47			7/50	8/54	3/58		
6240		NEW	12/44	7/47			1/50	10/54		7/58	8/60
6241		NEW	10/44			6/48	9/49	6/53	2/58		
6242		NEW	10/48?	5/47			7/49	10/53	4/57		
6243		NEW	12/43				6/49	2/54	11/57	10/58	12/59
6244		NEW	1/44	9/47		8/48	10/50	7/53	7/57	10/58	6/60
6245			NEW	10/47				4/53			12/57
6246			NEW	10/46	11/48			6/53	6/57	10/58	4/60
6247			NEW	6/47				2/54		7/59	5/58 + 1/61
6248			NEW	12/46	3/49			10/53			6/58
6249			NEW	11/47			9/50	10/54	8/57		
6250			NEW	9/47			5/50	10/52	11/57		
6251			NEW	8/47	5/49			2/55	9/57	11/58	11/60
6252			NEW		4/49			1/52	2/59		
6253				NEW				11/53	1/58		
6254				NEW			9/50	10/55	4/57	9/58	6/60
6255				NEW			8/50	1/53	11/57		
6256				NEW			5/51	6/54			5/58**
6257				NEW				12/52	1/58		

*experimental blue/grey (LMS)
#8/52 painted plain black
**BR Lined black 10/48

CORONATION standing on the east, departure side of Euston station, probably waiting to depart with the 'Coronation Scot' train. Notice that by this time, although the photograph is undated, the plate recoding the engine's parentage has been fixed below the nameplate.

This photograph was taken on the occasion of the record breaking run of 6220 from Euston to Crewe and back on 29 June 1938; this is confirmed by the reporting number W700 that was used on that occasion. It is difficult to say whether this is the up or down train and indeed where the picture was taken, but in hazarding a guess in view of the layout of the tracks, I would say it is the up train on the return trip to Euston not far north of Stafford.

Mechanical and Electrical Engineering Committee recommended fitting self-cleaning smokeboxes as well as *'proper ashpans and rocking grates on 33 class 7 4-6-2 passenger locomotives of the Coronation class'*. At that time there were actually thirty-six Coronations in service but 6253-6255 had already got the rocking grates and self-cleaning smokeboxes; 6256 and 6257, with the long-envisaged 'experimental features' were yet to be built.

The report continues: *'The fitting of rocking grates - a feature adopted as standard on all new engines - will assist in keeping the fire clean when the engines are working long distance expresses. Ashpans of the hopper type were already fitted to 20 of the engines and the remaining 13 would be similarly fitted as a necessary adjunct to the rocking grate. Controls inside the cab would also be provided to facilitate the emptying of the ashpans under varying operating conditions. The self cleaning smokebox keeps the lower row of tubes free from obstruction and assists disposal of the engines by avoiding the necessity to clean out the smokebox each day. Estimate £9,085. Approved'*.

Double Chimney

It is not always present, but many of the Record Cards have a reference, under Order No.6865, *'Double Blastpipe and Chimney'* at about £70. As an experiment, a double blastpipe and chimney had been fitted to 6234 DUCHESS OF ABERCORN; witness the engine's storming progress with twenty coaches from Crewe to Carlisle and back, described under the section

chronicling the 1938 building of 6225-6234. The engine had been tested a fortnight before on the same working, with its original single chimney, and had failed to keep steam and time. So the triumph with the double arrangement a couple of weeks later was all the more telling. No.6235, and all the engines after it, were given the new double chimney, and the earlier engines were modified as soon afterwards as maybe. Rowledge (*The LMS Pacifics*, David & Charles, 1987) has an amusing story of 6245 having a Kylchap exhaust when new in 1943, the story being that it had come from the LNER at Doncaster, though it had also been in the possession of the Southern at Eastleigh... It was removed when someone noticed that CITY OF LONDON didn't sound like the rest... Allen (*British Pacific Locomotives*) makes the point that the double chimney as fitted to the class as a whole was *not* a Kylchap arrangement. The Kylchap on the LNER was a series of petticoats, one below the other between the base of the chimney and the blast orifices. The arrangement on the Coronations was simpler, the blastpipe branching into two with the two chimneys, in line, sited above.

Bits and Pieces

A typical Record Card, under the heading 'Improvements, Etc.' might read (without quoting Order Nos.) something like: *(table below)*.

After this, improvement work is usually noted simply with the Crewe Order No., 'E4176, R7481' and so on. The Cards were maintained by different people at different times and there is no strict continuity to the entries. It *is* possible, by cross referencing, to discover what some of these Order Nos. are. 46225 for instance got its speed indicator under Order R7461 on 5.10.57 at the incredible cost of £322.19.3. (Some of the costings look a mite problematical; they are given as two sums, under Capital and Revenue accounts and sometimes the figures are added together to give the total, other times they are subtracted...) But to return to the detective work: 46224 for instance has no 'speedo' listed but has the same (anonymous) number R7461, the same date and more or less the same cost, so it is quite possible to date its speedo fitting, too.

Other references are more obscure, however, and often earlier improvements such as double chimneys and smoke deflectors are difficult to

Bits and Pieces (See above)	
2.9.44 New design valves, casing and filter for oil relief valves	£3.12.6
28.3.45 Flexible pipe to sand hopper	£1.14.0
13.7.46 Misc.	£103.0.0
29.11.47 Longer dis. Monel Stays	£12.0.0.
27.12.47 Fitting of small Radius Rocking Washers and new bottom frame bars	£47.7.7
15.5.48 Prov. of additional washout plugs	£1.15.0
29.11.52 Removal of sand guns and equipment	£1.7.0'

Whoever took the down 'Coronation Scot' a little south of Oxenholme has included a lady companion, perhaps his wife; whatever the case it makes for a nice study. It is however a pity about the platelayers hut masking part of the engine which, judging by the length of the nameplate, is 6220 CORONATION itself.

The up 'Coronation Scot' behind 6223 PRINCESS ALICE just south of Preston, probably during the summer of 1938. This is a classic shot by the master photographer Eric Treacy.

PRINCESS ALICE in the blue livery adopted for the 'Coronation Scot' engines and train. This is the down working about to leave Carlisle. Notice there is a full head of steam with the safety valves lifting. Either the driver has applied the steam sanding gear to be sure of a good level of adhesion as he gets the train underway, or the engine has just stopped slipping and sand is now being applied; this would account for a sudden lifting of the safety valves if the driver had attempted to start the train and then had to rapidly close the regulator to control a bout of slipping. Carlisle was the only intermediate stop made by this train in either direction. Photograph www.transporttreasury.co.uk

6226 DUCHESS OF NORFOLK, one of the second batch of engines and in this case painted in maroon, although with the same arrangement of lining as the earlier blue livered examples. This picture illustrates well the raised part of the casing to clear the outside cylinders and the open door in the tender (left open in this case) for ease of access when filling the tender from water columns. The art deco headlamps reserved for the streamlined engines are also noticeable in this photograph, taken at the very north end of Camden shed yard.

In red with gold lining a streamlined 6228 DUCHESS OF RUTLAND breasts Tring summit with the up 'Royal Scot' in the summer of either 1938 or 1939. Photograph C.R.L. Coles.

trace. 46228, for instance, has a listing '17.9.40 X6865 Double Blast Pipe & Chimney £62.3.9'. 46229 has the same Order No. and description but the date is 15.5.43 and the cost £126.0.0. On other Cards there is just the Order No. or no reference at all. Smoke deflectors are hard to find; there is no reference to them at all in most cards and the job did not have an Order No. to enable a cross reference. 6234 is noted getting its deflectors in the period ending 10.8.46, at £45, but the heading is that famous one, 'Misc.'.

Other, apparently minor jobs, are consistently recorded, and in some detail, such as 'removal of sand guns' and 'tell-tale device to give warning of excessive heating of inside big-ends'. The first was a steam jet operated by the crew, intended to 'free-up' the tubes from the firebox end. It directed a blast of sand through the tubes to clean them but the debris went up through the chimney, and onto Mrs Jones' washing! It proved ineffective and was taken out from the Coronations about 1952. The 'stink bomb' was just that, and gave off an unmistakable odour when the inside big end to which it was attached grew too hot. These were fitted about 1951.

'Additional clothing on inside cylinders' was another general entry; it was also one of the few jobs which can be matched to the LMS Engineering Minutes. There are few original references to, say, double chimneys or smoke deflectors, though certainly there would have been reports, assessments, approvals and all the rest. However, so far as the cylinders are concerned there is for once a Mechanical and Electrical Engineering Committee reference: '22 *March 1945 recommend 29 4-6-2 locomotives be fitted with additional cylinder clothing to the inside cylinders at an estimated cost of £810 to prevent the bad effect of cold air which was at present drawn up over the steam chest of the inside cylinder and which it was thought was partly responsible for certain amount of cracking in the cylinders'*.

AWS/ATC

Despite CITY OF LEICESTER's derailment at Polesworth in 1951 (see under the locomotive's separate entry), in which the Inspecting Officer once again recommended Automatic Train Control (or AWS-Automatic Warning System) it was nearly a decade before the big LM express engines got it. It was a prominent feature, for it had to be protected from the front screw coupling by a substantial shield; there were also vacuum reservoirs and battery box to be accommodated on the footplating. Some engines, no doubt, would have carried this long-overdue improvement for only three years or so.

A Note on Record Cards

Inconsistencies litter the Record Cards, or rather the Engine History Cards; dates are largely period ending, though the definition of period seems to have shifted at times. Dates sometimes appear to be 'actual' but it wouldn't do to take these as wholly gospel. This is hardly to be marvelled at, for the cards were kept over a quarter of a century, by different people in different places; there was a war on for much of the period and after 1948 the railway which had operated the Coronations from their construction was divided into two separate Regions, very much independent of each other. The Coronations appeared before the Second World War and the last of them came in the first year of BR. Much policy and practice changed over that time, a new form of card was devised, headings changed, emphasis varied. So a lot changed (though a lot didn't!) and many of the inconsistencies in the record seem to owe as much to accident as much as anything else. Mileages need a raised eyebrow, as we have read in Chapter 2. Some major items, such as smoke deflectors and double chimneys are altogether absent from some cards.

The records, anomalously, give *two* dates for removal of streamlining; one is taken from the day the engine came off Crewe at the end of the particular works visit in which the casing was removed and it is reported again (though not always...) under 'Improvements etc.'. This relates to 'period ending' and is by definition later. Except in one or two cases where it is obviously wrong, the first date is the one used in this book.

Boilers are fairly well detailed, but some cards begin the record (presumably as practice changed over the years) with the first boiler carried by the locomotive, other cards begin with the first *change* of boiler—

The summer of 1939 and an engine numbered 6229, with the name DUCHESS OF HAMILTON and painted blue; in actual fact it is the original 6220 CORONATION. The giveaway is the continuation of the streamlined casing below the raised section over the cylinders which covers the cylinder by-pass valves and drain cocks; only the first five engines had this. This locomotive had exchanged identity with 6229 so that one of the latest batch of engines could be sent on the American tour, with special attention paid to various items while under construction. When the engine came back to this country in 1942, the engines reverted to 'as built' as it were. The engine is clearing the outskirts of London with the down 'Coronation Scot', at the start of its long journey north.

comparison with the building date will reveal this. In the first years the records are more interesting, for when a new boiler is fitted the 'donor' locomotive (that is, the locomotive which previously bore the overhauled boiler) is also recorded. Other items are flatly incomprehensible. What does *'deleted from selected list 20.1.58'* mean, for instance, on Scottish ones only?

The record is often abandoned before the end—1955 in the case of 46220, when it clearly would have had several more boilers after that. Total mileage is recorded but not right to the bitter end. In any event it was an estimation, a minor miracle of paperwork and not mechanically recorded.

Prices quoted differ over the years, for it took a long time to build the Coronations. There are some amusing differences, however. The early engines were priced at £10,095, which seems specific enough, but 6222, apparently, cost 8/11d more!

Shed allocations in the original *Book of the Coronation Pacifics* were those given in the engine histories but these had the disadvantage of being less than perfectly recorded in the last three or four years from about 1960. This time, however, the estimable Peter Groom has tidied up the last few years of allocations, with reference to the SLS *Journal, The Railway Observer* and *Trains Illustrated*.

A couple of points; at the outbreak of war it was envisaged (somehow) that public passenger services would cease and to this end some Pacifics were recorded as sent to sheds such as Bletchley, Speke Junction, Rugby and so on, ostensibly for store. Some of these indeed took place; others probably never actually did. One or two of the unlikeliest 'transfers' have been omitted as well, a bit *too* unlikely. This was all soon rescinded as it dawned that the Pacifics were needed as never before and the Coronations returned to more natural haunts, if indeed they had ever left them in the first place.

Sometimes locomotives were noted officially on loan at a shed a week or two before its allocation proper. This 'loan' period is not listed separately in this volume and allocation is assumed to have begun with the arrival of the loco on the books of its new shed.

Disposal details are taken from the BR Record but much of this information has been cast into doubt in recent years. Any reader wanting to model a particular Coronation in a particular scrapyard should maybe delve a bit further...

A Note on Codes

Precisely what degree of work constituted a particular grade of repair varied over the years, especially between LMS and BR practice, and between pre-Group/early LMS and later LMS practice. LMS codes, in the time of the Coronations, were as follows:

HG Heavy General; **NC** Non Classified. **LS** and **HS** stood for Light Service and Heavy Service respectively. This 'Service' classification was replaced, broadly speaking, by the 'Intermediate' category. **LO** seems to stand for Light Overhaul; **TRO** it is believed, stands for 'Tender Repair Only'.

By BR days, **HI** and **LI** meant Heavy Intermediate and Light Intermediate, while **HG** still meant Heavy General. **NC** stood for Non Classified.

Below. An early example of the first batch of non-streamlined engines, 6234 DUCHESS OF ABERCORN, at Crewe North shed on 14 August 1938, just ten days after its official date of entering service. It certainly looks very new with burnished screw coupling, draw hook and hand rails. Could this photograph have been taken before the engine made its first run? This was the locomotive selected for the high power test runs and experiments with a double chimney in February 1939.

Below right. In the highly inauspicious year of 1939, a Coronation Pacific and a train of LMS stock built for the Coronation Scot journeyed across the Atlantic to be the British representative at the New York World's Fair. 6220 CORONATION looked bonny indeed with its light and bell, except of course, that the engine was in fact 6229 DUCHESS OF HAMILTON. CORONATION merely donated its plates and numbers, assuming the identity of 6229 for the duration, back in the home country. It wasn't that the engine was indisposed, it was just that the PR people (rightly) preferred a red and gold engine—and that is how 'CORONATION' came to run in red, and 'DUCHESS OF HAMILTON' in blue! The whole ensemble departed from Southampton, courtesy of the Southern Railway, to be delivered onto the Baltimore & Ohio. Obviously a suitably dramatic picture should be available at the earliest possible opportunity, to publicise its extensive tour from 21 March to 14 April, taking in Baltimore, Washington, Pittsburgh, Chicago and many other cities (prior to landing up at New York for the Fair). This photograph, taken from the air with a cunningly inserted four engined aircraft (pretty much out of scale) would fit the bill. That allotment shed, and the lack of the bell alerts us to the fact that the scene could hardly be *less* transAtlantic; it turns out to be near Watford, its allotments a far cry from the glamour of 'Over There'...

Above. This engine, 6244, was named CITY OF LEEDS when built in July 1940; this photograph shows it newly renamed KING GEORGE VI in April 1941. A later engine from the next, 1943 batch, took the CITY OF LEEDS name. As the later streamlined engines did not have cylinder by-pass valves below the cylinders there was no need for a continuation of the streamlined casing to hide them; notice the small air vent in the casing ahead of the cylinders, a feature of the later streamlined engines. The hollow axles which gave a saving of about nine cwt in weight can be clearly seen as can the speedometer drive arrangements on the trailing coupled axle. The coupling and connecting rods as well as the axles and some other highly stressed parts of the motion were made of 'Vibrac' steel, an alloy containing nickel, chrome, molybdenum and manganese developed by the English Steel Corporation and made by the acid open-hearth process. It had a very high tensile strength along with a substantial resistance to bending moments, enabling considerable weight saving and therefore, the amount of reciprocating balance required in the coupled wheel sets. The connecting rods on these engines were two feet longer than the earlier Princess Royal class and were marginally lighter, which demonstrates one of the benefits of the new grade of steel. This steel was first used on locomotives in this country by the Southern Railway for the Lord Nelson 4-6-0s. The valve gear parts, with the exception of the eccentric rod big ends, were fitted with grease lubricated needle roller bearings, although later engines (due to wartime restrictions) originally had plain bronze bearings. Nevertheless they were still grease lubricated as the use of soft grease reduced crew preparations time; it was only necessary for the shed maintenance staff to apply grease at the X day examinations.

OVER THERE

Truly Over There. A familiar picture, with '6220' posed with a Baltimore & Ohio diesel at Baltimore on 18 March 1939. Riddles was in charge of the tour, and apparently the coal provided came as something of a shock, for it was the sort of slack customarily supplied to US locomotives, with their vast maws and mechanical stokers. With the Driver (Freddie Bishop of Camden) going down with pneumonia, Riddles had taken a good share of the firing and was more than once engaged in frantic repair work. Riddles gave an address to the Junior Institution of Engineers in which he described burning eleven or twelve tons of coal ('or dirt!') in *one* day. Improvisation was the order of the day, turning up parts to fit and spending nights working on a fallen brick arch. Filthy and exhausted, it was then a case of negotiating entry into the hotel. Extricating a brick arch means manoeuvring something weighing (in its myriad parts) near enough a ton inside a fearsomely hot firebox. Riddles afterwards certainly deserved his *'bath, rump steak, bottle of champagne and bed'*.

Prior to the departure of 6229 to America in January 1939, masquerading as 6220 CORONATION, along with a brand new set of vehicles specially built for the purpose, the opportunity was taken to stage a number of publicity events, culminating, perhaps, in the 'Wings over Watford. This view at Euston on 9 January 1939 has Sir Josiah Stamp (Baron Stamp of Shortlands) Chairman and Chief Executive of the LMS, bidding farewell to the crew that went to the USA with the engine. Both Camden men, the driver is Fred C. Bishop and his fireman John McKinnon Carswell. Photograph R.S. Carpenter.

The origin of the visit of the engine and Coronation Scot train to America was an invitation to send an exhibit for the New York World's Fair, due to open on 30 April 1939. On arrival at Baltimore however, between 22 March and 12 April and prior to the exhibition opening, the engine and train went on a wide ranging tour of parts of North America. This included for example, visits to Washington, Philadelphia, Pittsburgh, Cincinnati, St Louis, Chicago, Cleveland, Buffalo and Boston, attracting a great deal of interest along the way. In total the train covered 3,121 miles over American railroads without any untoward problems. By the time the Fair closed war had been declared in Europe and rather than risk bringing the engine and train back it was placed in store by the Baltimore & Ohio Railway. However, while the coaches remained in the USA for the duration of the war, due to shortage of motive power it was eventually decided to risk bringing the engine back and it arrived safely at Cardiff docks on 16 February 1942. These two photographs taken in 1939 show the engine at the World's Fair exhibition.

Left. The British Railways Locomotive Interchange Trials of 1948 are well-chronicled, and so is the fact that the Stanier Pacific probably showed less well than it could. Certainly this was the case with 46236 CITY OF BRADFORD on the Southern at Waterloo. Driver Byford, it is said, was concerned with coal consumption rather than dramatic flourishes. Allen in his book *The Locomotive Exchanges 1870-1948* (Ian Allan, 1949) tells of all the Pacifics on the Southern testing ground, A4, Merchant Navy and 46236, being trounced by Royal Scot 46154 THE HUSSAR, so it was an LM victory of sorts! 46236 (seen here at Waterloo) was notable for the attachment of a WD tender, for greater water capacity on the Southern, which lacked troughs. The LMS had never owned such tenders but in despite of this, and the fact that CITY OF BRADFORD was already numbered in its BR sequence (something which seems to have been insisted upon) someone saw a loophole and hurriedly had the tender lettered LMS... The Record Card incidentally, shows it to have been off a Western Region WD, numbered A79294. Photograph C.C.B. Herbert.

Bottom left. One of the dynamometer car trains, behind 46236 CITY OF BRADFORD on 21 May 1948, near Ealing with the 8.30 am from Plymouth. It did well on some days on the Western Region and not so well on others. It was responsible for 'a most uninspiring run' on 19 May for instance, but elsewhere showed moments of brilliance. The Stanier Pacific proved its reliability at least, for it never had to be replaced, unlike the A4s, say. Originally, 46229 DUCHESS OF HAMILTON was selected to represent the LMS, but CITY OF BRADFORD must have been better suited. Photograph J.C. Flemons, www.transporttreasury.co.uk

Below. In that wonderful black during the trials, about to leave Wakefield with the 1pm to Kings Cross. How small that cab window does look, immediately post-streamlining.

46220 CORONATION

Built Crewe 1/6/37, cost £10,095 (engine), £1,546 (tender)
Renumbered 6229 ('verbal message CME') 20/12/38
Renumbered 6220 ('during repairs at Crewe') April 1943
Built streamlined, casing removed 6/11/46
Renumbered 6220 to 46220 week ending 3/7/48

Boilers

Fitted	No.	From
5/1/40	10637	new
1/5/43	9939	6223
6/11/46	10292	6243
26/1/50	10640	6242
29/8/52	10302	-
30/7/55	10295	-

No record after this date

Repairs LMS
1/11/37-18/11/37**LO**
4/4/38-14/4/38**LO**
22/9/38-19/10/38**LS**
27/3/39-6/4/39**LO**
29/11/39-5/1/40**HG**
22/2/40-19/3/40**LO**
3/8/40-24/8/40**LO**
5/11/40-10/12/40**LO**
5/3/41-22/3/41**LO**
21/7/41-16/8/41**HS**
7/1/42-5/2/42**LO**
10/9/42-3/10/42**LS**
16/4/43-14/5/43**HG**
11/2/44-11/3/44**HS**
20/4/44-19/5/44**LO**
30/4/45-2/6/45**LS**
4/10/45-9/11/45**LO**
26/9/46-6/11/46**LO**
3/6/48-3/7/48**LS**
20/7/48-3/7/48**TRO**
10/1/49-12/2/49**HC**
12/12/49-26/1/50**HG**
18/7/50-18/8/50**LC**

Repairs BR
Dates in the first column are from out of traffic to return to traffic; A = 'Weekdays Waiting', B= 'Weekdays on Works'. The two mileage figures represent, firstly, the miles accumulated since the previous General or Intermediate (C) and secondly (the lower figure) the miles run up from January 1st of the year of shopping - D. All work is recorded as taking place at Crewe unless otherwise noted. StR=St Rollox

Dates	A	B	C	D
19/4/51-19/5/51**LI**	3	23	85,096	18,190
15/5/52-29/8/52**G**	10	81	67,479	23,647
23/4/53-21/5/53**LC***	6	19	46,771	21,059
12/10/53-11/11/53**LI**	6	20	73,331	47,711
1/9/54-1/9/54**NC**	-	1(StR)	52,905	44,530
22/9/54-4/11/54**LC***	12	25	56,504	48,129
24/5/55-30/7/55**G**	9	49	79,668	15,778
2/8/55-25/8/55**NC***	-	20	nil	15,778
12/2/57-22/3/57**LI**	6	27	93,572	7,472
25/11/57-28/11/57**NC**	-	3	-	-
19/5/58-26/6/58**HI**	1	34	72,235	21,295

record ends
*='(EO)' - 'Engine Only'

Sheds

Camden	
Rugby	16/9/39*
Camden	21/10/39
Polmadie	21/12/39
Crewe North	13/7/58
Upperby (loan)	2/4/60
Crewe North	23/4/60
Upperby	2/61

*stored 19/9/39-2/10/39

Tenders

No	Fitted
9703	1/6/37
9803	23/6/44
9703	6/8/44
9804	9/1/46
9705	3/8/49

LMS 'Summary' *(this became 'Annual Statistics' from 1951)*

Year	Mileage	Weekdays out of service			
		wks	shed	n/req	total
1937	36,210	9	31	21	61
1938	66,809	34	52	22	108
1939	67,907	37	60	24	133#
1940	54,901	78	37	22	137
1941	54,705	42	91	11	144
1942	71,104	47	36	10	93
1943	74,633	25	52	3	80
1944	40,435	52	93	2	147
1945	54,957	61	81	-	142
1946	48,435	36	117	1	154
1947	59,505	-	65	-	65
1948	46,006	27	80	2	109
1949	55,214	48	65	2	117
1950	66,906	47	48	-	95
1951	62,022	26	71	-	97
1952	49,359	91	38	-	129
1953	56,086	51	52	2	105
1954	55,535	37	44	-	81
1955	40,828	78	67	1	146
1956	61,050	-	62	1	63
1957	58,412	33	42	2	77

#includes 12days 'stored unserviceable'
record ends
wks=heavy and light repairs at main works
shed=shed repairs and examinations
n/req= not required

Total Recorded Mileage 1,178,019
Withdrawn week ending 20/4/63
Cut up Crewe Works 5/63

Pioneer 6220 CORONATION passing Hemel Hempstead on the down 'Coronation Scot' on 22 March 1938. This train, for which these engines were originally built, started to run on its six and a half hour schedule between Euston and Glasgow on 5 July the previous year with a limited nine coach load. Photograph Ken Nunn Collection, Locomotive Club of Great Britain.

6220 CORONATION on shed at Polmadie towards the end of its life with the LMS. Painted in the fully lined black livery with straw lining applied in October 1946, the engine retains the casting for housing the Fowler-Anderson cylinder by-pass valves although by this date they would have long since been blanked off. Interesting paint style of the cab number on the Class 5 alongside. Photograph www.transporttreasury.co.uk

During the year of the Coronation of our present Queen Elizabeth II, the Scottish Region arranged for 'The Royal Scot' to be additionally adorned with the crown headboard seen here, on this occasion very fittingly, on 46220 CORONATION. This is the up train on 6 June 1953 just south of Carstairs. The engine shed is to the right and notice that row of livestock wagons to the left, recalling days when the railways carried cattle and sheep; all livestock indeed. Photograph J. Robertson,www.transporttreasury.co.uk

Left. A brooding 46220 at Polmadie. The large diameter pipe disappearing behind the cab side sheet is the exhaust steam pipe from the blast-pipe to the exhaust injector, itself seen just aft the trailing truck. Notice the single brake block for each coupled wheel; the first five had this arrangement while all the later ones had smaller twin blocks, albeit carried in a single hanger. Apart from 46224 which was modified to the later arrangement, the others were never similarly altered and retained the design as seen here. Photograph R. Bruce, www.transporttreasury.co.uk

Bottom left. Polmadie's 46220 CORONATION at Shrewsbury; while it was the practice to use engines arriving at Crewe from the north on fill-in turns to Shrewsbury with West of England trains, which served the double purpose of turning them round for a trip north again, I do not think this is what has happened in this case. It was not the normal procedure for engines on fill-in turns to visit the shed at Shrewsbury; rather, they turned on the Severn Bridge triangle and proceeded to Crewe Bank, north of the station, to await the return working, sometimes whiling away time in the bay platform. Notice in this case the engine has taken on some coal, so it may have been sent here on a running-in turn after attention at Crewe. The engine is in forward gear with a crew, so it is probably waiting to leave the shed. Photograph David Montgomery.

Below. CORONATION on Crewe North shed some time after August 1952 when it received the BR green livery and December 1955 when the smokebox was modified. The engine will have worked south from its home shed at Polmadie and be waiting for its return working. While turned ready it has not yet been coaled which is unusual as normal practice was to fill the tenders on arrival. Could it have just returned from a fill-in turn to Shrewsbury? Photograph David Montgomery.

46221 QUEEN ELIZABETH

Built Crewe 14/6/37 cost £10,095 (engine), £1,546 (tender)
Built streamlined, casing removed 28/6/46
Renumbered 6221 to 46221 week ending 23/10/48

Boilers

Fitted	No.	From
6/11/40	10303	6232
17/7/43	10637	6220
28/6/46	10294	6234
30/3/50	10694	6241
16/12/52	10292	-
5/11/55	10694	-
7/9/61	10298	-

No record after this date

Repairs LMS

17/2/38-1/3/38**LO**
27/6/38-1/7/38**TO**
24/10/38-15/11/38**LS**
18/4/39-27/4/39**LO**
7/8/39-29/8/39**LS**
24/9/40-6/11/40**HG**
17/12/40-14/1/41**LO**
7/7/41-9/8/41**LO**
11/2/42-11/3/42**LS**
26/9/42-31/10/42**HS**
9/6/43-17/7/43**HG**
15/6/44-29/7/44**LS**
17/4/45-12/5/45**LS**
22/5/46-28/6/46**HG**
24/1/47-1/2/47**LO**
21/3/47-5/5/47**LO**
1/12/47-6/12/47**NC**
16/9/48-22/10/48**HS**
8/1/49-1/2/49**LC**
13/5/49-17/6/49**LC**
28/9/49-29/10/49**LC**
13/2/50-30/3/50**HG**

Repairs BR
Dates in the first column are from out of traffic to return to traffic; A = 'Weekdays Waiting', B= 'Weekdays on Works'. The two mileage figures represent, firstly the miles accumulated since the previous General or Intermediate (C) and secondly (the lower figure) the miles run up from January 1st of the year of shopping - D. All work is recorded as taking place at Crewe unless otherwise noted. StR=St Rollox

Dates	A	B	C	D
26/2/51-5/4/51**LI**	5	28	81,258	15,139
12/2/52-7/4/52**HI**	3	44	69,343	8,843
2/7/52-20/8/52**LC***	15	27	17,933	26,776
30/10/52-16/12/52**HG**	5	35	29,521	38,364
23/2/54-3/4/54**HI**	7	27	69,174	5,691
24/12/54-24/12/54**NC***	-	(StR)	-	57,706
24/2/55-24/2/55**NC**	-	(StR)	-	46,005
24/9/55-5/11/55**HG**	5	31	90,412	43,811
23/7/56-1/9/56**LC***	12	23	42,573	36,016
28/9/57-9/11/57**LI**	4	32	102,387	39,459
17/11/58-1/1/59**HI**	4	33	69,566	63,922
10/9/59-30/10/59**LC**	16	27	59,885	59,885
1/5/60-7/6/60**HI**	3	28	105,310	33,288
19/6/61-7/9/61**HG**	30	39	66,618	22,263

record ends
*='(EO)' - 'Engine Only'

LMS 'Summary' *(this became 'Annual Statistics' from 1951)*

Year	Mileage	Weekdays out of service			
		wks	shed	n/req	total
1937	30,945	-	37	20	57
1938	67,705	36	39	15	90
1939	66,484	29	46	29	128#
1940	74,123	49	43	31	123
1941	61,882	43	73	12	128
1942	68,199	56	38	5	99
1943	68,945	34	61	2	97
1944	71,847	39	63	3	105
1945	53,202	22	110	2	134
1946	67,947	33	80	2	115
1947	52,165	47	68	2	117
1948	57,948	32	66	1	99
1949	49.494	80	51	2	133
1950	71,441	39	46	-	85
1951	75,639	33	69	-	102
1952	40,424	129	30	1	160
1953	61,423	-	80	-	80
1954	52,292	34	88	3	125
1955	50,368	36	54	12	102
1956	56,371	35	43	1	79
1957	45,103	35	80	2	117
1958	63,922	34	38	-	72
1959	72,022				

#includes 24 days 'stored serviceable'
record ends
wks=heavy and light repairs at main works
shed=shed repairs and examinations
n/req= not required

Total Recorded Mileage 1,387,893
Withdrawn week ending 18/5/63
Cut up Crewe Works 7/63

Sheds

Camden	
Crewe North	16/9/39
Camden	21/10/39
Polmadie	25/11/39
Crewe North	5/7/58
Camden	20/6/59
Crewe North	1/10/60
Carlisle Upperby	11/2/61
Carlisle Kingmoor	11/4/61
Carlisle Upperby	7/4/62

Stored 10/9/39-2/10/39, and 29/10/62 to we 2/2/63

Tenders

No	Fitted
9704	14/6/37
9816	17/11/61
9359	18/10/62

A lovely portrait of the second engine of the class, 6221 QUEEN ELIZABETH on Polmadie shed in the original light blue livery introduced for the 'Coronation Scot' train. The engine looks quite new so I would suggest the photograph dates from some time in 1937; it was new in June. I have not been able to trace the W27 reporting number in contemporary timetables; it was not the number for either the Coronation Scot, Royal Scot or Mid-Day Scot, which might otherwise be the trains this engine would work. Points to note are the special art deco headlamps provided for these engines with *Hermes*-style wings, the speedometer drive off the trailing coupled axle, the sand box filler lids protruding from the streamline casing just below the nameplate line and the door at the top rear of the tender to assist in taking-on water.

Polmadie in the early 1950s with 46221 QUEEN ELIZABETH already coaled and taking water prior to its next diagram. By this time painted in the BR green livery the engine still has the sloping smokebox top, which was modified to the circular arrangement in September 1952. The engine retains the casting beneath the cylinder that formerly bore the Fowler-Anderson cylinder by-pass valves; the replacement anti-vacuum valve, albeit in this case for the inside cylinder, can just be discerned mounted on the frames below the smoke deflector. That is the shed ash handling plant to the right background. Photograph J. Robertson, www.transporttreasury.co.uk

QUEEN ELIZABETH at Crewe North, coaled and facing north ready for its next turn of duty in September 1952. I cannot find the reporting number W549 in any of the contemporary working timetables in my collection, though it was the highest of a batch allotted to trains heading south from Scotland. The W indicates the Western Division, at that time of the London Midland Region, but the system of numbering was a continuation of the former LMS practice and remained in use until the four character codes were introduced by BR. As 46221 is a Crewe the engine the number must refer to its previous working. Photograph J.T. Clewley, www.transporttreasury.co.uk

46222 QUEEN MARY

Built Crewe 22/6/37, cost £10,095 8s 11d (engine), £1,546 (tender)
Built streamlined, casing removed 10/7/46
Renumbered 6222 to 46222 week ending 25/9/48

Boilers

Fitted	No.	From
24/1/40	10638	new
28/7/43	10298	6227
28/7/45	10287	6233
9/8/47	10296	6242
28/10/50	12471	6254
12/8/53	10295	-
16/4/55	12472	-

No record after this date

Repairs LMS

15/6/38-28/6/38**LO**
5/12/38-22/12/38**LS**
2/12/39-24/1/40**HG**
25/1/41-20/2/41**LS**
21/5/42-20/6/42**HS**
11/6/43-28/7/43**HG**
6/7/44-5/8/44**LS**
11/6/45-28/7/45**HG**
1/3/46-16/3/46**LO**
10/4/46-24/5/46**LS**
14/1/47-28/2/47**LO**
5/5/47-31/7/47**HS**
11/8/47-14/8/47**NC**
7/10/47-11/10/47**NC**
17/8/48-21/9/48**LS**
22/7/49-15/9/49**LI**
16/9/49-22/9/49**NC**
20/2/50-17/3/50**LC**
29/8/50-28/10/50**G**

Repairs BR

Dates in the first column are from out of traffic to return to traffic; A = 'Weekdays Waiting', B= 'Weekdays on Works'. The two mileage figures represent, firstly the miles accumulated since the previous General or Intermediate (C) and secondly (the lower figure) the miles run up from January 1st of the year of shopping - D. All work is recorded as taking place at Crewe unless otherwise noted. StR=St Rollox

Dates	A	B	C	D
20/11/51-29/12/51**LI**	6	28	87,165	70,835
30/4/52-27/6/52**LC**	6	44	26,008	26,008
4/6/53-12/8/53**G**	12	47	77,762	20,569
20/8/53-22/8/53**NC**	-	2	672	21,241
27/4/54-27/4/54**NC***	-	1(StR)	38,706	21,871
7/9/54-8/9/54**NC**	-	1(StR)	61,835	45,000
26/2/55-16/4/55**G**	7	34	87,356	6,097
11/4/56-12/4/56**NC**	-	1(StR)	62,494	18,520
20/4/56-25/5/56**HI**	9	21	63,966	19,992
19/4/57-1/6/57**HI**	8	29	59,055	18,418
†4/6/57-10/6/57**NC***	-	5	-	-
†4/6/57-19/6/57**NC***	-	13	192	18,610
21/6/57-3/7/57**NC***	-	10	248	18,666
2/12/57-4/12/57**NC***	-	2	-	-
5/12/58-27/1/59**G**	14	29	72,472	45,726
14/7/59-13/11/59**LC**	23	33	39,464	39,464
5/9/60-19/10/60**HI**	6	32	93,401	46,321
26/4/61-17/6/61**HC**	10	35	34,697	19,746
26/3/62-28/7/62**G**	9	98	-	-

†dates conflict; pres. Clerical error
Record ends
*(EO)'-'EngineOnly'

LMS 'Summary' *(thisbecame 'Annual Statistics' from 1951)*

Year	Mileage	Weekdays out of service			
		wks	shed	n/req	total
1937	33,300	-	24	23	47
1938	69,163	28	37	28	93
1939	67,299	24	76	9	109
1940	83,546	21	51	28	100
1941	50,329	23	100	6	129
1942	61,516	27	62	5	94
1943	56,720	41	109	3	153
1944	70,665	27	96	6	129
1945	58,493	42	96	2	140
1946	55,946	53	112	3	168
1947	42,531	120	30	-	150
1948	61,078	31	52	-	83
1949	61,093	54	49	1	104
1950	55,828	74	38	1	113
1951	70,835	34	40	-	74
1952	67,193	50	59	-	109
1953	37,404	59	103	-	162
1954	64,424	-	50	-	50
1955	50,071	41	64	-	120
1956	60,629	30	53	-	86
1957	45,164	37	49	-	101
1958	45,726	20	93	-	113
1959	47,080	*recordends*			
1960	61,272				
1961	50,443				
1962	30,612				

wks = heavy and light repairs at main works
shed = shed repairs and examinations
n/req = not required

Total Recorded Mileage 1,458,368
Withdrawn week ending 26/10/63
Cut up Crewe Works 11/63

Sheds
Camden
Polmadie 21/11/39

Tenders

No	Fitted
9705	22/6/37
9804	3/8/49

Polmadie, home for most of their lives of the first few members of the class; 46222 QUEEN MARY in the BR blue livery that was used for a period on the principal express passenger locomotives of all Regions. This view is dated 8 March 1952; the engine is prepared for a run south and, in forward gear, is doubtless about to move off the shed and head for Glasgow Central. The large building to the right is the former LMS Repair Shop, still in use at the time and indeed retained well into diesel days as a Regional Repair Shop, to help out the Scottish depots with the heavier levels of repairs. Photograph
www.transporttreasury.co.uk

What a lovely portrait; never mind the grime for it cannot mask the dignity of this magnificent High Born Lady. 6222 QUEEN MARY is about to enter Dalry Road shed in Edinburgh, where engines of this class were by no means regular visitors. The engine bears the LMS lined black livery introduced after the war, but seems to have a non-standard position for the lettering on the tender and nameplates picked out in white – they were of course brass. The rather small cab front window as seen here was a feature of those engines that were formerly streamlined; they were later enlarged to bring them into line with the non-streamlined engines and of course, improve forward vision. This modification dates from September 1948, after which the engines were altered as they went through Crewe Works. Unfortunately this photograph is undated but judging by the position of the sun, it is tempting to suggest that the engine may have come north on one of the overnight trains and worked through with the Edinburgh portion. QUEEN MARY was a Polmadie engine for almost all its life. Photograph W. Hermiston, www.transporttreasury.co.uk

QUEEN MARY at Carlisle at an unknown date, though the tender has the early BR emblem which was replaced by the later version from 1956 onwards. There is no AWS equipment and Citadel still has its full overall roof. The engine is standing at the south end of the station and is just moving off in back-gear; being a Polmadie engine it has probably arrived on an up train and is on its way to Kingmoor shed. Photograph Paul Chancellor Collection.

Bottom left. The smokebox was restored to conventional outline in August 1953 and by now 46222 is painted in the later green livery used for all express locomotives. This is Polmadie and QUEEN MARY, coaled for its return journey, has yet to be turned to head south. The former Caledonian Railway McIntosh 3F 0-6-0 alongside, 57581, was a Polmadie engine for just about all its life with BR; it was withdrawn in November 1963. Photograph N. Lester, www.transporttreasury.co.uk

Below. One last view of QUEEN MARY, in this case on the morning of 14 April 1956, arriving at Glasgow Central with one of the overnight sleeping car trains. Behind the two GUVs are four former LMS twelve-wheel sleeping cars. It looks as if the driver has just opened the regulator having cleared the maze of point work, to take the train to the platform end, causing the exhaust injector to 'knock off'. If this engine has hauled the train from Carlisle, as would seem to be the case, there is a surprising amount of coal visible in the tender. Photograph J. Robertson, www.transporttreasury.co.uk

46223 PRINCESS ALICE

Built Crewe 28/6/37, cost £10,095 (engine), £1,546 (tender)
Built streamlined, casing removed 6/8/46
Renumbered 6223 to 46223 week ending 19/3/49

Boilers

Fitted	No.	From
17/4/40	9939	6222
1/11/41	9938	6221
30/5/42	10642	new
13/7/45	10301	6232
5/12/47	10297	6233
14/4/50	10292	6220
10/10/52	10297	-
25/8/55	9940	-
2/7/60	10299	-

No record after this date

Repairs LMS

6/1/38-19/1/38**LO**
11/7/38-25/7/38**LS**
17/11/38-2/12/38**LO**
18/4/39-3/5/39**LS**
4/3/40-17/4/40**HG**
6/12/40-2/1/41**HS**
25/8/41-20/9/41**LO**
3/10/41-1/11/41**HG**
23/4/42-30/5/42**HO**
21/9/42-5/11/42**LO**
6/5/43-28/5/43**LS**
13/12/43-22/1/44**LS**
22/8/44-16/9/44**LS**
28/5/45-13/7/45**HG**
24/9/45-3/11/45**HO**
10/6/46-6/8/46**LS**
12/12/46-31/12/46**LO**
27/2/47-10/3/47**LO**
14/5/47-20/6/47**LS**
8/9/47-5/12/47**HO**
14/2/49-14/3/49**LI**
11/10/49-17/11/49**LC**
24/11/49-2/12/49**NC**
20/2/50-14/4/50**HG**

Repairs BR

Dates in the first column are from out of traffic to return to traffic; A = 'Weekdays Waiting', B= 'Weekdays on Works'. The two mileage figures represent, firstly the miles accumulated since the previous General or Intermediate (C) and secondly (the lower figure) the miles run up from January 1st of the year of shopping - D. All work is recorded as taking place at Crewe unless otherwise noted. StR=St Rollox

Dates	A	B	C	D
23/7/51-28/8/51**HI**	7	24	92,743	36,636
22/8/52-10/10/52**HG**	5	37	78,223	44,097
23/12/53-2/2/54**HI**	6	27	77,688	nil
31/5/54-5/6/54**NC***(StR)	-	-	-	-
18/2/55-18/2/55**NC**(StR)	-	-	-	-
27/4/55-28/4/55**NC**(StR)	-	-	-	-
17/6/55-25/8/55**HG**	27	32	80,715	19,501
27/8/56-11/10/56**LC***	4	35	62,560	41,036
8/4/57-17/5/57**HI**	3	31	92,519	16,246
9/11/57-14/12/57**LC**	5	26	35,288	51,534
30/9/58-15/11/58**HI**	11	29	85,536	49,014
26/4/60-2/7/60**HG**	30	28	80,007	12,752
22/8/60-19/11/60**LC**	4	73	-	-
15/11/61-5/1/62**HI**	14	28	78,035	44,204

*(EO)'-'EngineOnly'

LMS 'Summary' *(this became 'Annual Statistics' from 1951)*

Year	Mileage	Weekdays out of service			
		wks	shed	n/req	total
1937	29,875	-	37	20	57
1938	66,968	39	43	27	109
1939	69,267	14	81	32	127
1940	61,786	58	37	18	113
1941	53,227	53	68	6	127
1942	51,886	73	48	4	125
1943	80,192	32	55	-	87
1944	70,930	46	66	6	118
1945	49,247	77	91	3	171
1946	73,524	65	44	1	110
1947	36,378	122	23	4	149
1948	71,435	-	79	-	79
1949	49,983	66	61	3	130
1950	69,358	46	50	-	96
1951	70,505	31	59	-	90
1952	59,084	42	46	-	88
1953	62,958	8	57	-	65
1954	61,214	25	39	1	65
1955	41,025	59	53	15	127
1956	54,310	39	58	-	97
1957	52,736	63	41	1	105
1958	55,825	40	147	1	85
1959	60,508	*record ends*			
1960	46,583				
1961	44,204				
1962	49,708				

wks=heavy and light repairs at main works
shed=shed repairs and examinations
n/req= not required

Total Recorded Mileage 1,492,619
Withdrawn. Curiously, no note made, but the tender 'attached to 46223' is recorded instead, 'withdrawn period ending 5/10/63'. 46223 was indeed withdrawn in October that year.
Cut up Crewe Works 10/63

Sheds
Camden
Polmadie   25/11/39

Tenders

No	Fitted
9706	28/6/37
9748	6/5/46

PRINCESS ALICE again, this time defrocked and rather unkempt, at Glasgow St Enoch on 29 March 1952, about to leave on a southbound train piloted by what would in all probability be a Class 2 4-4-0 of Midland Railway parentage. One is tempted to think this would be a main line train routed over the Glasgow & South Western Route, but the first vehicle in a non-corridor one, so in all probability this is a local train, with the Class 2 perhaps being worked home to Kilmarnock, or wherever, to save a light engine move. Whatever the case we can but guess. The engine is in the blue livery, which it retained until October 1952. Photograph www.transporttreasury.co.uk

6223 PRINCESS ALICE, in its original streamlined form, standing at the south end of No.5 platform at Crewe, with a Great Western through coach. The engine would have been waiting to attach this vehicle to a Liverpool/Manchester to the West of England train, which it would work forward to Shrewsbury, where the GWR would take over. Diagrams like this were a regular part of Pacific working from the initial introduction of the class until the diesels arrived, a sort of filling in job between other duties, which also served to have the engines turned ready for a journey back north on an overnight train. At the time Crewe North did not have a turntable long enough and engines used the Severn Bridge triangle at Shrewsbury before returning on a similar train. Although the engines could be turned at Crewe South, or on the Gresty Lane triangle, this was another way of achieving the same goal while at the same time improving the utilisation of the class. The photograph is dated September 1937, so the engine is quite new; it entered traffic in July, and would be in the blue livery that the first five carried. Notice the fellow in the tender – one wonders what he was doing? Photograph www.transporttreasury.co.uk

The down 'Royal Scot' just starting to leave Glasgow Central on 28 May 1959 with a rather clean Polmadie Pacific 46223 PRINCESS ALICE. It looks as if the fireman has just put a round on the fire; the safety valves are sizzling nicely so the injector, which had probably been keeping them quiet, has just been turned off and the cylinder cocks are open. Clearly here is a crew who know what they are about and there is the driver looking back to ensure all is well. The headboard looks as if its background is painted Caledonian blue; the Scottish Region often did this. What a lovely composition and so typical of these magnificent engines. Photograph R.C. Riley, www.transporttreasury

46224 PRINCESS ALEXANDRA

Built Crewe 13/7/37, cost £10,095 (engine), £1,546 (tender)
Built streamlined, casing removed 27/6/46
Renumbered 6224 to 46224 week ending 8/5/48

Boilers

Fitted	No.	From
29/5/40	9937	6220
5/11/40	10300	6228
16/10/43	10289	6237
28/3/45	10290	6225
27/6/46	10305	6229
3/5/48	10301	6223
26/8/50	10303	6250
20/5/52	10643	-
23/10/54	10293	-
24/9/57	9941	-
6/1/62	10288	-

Repairs LMS

26/8/37-1/9/37**LO**
26/1/38-10/2/38**LO**
2/9/38-22/9/38**LS**
10/3/39-27/3/39**LO**
14/7/39-31/7/39**LS**
25/4/40-29/5/40**HG**
10/9/40-5/11/40**HO**
29/3/41-19/4/41**HS**
24/3/42-14/4/42**LS**
15/3/43-15/4/43**LS**
10/9/43-16/10/43**HG**
10/7/44-17/8/44**LS**
17/2/45-28/3/45**HG**
14/5/46-27/6/46**HS**
4/10/47-22/11/47**HS**
9/3/48-3/5/48**HG**
19/5/48-31/5/48 'NIL'
21/11/48-21/12/48**LO**
8/6/49-8/8/49**LI**
29/6/50-26/8/50**HG**

Repairs BR

Dates in the first column are from out of traffic to return to traffic; A = 'Weekdays Waiting', B= 'Weekdays on Works'. The two mileage figures represent, firstly the miles accumulated since the previous General or Intermediate (C) and secondly (the lower figure) the miles run up from January 1st of the year of shopping - D. All work is recorded as taking place at Crewe unless otherwise noted. StR=St Rollox

Dates	A	B	C	D
5/9/50-15/9/50**NC**	-	9	404	31,573
8/3/51-25/4/51**HI**	18	23	47,646	18,646
7/4/52-20/5/52**HG**	3	34	70,717	13,668
26/5/52-31/5/52**NC**	-	5	460	14,128
12/5/53-19/6/53**HI**	8	25	71,083	27,589
14/9/54-23/10/54**HI**	7	27	81,198	40,252
4/5/54-4/5/54**NC**(StR)	-	1	61,592	20,646
1/2/56-14/3/56**LI**	10	26	71,014	4,559
16/5/56-16/5/56**NC**(StR)	-	1	5,370	9,929
8/10/56-10/11/56**LC***	9	20	32,472	37,031
14/11/56-16/11/56**NC***	-	2	32,567	37,126
27/7/57-24/9/57**HG**	14	36	73,626	32,419
3/4/59-20/5/59**LI**	11	29	93,262	12,320
5/10/59-4/12/59**LC***	22	30	25,640	37,709
10/3/60-7/5/60**LI**	17	32	43,358	13,731
4/11/61-3/1/61**HC***	14	35	32,367	46,098
25/10/61-5/1/62**HG**	22	38	67,136	34,769

Record ends
*'(EO)'-Engine Only

LMS 'Summary' (this became 'Annual Statistics' from 1951)

Year	Mileage	Weekdays out of service			
		wks	shed	n/req	total
1937	31,149	6	19	11	36
1938	63,289	32	63	19	114
1939	60,093	30	55	24	109
1940	63,147	79	53	26	158
1941	67,276	19	52	8	81
1942	75,354	19	64	-	83
1943	63,994	60	51	3	114
1944	68,979	34	59	6	99
1945	70,768	34	64	-	98
1946	57,484	39	86	5	130
1947	53,445	43	65	-	108
1948	55,145	82	43	2	127
1949	67,583	53	46	2	101
1950	60,169	59	38	1	98
1951	75,695	41	55	-	96
1952	57,162	42	53	1	96
1953	68,535	33	36	2	71
1954	51,486	34	52	-	86
1955	55,008	-	80	12	92
1956	44,865	67	61	-	128
1957	47,772	50	48	2	100
1958	66,379	*record ends*			
1959	41,947				
1960	46,098				
1961	34,769				
1962	42,899				

wks=heavy and light repairs at main works
shed=shed repairs and examinations
n/req= not required

Total Recorded Mileage 1,490,488
Withdrawn week ending 19/10/63
Cut up Crewe Works 10/63

Sheds

Camden
Polmadie   30/12/39

Tenders

No	Fitted
9707	13/7/37
9748	14/8/45
9706	6/5/46

On the ash pits at Polmadie, 46224 PRINCESS ALEXANDRA, in April 1957. The driver would appear to be keeping an eye on his young fireman as he removes the residual ash from the front of the engine, left there by the disposal crew when they emptied the smokebox. The driver would be anxious to have it removed as otherwise it would blow back towards the cab as they gather speed on their way south - clearly an experienced man! Photograph R.E. Vincent, www.transporttreasury.co.uk

An aristocrat of a locomotive; 46224 PRINCESS ALEXANDRA on Carlisle Kingmoor shed, in the period before October 1954, when its smokebox was altered. The engine would have worked the up 'Royal Scot' south from Glasgow earlier in the day, arrived about mid-day, and would be waiting to take the down train north in the early afternoon. For much of their existence the Scottish Region engines shuttled between Glasgow and Carlisle, such that the mileages they accumulated were less than their English brethren. One of the anti-vacuum valves is clearly visible; it is the circular object with a series of small holes in front of the cylinder. The valve on the front cover of the cylinder is the pressure relief valve. The Class 5 to the left, 45499, the highest numbered of the class, was allocated to St Rollox shed in Glasgow, where the staff were clearly conscious of spring snowfalls on the West Highland lines where it might otherwise be used – hence the miniature snow plough. Photograph W. Hermiston, www.transporttreasury.co.uk

Above. 46224 PRINCESS ALEXANDRA, departing from Shrewsbury on its way back to Crewe in the early 1950s and certainly prior to October 1954, when the smokebox was modified. A Polmadie engine for much of its life and is doubtless on a running-in turn after attention in Crewe Works. Photograph David Montgomery.

Top right and right. Two excellent views of 46224 PRINCESS ALEXANDRA at Glasgow St Enoch on 28 May 1960. In the first the engine is backing down towards the station to attach to its train; in the second it is on its way south. Unfortunately we know nothing of the train itself, but it is probably not a long distance one as the first vehicle is a BR built non-corridor coach. Once the diesels arrived on the scene Polmadie often used its Pacifics on semi-fast trains over the Glasgow & South Western route to and from St Enoch. Notice in the first photograph the engine has been modified to take the twin brake blocks; it was the only one of the first five engines with the earlier arrangement to be thus modified. But the engine retains the Fowler-Anderson cylinder by-pass valve castings, visible underneath the cylinder. Photograph J. Robertson, www.transporttreasury.co.uk

46225 DUCHESS OF GLOUCESTER

Built Crewe 11/5/38, cost £10,136 (tender £1,601)
Built streamlined, casing removed 24/3/47
Renumbered 6225 to 46225 week ending 19/6/48

Boilers

Fitted	No.	From
27/8/40	10302	6331
22/8/42	10290	6238
22/9/44	10291	6239
24/3/47	10638	6248
28/3/50	10642	-
21/3/53	12472	-
20/1/55	10645	-
7/8/58	10301	-
7/10/61	10693	-

No record after this date

Repairs LMS
12/8/38-1/9/38**LO**
18/4/39-4/5/39**LS**
19/7/40-29/8/40**HG**
23/9/41-11/10/41**LS**
7/3/42-21/3/42**LO**
30/7/42-22/8/42**HG**
1/6/43-24/6/43**HS**
15/3/44-7/4/44**HS**
16/5/44-22/7/44**HG**
10/2/45-28/3/45**HS**
6/3/46-5/4/46**LS**
11/2/47-24/3/47**HG**
26/10/47-4/11/47**NC**
22/5/48-19/6/48**LS**
7/2/49-11/3/49**HI**
11/6/49-16/6/49**NC**
7/2/50-28/3/50**HG**

Repairs BR
Dates in the first column are from out of traffic to return to traffic; A = 'Weekdays Waiting', B= 'Weekdays on Works'. The two mileage figures represent, firstly the miles accumulated since the previous General or Intermediate (C) and secondly (the lower figure) the miles run up from January 1st of the year of shopping - D. All work is recorded as taking place at Crewe unless otherwise noted. StR=St Rollox

Dates	A	B	C	D
31/3/50-21/4/50**LC**	-	17	198	4,787
13/12/50-21/1/51**LC**	3	22	50,734	55,323
22/9/51-24/10/51**HI**	6	21	105,206	54,472
26/3/52-4/4/52**NC***	3	5	33,613	19,452
18/5/52-28/6/52**LI**	7	28	46,580	32,419
24/1/53-21/3/53**HG**	3	46	49,283	3,102
25/3/53-26/3/53**NC***	-	1	140	3,242
9/10/53-10/11/53**LC***	9	18	48,507	51,609
12/1/54-16/1/54**NC***	3	1	62,559	3,132
11/11/54-20/1/55**HG**	3	55	115,776	56,349
23/6/55-1/7/55**NC***	1	6	10,339	10,339
17/2/56-10/3/56**HI**	2	17	65,762	11,547
9/5/56-18/5/56**NC***	-	8	5,409	16,956
16/4/57-18/4/57**NC***	-	2	76,141	22,727
15/8/57-28/9/57**HI**	5	33	102,826	49,412
13/6/58-7/8/58**HG**	6	41	56,532	34,956
6/11/59-1/1/60**LI**	12	34	93,836	61,923
11/3/60-14/4/60**LC***	16	13	20,436	20,205
2/8/61-9/10/61**HG**	6	52	106,356	28,668

*='(EO)'-'EngineOnly'

Sheds

Camden	21/5/38
Holyhead	21/10/39
Crewe North	6/4/40
Polmadie (loan)	11/5/40
Crewe North	15/6/40
Camden	22/5/43
Crewe North	12/10/46
Camden	11/10/47
Crewe North	1/10/49
Camden	5/7/52
Crewe North	20/9/52
Rugby Test Station	22/1/55
Crewe North	4/6/55
Carlisle Upperby	27/6/59

stored 2/1/64 - 27/1/64

Tenders

No	Fitted
9743	11/5/38
9749	9/8/45
9799	11/3/49

LMS 'Summary' *(this became 'Annual Statistics' from 1951)*

Year	Mileage	Weekdays out of service			
		wks	shed	n/req	total
1938	53,126	18	24	2	44
1939	78,386	15	86	11	112
1940	61,957	34	50	17	101
1941	79,372	17	47	1	65
1942	70,079	34	48	-	82
1943	78,942	21	53	1	75
1944	63,028	80	51	-	131
1945	69,800	40	110	-	150
1946	82,352	27	40	4	71
1947	70,803	36	50	-	86
1948	68,077	25	70	3	98
1949	76,794	29	42	5	76
1950	55,323	74	49	6	129
1951	68,633	37	44	-	81
1952	78,600	35	61	-	96
1953	62,529	77	41	2	120
1954	56,349	43	63	-	106
1955	54,215#	15	26	109	150
1956	64,961	19	55	-	74
1957	70,988	38	32	-	70
1958	66,869	47	51	-	98
1959	62,154	*record ends*			
1960	77,457				
1961	41,982				
1962	58,491				
1963	40,757				
1964	35,000##				

 # 'includes miles run at Rugby Test Station'
'estimate'
wks=heavy and light repairs at main works
shed=shed repairs and examinations
n/req= not required

Total Recorded Mileage 1,609,518
Withdrawn week ending 12/9/64
Cut up West of Scotland
Shipbreaking Co. Troon 12/64

Upperby's 46225 DUCHESS OF GLOUCESTER, towards the end of its life, arriving at Preston from the south with a parcels and van train on 14 April 1964. I well recall from my days at Crewe North that Carlisle had a number of diagrams of this nature at the time, and the surviving Pacifics were their staple motive power. Photograph A.W. Battson, www.transporttreasury.co.uk

DUCHESS of GLOUCESTER turning on the Severn Bridge triangle at Shrewsbury. The engine is in back gear and would appear, having arrived off a train from Crewe, to be waiting to proceed round the triangle so as to face the correct way for its return journey. If this is the case the engine is doubtless on a running-in turn after a visit to Crewe Works. Only a few of the engines that were painted by BR in maroon livery had the BR style of lining rather than the LMS style that became standard. This was one of those that received the BR style and is probably running-in after a general repair in August 1958, when this livery was applied. Notice that the engine has been fitted with a Smith-Stone speedometer; the equipment can be seen on the trailing coupled axle. Photograph David Montgomery.

93

46226 DUCHESS OF NORFOLK

Built Crewe 23/5/38 cost £9,372 (engine), £1,570 (tender)
Built streamlined, casing removed 27/11/48
Renumbered 6226 to 42226 week ending 25/9/48

Boilers

Fitted	No.	From
23/5/38	10298	new
14/9/40	9941	6224
3/1/42	9940	6228
25/7/42	10304	6233
20/10/45	10302	6230
23/9/48	9939	6235
1/6/51	10306	46245
14/5/54	10296	-
10/5/57	10638	-
18/6/60	10640	-

No record after this date

Repairs LMS
2/1/39-17/1/39**LO**
4/5/39-19/5/39**LS**
14/5/40-24/5/40**TRO**
5/8/40-14/9/40**HG**
12/2/41-8/3/41**LO**
28/8/41-30/9/41**LS**
6/12/41-3/1/42**HO**
20/6/42-25/7/42**HG**
10/5/43-2/6/43**HS**
17/4/44-12/5/44**LS**
5/12/44-30/1/45**LS**
19/9/45-20/10/45**HG**
30/7/46-30/8/46**HS**
15/10/47-21/11/47**LS**
2/12/47-16/12/47**NC**
20/7/48-23/9/48**HG**
4/7/49-10/8/49**LI**
15/4/50-16/5/50**HI**

Repairs BR
Dates in the first column are from out of traffic to return to traffic; A = 'Weekdays Waiting', B= 'Weekdays on Works'. The two mileage figures represent, firstly the miles accumulated since the previous General or Intermediate (C) and secondly (the lower figure) the miles run up from January 1st of the year of shopping - D. All work is recorded as taking place at Crewe unless otherwise noted. StR=St Rollox

Dates	A	B	C	D
20/4/51-1/6/51**HG**	3	33	59,870	14,952
12/9/52-8/10/52**LI**	2	20	96,668	50,607
23/3/54-14/5/54**HG**	2	42	95,791	14,838
12/10/55-12/11/55**HI**	4	23	105,754	56,637
28/3/57-10/5/57**HG**	9	27	103.098	14,163
23/10/57-6/11/57**NC***	8	4	37,959	52,122
15/10/58-28/11/58**HI**	6	32	103,337	56,503
24/3/60-18/6/60**HG**	15	58	93,967	11,929

record ends
*(EO)' - 'Engine Only'

Sheds
Camden	
Speke Jct	16/9/39
Holyhead	21/10/39
Camden	9/12/39
Crewe North	6/4/40
Camden	22/5/43
Carlisle Upperby	12/10/46
Camden	23/6/51
Carlisle Upperby	15/9/51
Edge Hill	14/11/53
Carlisle Upperby	12/12/53
Edge Hill	22/1/55
Carlisle Upperby	5/3/55
Crewe North	29/9/56
Carlisle Upperby	20/10/56

stored 16/9/39 - 2/10/39

Tenders
No	Fitted
9744	23/5/38

LMS 'Summary' *(this became 'Annual Statistics' from 1951)*

Year	Mileage	Weekdays out of service			
		wks	shed	n/req	total
1938	61,341	-	46	1	47
1939	69,456	28	53	13	108#
1940	65,229	46	63	5	114
1941	53,227	69	50	-	119
1942	71,862	37	39	-	76
1943	73,235	21	57	-	78
1944	72,909	45	52	-	97
1945	71,171	54	45	2	101
1946	73,777	28	70	2	100
1947	51,342	46	83	7	136
1948	53,942	57	58	3	118
1949	70,735	41	45	3	89
1950	67,085	26	53	2	81
1951	61,013	36	77	1	114
1952	65,765	22	55	6	83
1953	65,795	-	85	8	93
1954	63,955	44	49	4	97
1955	63,953	27	57	9	93
1956	81,619	-	57	8	65
1957	60,997	36	62	11	109
1958	63,489	38	64	11	113
1959	75,052				

#incudes 14 days 'stored serviceable'
wks=heavy and light repairs at main works
shed=shed repairs and examinations
n/req= not required

Total Recorded Mileage 1,456,949
Withdrawn week ending 12/9/64
Cut up West of Scotland
Shipbreaking Co. Troon 2/65

Royal Train duty for 6226 DUCHESS OF NORFOLK, resplendent in the maroon livery, speeding north at Headstone Lane on 2 July 1938. The train is the former LNWR one, retaining its plum and spilt milk livery at the special request of the late King George V. The four headlamp code would indicate that the King himself was travelling, by this time George VI, and the shadows would indicate a late evening shot, so the family was doubtless heading for Balmoral and the summer break.

Minus its streamlining and looking a little travel worn, 46226 DUCHESS OF NORFOLK again, this time on the turntable in the roundhouse at Carlisle Upperby at an unknown date. The records indicate that this locomotive retained its 'semi' smokebox until November 1955, and this blue livery until April 1951. Photograph www.transporttreasury.co.uk

Inset right. A much later view of 46226 DUCHESS OF NORFOLK, at Carlisle on 23 April 1962, by this time sporting the maroon livery that a few members of the class received, as events turned out, in their twilight years. I would wager the engine has arrived with a train from the north; notice no coal showing in the tender. It will be heading light engine for Kingmoor shed where it was allocated at the time – it is in backward gear. The fireman's attention is on the exhaust injector which is losing water, though he does not seem to be doing anything about it. I would like a pound for every repair card I have seen endorsed 'exhaust injector losing water'! The twin brake blocks referred to in earlier captions and fitted to the later engines of the class are clearly visible. Photograph Paul Chancellor Collection.

Main photograph. A melancholy 46226 DUCHESS OF NORFOLK, its life's work complete. Here is the great lady at Carlisle Kingmoor in August 1964, shorn of nameplates and dumped, motion partly removed, awaiting its last journey to the breakers. Although the actual withdrawal date is recorded as 12 September, clearly Kingmoor had no further use for the engine; another of its stable mates lies behind. Notice the yellow stripe on the cab side, indicating the engine should not be used south of Crewe on the electrified lines due to clearances under the overhead line equipment. Photograph J.G. Walmsley, www.transporttreasury.co.uk

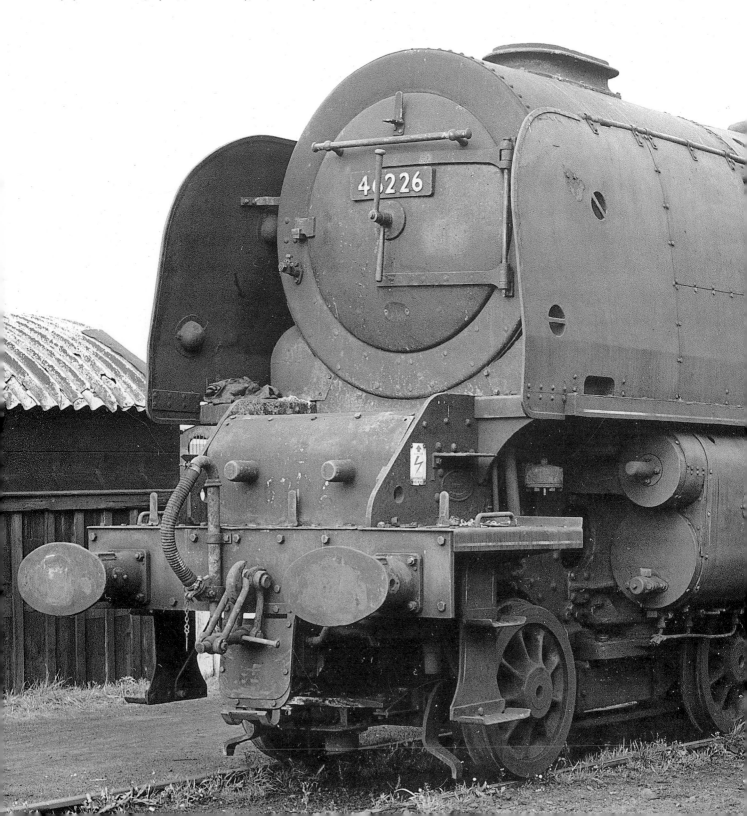

46227 DUCHESS OF DEVONSHIRE

Built Crewe 7/6/38, cost £9,732 (engine), £1,570 (tender)
Built streamlined, casing removed 26/8/46
Renumbered 6227 to 46227 week ending 8/5/48

Boilers

Fitted	No.	From
31/12/40	10298	6226
17/12/42	10288	6236
22/8/45	10642	6223
26/3/47	10299	6235
23/8/50	10638	6225
18/4/53	10637	-
11/8/56	10298	-
18/5/61	9938	-

No record after this date

Repairs LMS

16/1/39-31/1/39**LO**
15/5/39-27/5/39**LS**
22/11/40-31/12/40**HG**
29/12/41-31/1/42**LS**
20/6/42-17/7/42**LO**
5/11/42-17/12/42**HG**
26/6/43-27/7/43**LO**
25/10/43-11/12/43**LS**
14/3/44-31/3/44**LO**
12/9/44-4/10/44**LS**
6/7/45-22/8/45**HG**
12/1/46-13/2/46**LO**
16/7/46-26/8/46**HS**
22/2/47-26/3/47**HO**
11/8/47-24/9/47**LS**
5/3/48-6/4/48**LO**
13/4/48-3/5/48**NC**
14/3/49-14/4/49**LI**
26/6/50-23/8/50**HG**

Repairs BR

Dates in the first column are from out of traffic to return to traffic; A = 'Weekdays Waiting', B= 'Weekdays on Works'. The two mileage figures represent, firstly the miles accumulated since the previous General or Intermediate (C) and secondly (the lower figure) the miles run up from January 1st of the year of shopping - D. All work is recorded as taking place at Crewe unless otherwise noted. StR=St Rollox

Dates	A	B	C	D
5/2/52-10/3/52**HI**	2	27	90,525	5,526
29/9/52-11/11/52**LC***	12	25	35,589	41,115
16/2/53-18/4/53**'GEN'**	10	43	51,982	8,915
5/2/54-13/3/54**LC***	8	23	54,625	5,502
18/5/54-18/5/54**NC***(StR)	-	-	57,329	8,206
21/5/55-19/2/55**HI**	3	22	102,246	4,004
23/3/56-24/3/56**NC**(StR)	-	-	59,944	12,236
16/6/56-11/8/56**HG**	7	41	72,097	24,389
24/10/56-29/11/56**LC***	11	20	9,600	33,990
24/6/57-17/8/57**LC***	2	45	37,947	22,366
13/11/57-8/2/58**LI**	32	41	54,288	38,707
16/2/59-4/4/59**LI**	7	33	64,216	7,705
16/3/60-21/5/60**HI**	18	38	57,061	8,936
1/3/61-18/5/61**HG**	29	37	50,615	9,451

Record ends
*='(EO)'-'EngineOnly'

Sheds

Camden	
Holyhead	21/10/39
Crewe North	6/4/40
Camden	22/5/43
Carlisle Upperby	12/10/46
Camden	24/5/47
Crewe North	21/6/47
Polmadie	12/6/48

Tenders

No	Fitted
9745	7/6/38

LMS 'Summary' *(this became 'Annual Statistics' from 1951)*

Year	Mileage	Weekdays out of service			
		wks	shed	n/req	total
1938	58,007	-	31	1	32
1939	77,944	26	51	23	100
1940	72,530	31	43	28	102
1941	73.539	2	72	-	74
1942	57,222	91	47	-	138
1943	61,277	69	67	-	136
1944	77,781	36	37	-	73
1945	73,925	41	77	2	120
1946	72,472	64	32	2	98
1947	63,260	67	21	1	89
1948	51,376	45	79	1	125
1949	57,912	28	75	2	105
1950	49,667	50	69	-	119
1951	62,062	-	91	1	92
1952	48,593	66	70	3	139
1953	58,038	53	58	2	113
1954	49,119	31	66	-	97
1955	51,452	25	65	9	103
1956	39,526	79	60	1	140
1957	39,151	76	50	-	126
1958	56,511	33	57	-	90
1959	55,830	record ends			
1960	50,100				
1961	44,175				
1962	42,170				

wks=heavy and light repairs at main works
shed=shed repairs and examinations
n/req= not required

Total Recorded Mileage 1,443,639
Withdrawn week ending 29/12/62
Cut up Crewe Works 11/63

Written on the reverse of this print is 'Auchlochan?' and the question mark is well-warranted, for I can find no such place on any railway map of Scotland. My guess is that 46227 DUCHESS OF DEVONSHIRE, a Polmadie engine, had worked a train to Aberdeen, and Ferryhill shed was using it on a fill-in turn before going back south – notice the local passenger train head lamp code. The photograph is undated, but this is quite late in the engine's life. It is fitted with Automatic Warning System (AWS); that is the protection plate for the receiver behind the screw coupling. The outside cylinder anti-vacuum valve is very noticeable in this view, nicely caught by what would appear to be a late afternoon sun which, in view of the shadow, probably means the train is heading north. AWS was fitted to the engines from 1959 onwards as they went through Crewe Works for attention of any sort. Photograph Great North of Scotland Railway Association [Forrest], www.transporttreasury.co.uk

46228 DUCHESS OF RUTLAND

Built Crewe 17/6/38, cost £9,732 (engine), £1,601(tender)
Built streamlined, casing removed 16/10/47
Renumbered 6228 to 46228 week ending 31/7/48

Boilers

Fitted	No.	From
31/8/40	9940	6223
2/8/41	9937	6224
16/5/44	10295	6243
16/10/47	9941	6239
2/10/50	10693	6239
27/2/53	10694	-
6/6/55	10288	-
2/9/59	10291	-

No record after this date

Repairs LMS
4/2/39-22/2/39**LO**
19/6/39-29/6/39**LS**
29/7/40-31/8/40**HG**
5/9/40-17/9/40**LO**
28/12/40-9/1/41**LO**
20/2/41-18/3/41**LO**
26/6/41-2/8/41**HO**
15/1/42-21/2/42**LS**
26/11/42-2/1/43**HS**
4/8/43-25/8/43**LO**
24/4/44-16/5/44**HG**
14/8/44-25/8/44**LO**
14/3/45-14/4/45**HS**
14/8/45-27/9/45**LO**
26/5/46-20/6/46**LS**
19/6/47-16/10/47**HG**
5/6/48-26/7/48**LO**
4/1/49-28/1/49**LI**
15/3/49-1/7/49**HC**
31/1/50-7/3/50**LC**
9/5/50-27/5/50**NC**
21/8/50-2/10/50**HG**

Repairs BR
Dates in the first column are from out of traffic to return to traffic; A = 'Weekdays Waiting', B= 'Weekdays on Works'. The two mileage figures represent, firstly the miles accumulated since the previous General or Intermediate (C) and secondly (the lower figure) the miles run up from January 1st of the year of shopping - D. All work is recorded as taking place at Crewe unless otherwise noted. StR=St Rollox

Dates	A	B	C	D
5/12/51-5/1/51**LI**	4	21	90,497	71,396
3/1/53-27/2/53**HG**	15	32	68,403	444
9/3/53-27/3/53**HC***	-	16	289	733
11/11/53-10/12/53**HC***	8	17	39,777	40,221
23/4/55-6/6/55**HG**	3	34	135,099	23,454
1/12/56-17/1/57**HI**	13	25	115,094	67,905
29/9/57-2/10/57**NC***	-	2	49,759	49,759
9/5/58-21/6/58**HI**	2	35	99,198	29,217
3/7/59-2/9/59**HG**	21	31	86,101	43,456
29/12/60-18/2/61**LI**	12	32	106,359	127

record ends
*(EO)' - 'Engine Only'

Sheds

Camden	
Longsight	16/9/39
Rugby	30/9/39
Holyhead	21/10/39
Crewe North	6/4/40
Camden	22/5/43
Carlisle Upperby	12/10/46
Camden	7/7/51
Carlisle Upperby	15/9/51
Edge Hill	5/6/54
Carlisle Upperby	19/6/54
Edge Hill	25/9/54
Carlisle Upperby	16/10/54
Crewe North	21/9/57
Carlisle Upperby	20/6/59
Crewe North	27/6/69

stored 15/9/39-21/9/39, 27/9/39-2/10/39, 24/9/63-12/12/63

Tenders

No	Fitted
9746	17/6/38

LMS 'Summary' *(this became 'Annual Statistics' from 1951)*

Year	Mileage	Weekdays out of service			
		works	shed	n/req	total
1938	52,124	-	27	4	31
1939	78,276	26	43	17	107#
1940	53,082	42	61	35	138
1941	70,920	66	34	-	100
1942	58,100	59	57	1	117
1943	64,908	25	73	-	98
1944	72,918	31	59	-	90
1945	56,651	67	67	1	135
1946	79,242	22	68	1	91
1947	41,377	103	54	5	162
1948	70,947	44	45	1	89
1949	36,865	115	64	3	182
1950	56,737	82	31	3	116
1951	71,396	20	67	1	88
1952	67,659	5	61	9	75
1953	43,428	88	52	11	151
1954	68,661	-	62	9	71
1955	70,643	37	47	3	87
1956	67,905	23	71	11	105
1957	69,981	15	57	6	78
1958	71,862	37	43	1	81
1959	70,412	*record ends*			

 # 'includes 11 days stored serviceable'
works=heavy and light repairs at main works
shed=shed repairs and examinations
n/req= not required

Total Recorded Mileage 1,337,772
Withdrawn week ending 12/9/64
Cut up J.Cashmore, Great Bridge, 12/64

46228 DUCHESS OF RUTLAND at Shrewsbury probably on a filling-in turn from Crewe and in the process of turning on the Severn Bridge triangle so as to face the correct way for the journey back to Crewe on one of the West of England trains. We have no date for this photograph but as the engine has the BR green livery with the earlier emblem on the tender, it is probably somewhere between June 1955 when it received this livery and its next shopping eighteen months later when it would doubtless have received the later BR emblem. During this period the engine was allocated to Carlisle Upperby so quite why Crewe was using it on a filling-in turn is a mystery. It is not obvious here but the nameplate has a red background which quite a few Carlisle engines sported at this time thanks to a local custom; Crewe would never have turned out an engine so adorned! Photograph David Montgomery.

Standing on No.4 up through road at Crewe on 14 September 1961, Crewe North's 46228 DUCHESS OF RUTLAND has what appears to be a van train of some sort, although the headlamp code is that of a local passenger train. An aspect of the BR maroon livery, one rarely commented on, was the straw line round the buffer beams; those that retained the green livery had no such nicety. Photograph A.H. Roscoe, www.transporttreasury.co.uk

46229 DUCHESS OF HAMILTON

Built Crewe 7/9/38, cost £9,732 (engine), £1,570 (tender)
Built streamlined, casing removed 10/1/48
Renumbered and renamed 6220 CORONATION for America - shipped 20/1/39
Returned to Traffic 18/3/42
Renumbered 6229 during repairs completed 20/4/43
Renumbered 6229 to 46229 week ending 3/7/48

Boilers

Fitted	No.	From
25/9/43	10305	6233
25/1/46	10298	6222
10/1/48	10645	6252
23/2/50	9938	6237
23/2/50	9938	-
26/4/52	10639	-
19/3/54	9939	-
17/2/56	10302	-
8/10/59	10297	-
Record ends

Repairs LMS
9/12/38-7/1/39**LO**
23/2/42-18/3/42**LO**
USA
17/10/42-11/11/42**LS**
12/3/43-20/4/43**LO**
28/8/43-25/9/43**HG**
30/10/44-23/11/44**LS**
4/12/45-25/1/46**HG**
15/10/46-6/11/46**LS**
24/4/47-19/5/47**LO**
23/10/47-10/1/48**HG**
3/4/48-9/4/48**NC**
29/6/48-1/7/48 **'Nil'**
25/5/49-24/6/49**LI**

Repairs BR
Dates in the first column are from out of traffic to return to traffic; A = 'Weekdays Waiting', B= 'Weekdays on Works'. The two mileage figures represent, firstly the miles accumulated since the previous General or Intermediate (C) and secondly (the lower figure) the miles run up from January 1st of the year of shopping - D. All work is recorded as taking place at Crewe unless otherwise noted. StR=St Rollox

Dates	A	B	C	D
16/1/50-23/2/50**HG**	-	-	-	-
6/1/51-7/2/51**LI**	4	23	76,648	1,272
17/3/52-26/4/52**HG**	1	33	90,472	16,441
23/3/53-8/5/53**HI**	15	24	85,132	20,324
22/1/54-19/3/54**HG**	6	42	63,414	4,999
6/11/54-11/12/54**LC**	1	29	63,875	68,874
5/5/55-23/5/55**LC**	1	14	100,154	32,115
31/12/55-17/2/56**HG**	1	40	140,906	Nil
21/1/57-2/3/57**HI**	9	26	92,920	5,712
16/9/57-19/9/57**NC***	-	3	49,208	54,920
14/7/58-10/9/58**HI**	16	34	122,608	45,170
17/8/59-8/10/59**HG**	6	39	95,669	66,006
21/3/60-7/5/60**NC***	24	16	42,472	17,484
12/7/60-26/8/60**LC***	13	26	57,365	32,377
13/5/61-13/6/61**HI**	2	24	101,339	19,293
Record ends
*(EO)' - 'Engine Only'

Sheds
Crewe North
Camden	15/5/43
Crewe North	21/6/47
Camden	24/4/48
Crewe North	1/10/49
Carlisle Upperby	by 3/50
Crewe North	by 5/51
Camden	6/752
Crewe North	1/10/60
Edge Hill	11/4/61
stored 8/10/62-we 2/2/63, 14/10/63-23/12/63, 30/12/63-10/2/64

Tenders
No	Fitted
9747	7/9/38
9802	22/11/45

LMS 'Summary' *(this became 'Annual Statistics' from 1951)*

Year	Mileage	Weekdays out of service			
		wks	shed	n/req	total
1938	15,131	20	20	-	40
1939	USA	6	1	-	7
1940	USA	-	-	-	-
1941	USA	-	-	-	-
1942	61,368	43	23	1	67
1943	72,667	59	33	-	92
1944	79,805	22	45	1	68
1945	81,223	22	142	3	167
1946	77,910	43	63	2	108
1947	55,603	78	41	-	119
1948	78,285	12	63	1	76
1949	66,107	27	76	5	108
1950	78,954	33	17	11	61
1951	75,303	42	27	-	69
1952	81,249	34	60	-	94
1953	78,739	39	59	-	98
1954	73,038	78	35	-	113
1955	72,867	16	88	9	113
1956	87,208	40	59	-	99
1957	83,150	35	55	-	90
1958	74,833	50	58	-	108
1959	90,994	*record ends*			
1960	55,058				
1961	47,990				
1962	27,758				
1963	16,596				

wks=heavy and light repairs at main works
shed=shed repairs and examinations
n/req= not required

Total Recorded Mileage 1,454,892
Withdrawn week ending 15/2/64
Preserved at Butlins, then NRM – now streamlined!

A very grimy 46229 DUCHESS OF HAMILTON about to leave Glasgow Central for the south, a photograph probably taken shortly after hostilities ceased in 1945. This engine had its streamlined casing removed in November 1947, so the photograph predates this; it is also recorded as having had the rear top casing removed from the tender, as seen here, in January 1946, which narrows the date to the period between then and November 1947. It would appear the fireman has just put a round on the fire ready for departure and the safety valves are lifting. The engine is in the wartime black livery without lining with the large cabside numbers used at the time. For a short period in 1947, from June until November when it went into works, this was a Crewe North engine and if this is the case here the train is probably the 'Mid-Day Scot', the 1.15 departure. Photograph David Montgomery.

Carlisle Citadel in the days when it had an all-over roof, in June 1948, with 46229 DUCHESS OF HAMILTON standing on the up through road at the south end of the station. In all probability it is waiting for a train from the north to arrive, which it will take forward to London. A Camden engine at the time it is in the LMS post-war lined black livery, albeit renumbered into the BR list, with the early style of smokebox number plate; it retains the small cab front windows. Personally I always feel that the sloping smokebox top, a legacy of the former streamlined casing, detracted from the otherwise impressive bulk of these engines, especially when viewed from the front. Photograph W. Hermiston, www.transporttreasury.co.uk

Heading south from Crewe, having just passed Basford Hall Junction, 46229 DUCHESS OF HAMILTON heads for the capital. No coal visible in the tender, so this Camden engine is probably working through from Carlisle. The bridge carries what was then the A52, Newcastle-under-Lyme to Nantwich road and as can be seen, the CWS had a creamery alongside it. Photograph www.transporttreasury.co.uk

Camden shed had 46229 DUCHESS OF HAMILTON for a long period, between June 1952 and September 1960 when it moved to Crewe North. Here it is at Polmadie shed on 27 June 1953, turned with its tender topped up ready for the journey south. The valve gear is set in forward, so unless it is about to move off somebody should be due for a dressing down! It was always drilled into enginemen; *regulator closed, engine in middle gear, handbrake on, boiler full, taps open, dampers shut* when leaving engines. The Royal Scot behind, 46154 THE HUSSAR, was also Camden based at the time and while the Pacific might have come north on a through working from London, it is doubtful if the Scot would have done, so this engine could well have been on a cyclic diagram. One of the sheds grimy Austerity 2-8-0s is visible to the right. Photograph W. Hermiston, www.transporttreasury.co.uk

A not very clean Camden Pacific, 46229 DUCHESS OF HAMILTON with the up 'Royal Scot' on 3 June 1959, running from Carlisle to Euston through Preston without stopping. Somebody seems to have borrowed a Scottish Region headboard, as it has a light (Caledonian) blue background, usually only seen north of the border, but it does help brighten up this otherwise grimy Duchess! Notice that the exhaust injector is losing water, as was often their wont! Photograph A.W. Battson, www.transporttreasury.co.uk

This photograph is not dated but it would almost certainly be in the very late days of the class; the train is leaving Chester on the North Wales route where the engines were relatively infrequent visitors in their heyday. DUCHESS OF HAMILTON is crossing the River Dee with the famous Chester racecourse to the right, and the Cathedral on the skyline. A Camden engine still, working through from Euston to Holyhead perhaps, maybe deputising for a diesel, Holyhead having lost its Britannias and its share in these working with the onset of the EE Type 4 diesels. As an aside, we can spare a thought for some of the Holyhead men; having shovelled the best part of 20 tons of coal for years on end on the double-home jobs to Euston, when the diesels arrived they lost their lodging turns, and only went out and home to Crewe! Photograph S.D. Wainwright.

46230 DUCHESS OF BUCCLEUCH

Built Crewe 27/6/38 cost £9,181(engine), £1,478 (tender)
Built without streamlining
Renumbered 6230 to 46230 week ending 15/5/48

Boilers

Fitted	No.	From
1/11/41	10299	6227
9/2/43	10302	6225
30/6/45	10641	6238
21/2/48	9940	6245
2/5/52	10305	-
30/6/55	10644	-
8/4/60	10302	-
27/1/62	10694	-

No record after this date

Repairs LMS
6/6/39-21/6/39**LS**
11/9/40-11/10/40**HS**
22/1/41-15/2/41**LO**
22/9/41-11/11/41**HG**
17/1/42-31/1/42**LO**
28/12/42-9/2/43**HS**
1/9/43-15/10/43**LO**
20/11/43-11/1/44**LS**
4/10/44-3/11/44**HS**
25/5/45-30/6/45**HG**
24/8/46-14/9/46**HS**
7/11/47-21/2/48**HG**
28/2/48-11/3/48**NC**
11/5/48-27/5/48**#**
#'no repairs - special painting for liveries'

Repairs BR
Dates in the first column are from out of traffic to return to traffic; A = 'Weekdays Waiting', B= 'Weekdays on Works'. The two mileage figures represent, firstly the miles accumulated since the previous General or Intermediate (C) and secondly (the lower figure) the miles run up from January 1st of the year of shopping - D. All work is recorded as taking place at Crewe unless otherwise noted. StR=St Rollox

Dates	A	B	C	D
4/4/49-6/5/49**LI**	-	29	66,323	3,275
15/10/49-11/11/49**LC**	-	24	27,985	31,260
25/5/50-23/6/50**LI**	1	24	67,164	29,981
13/11/50-29/12/50**LC**	16	24	35,843	65,824
19/5/51-2/7/51**HI**	14	23	57,307	21,464
17/3/52-2/5/52**HG**	7	33	50,708	10,156
5/5/52-24/5/52**LC**	-	17	68	10,224
27/5/52-5/6/52**NC**	-	8	209	10,365
31/8/53-2/10/53**HI**	7	21	93,589	42,949
20/5/55-30/6/55**HG**	6	29	94,502	22,000
6/12/54**NC** (StR)	-	-	80,409	54,103
7/1/57-16/2/57**HI**	15	20	87,855	992
2/12/57-7/12/57**NC***	-	5	?	?
4/8/58-17/9/58**HI**	9	29	79,962	27,096
17/8/59-6/11/59**HC***	24	46	52,571	37,013
1/2/60-8/4/60**HG**	14	44	70,293	7,836
6/12/61-26/1/62**HG**	4	38	10,095	47,873
7/2/62-26/2/62**NC**	-	16	?	?
4/3/63**LC**		*record ends*		

*(EO)' - 'Engine Only'

Sheds
Camden
Polmadie   10/2/40
stored 3/12/62-29/12/62

Tenders

No	Fitted
9748	27/6/38
9707	14/8/45

LMS 'Summary' *(this became 'Annual Statistics' from 1951)*

Year	Mileage	Weekdays out of service			
		wks	shed	n/req	total
1938	47,941	-	31	1	32
1939	95,917	14	50	3	67
1940	80,816	28	44	13	85
1941	51,293	58	56	7	121
1942	68,121	15	63	7	85
1943	60,644	107	35	-	142
1944	65,576	39	74	6	119
1945	68,558	32	76	3	111
1946	72,551	19	68	-	87
1947	48,250	44	68	-	112
1948	63,048	47	60	1	108
1949	40,458	53	108	7	168
1950	65,824	65	21	-	86
1951	62,016	37	75	1	113
1952	60,796	57	49	-	106
1953	59,017	28	56	2	86
1954	56,434	-	80	-	80
1955	48,094	35	62	2	99
1956	59,992	-	74	3	77
1957	53,735	35	41	3	79
1958	42,654	38	93	2	133
1959	47,146		*record ends*		
1960	60,958				
1961	47,873				
1962	36,526				

wks=heavy and light repairs at main works
shed=shed repairs and examinations
n/req= not required

Total Recorded Mileage 1,464,238
Withdrawn week ending 9/11/63
Cut up Crewe Works 12/63

You won't find many photographs of locomotives in absolutely pristine condition in this book, and who could resist this one – 6230 DUCHESS of BUCCLEUCH, immediately on completion at Crewe in June 1938, and the first built without streamlining. Notice that the non-streamlined engines had the larger cab front windows from new, although the double chimney and smoke deflectors were later additions. A High Born Lady at Home, if ever there was one!

For most of its life 46230 was allocated to Polmadie shed in Glasgow so it was frequently used on 'The Royal Scot' to and from Carlisle. Here it is at the north end of Carlisle station on 23 April 1953 waiting for the down train to arrive which it will work forward; it would almost certainly have arrived in the Border City earlier in the day with the up working, visiting Kingmoor shed in the interim. This view shows well the proportions of the double chimney. Photograph J.L. Stevenson, courtesy Hamish Stevenson.

The down 'Royal Scot' leaving Carstairs on 12 July 1952, embarking on the last stage of its journey to the Scottish capital. By this time the train consisted of a complete rake of the newly introduced BR Mk 1 coaches, at this stage in their careers painted in the red and cream livery. This was another member of the class that spent its entire life with BR allocated to Polmadie, and thus somewhat of a rare visitor south of Carlisle. Whatever criticisms could be levelled at Polmadie, and my new found workmates at Crewe North had plenty, in the 1950s the staff there always managed to keep their Pacifics clean. Photograph J. Robertson, www.transporttreasury.co.uk

What is going on here then? The north end at Carlisle, with a grimy 46230 DUCHESS OF BUCCLEUCH; a close study of the original photograph reveals it to be a light engine and not attached to the coaches behind, which are actually on the centre road. In the bay is 60093 CORONACH, a Carlisle Canal A3 for many years, used on the Waverley route to Edinburgh and apparently engaged in a little shunting. It was withdrawn in April 1962. Canal shed by the way, formerly on the Scottish Region, had been transferred to the London Midland in 1958. Photograph www.transporttreasury.co.uk

46231 DUCHESS OF ATHOLL

Built Crewe 28/6/38 cost £9,181 (engine), £1,478 (tender)
Built without streamlining
Renumbered 6231 to 46231 week ending 29/5/48

Boilers

Fitted	No.	From
1/6/40	10639	new
27/11/43	10300	6224
2/9/45	10643	6236
20/12/47	10644	6249
19/1/51	9941	46228
9/12/53	10301	-
31/3/58	10287	-

No record after this date

Sheds

Camden
Polmadie   6/1/40
stored 13/8/62 - 29/12/62

Tenders

No	Fitted
9749	28/6/38
9812	23/1/45

LMS 'Summary' (this became 'Annual Statistics' from 1951)

Year	Mileage	wks	shed	n/req	total
1938	47,786	-	30	1	31
1939	88,155	22	63	1	86
1940	78,079	30	45	18	93
1941	64,075	31	54	19	104
1942	73,241	32	49	4	85
1943	61,556	86	39	1	126
1944	81,872	28	57	8	93
1945	69,932	65	40	2	107
1946	93,228	19	46	-	65
1947	39,336	92	69	1	162
1948	58,797	25	56	-	81
1949	61,850	42	56	1	99
1950	49,964	77	37	4	118
1951	69,906	29	62	1	92
1952	44,163	46	70	-	116
1953	40,053	84	70	2	156
1954	55,038	3	82	2	87
1955	48,953	76	19	14	109
1956	49,280	37	84	-	121
1957	56,898	25	41	2	68
1958	59,842	46	64	-	110
1959	56,412	*record ends*			
1960	54,673				
1961	44,221				
1962	25,129				

Weekdays out of service — columns: wks, shed, n/req, total

wks=heavy and light repairs at main works
shed=shed repairs and examinations
n/req= not required

Total Recorded Mileage 1,472,439
Withdrawn week ending 29/12/62
Cut up Crewe Works 11/63

Repairs BR

Dates in the first column are from out of traffic to return to traffic; A = 'Weekdays Waiting', B= 'Weekdays on Works'. The two mileage figures represent, firstly the miles accumulated since the previous General or Intermediate (C) and secondly (the lower figure) the miles run up from January 1st of the year of shopping - D. All work is recorded as taking place at Crewe unless otherwise noted. StR=St Rollox

Dates	A	B	C	D
15/11/50-19/1/51HG	12	42	32,404	49,964
29/1/51-15/2/51NC	-	15	467	467
27/2/51-12/3/51NC	-	11	1,203	1,203
27/6/52-20/8/52LI	4	42	12,557	22,651
25/3/53-5/5/53LC	16	19	33,973	12,461
8/7/53-11/7/53LC(StR)	1	2	44,662	23,150
10/8/53-12/8/53NC	-	2	51,337	29,825
18/8/53-22/8/53NC	-	4	51,343	29,831
16/10/53-9/12/53G	14	32	58,477	36,965
19/8/54-19/8/54NC(StR)	-	1	39,342	36,254
20/12/54-23/12/54LC*	2	1	57,793	54,705
28/2/55-16/4/55LI	12	28	67,088	8,962
16/11/55-16/11/55NC*(StR)	-	1	39,345	48,307
21/11/55-6/1/56LC*	14	24	39,991	48,953
26/1/56-17/2/56NC*	-	19	40,288	297
12/12/56-26/1/57LI	14	23	89,271	49,280
18/11/57-18/11/57NC(StR)	-	1	-	-
24/12/57-28/12/57LC*	-	4	56,989	56,898
31/3/58-23/5/58G	8	38	66,208	10,010
16/1/58-27/1/58NC*	-	9	-	-
22/7/59-12/9/59HI	19	26	87,461	37,629
4/5/60-18/6/60LC	16	19	39,351	20,568
23/1/61-5/4/61G	-	62	76,195	2,739
11/1/62-2/3/62LC	13	30	*Record ends*	

'(EO)'-'EngineOnly'

Repairs LMS

30/6/39-25/7/39LS
29/4/40-1/6/40HG
7/6/41-12/7/41LS
19/6/42-25/7/42HS
1/1/43-17/2/43LO
6/10/43-27/11/43HG
16/9/44-18/10/44LS
23/7/45-22/9/45HG
27/11/45-8/12/45LO
1/8/46-22/8/46LS
22/4/47-30/5/47LS
14/8/47-21/8/47NC
15/10/47-20/12/47HG
8/5/48-25/5/48#
27/11/48-31/12/48LO
25/2/49-8/4/49LI
19/4/50-1/6/50HI

#'no repairs - special painting - new liveries'

Yet another of the class permanently based at Polmadie throughout the BR period was DUCHESS OF ATHOLL, seen here as LMS 6231, in the pretty unkempt condition of many of the class in the immediate post-war years. Taking coal at its home shed on 11 April 1948, it was another of the original members of the class that were never streamlined. On these engines the footplating at the front was continuous between the buffer beam and the smoke deflectors. The fellow in the tender is trimming the last stages of coal delivery to ensure the maximum load; notice the wagon to the right with the painted legend CARDIFF COLLIERIES LIMITED LLANBRADAN; ostensibly a long way from home but of course, from early in the war years all private owner coal wagons were pooled, and with nationalisation of the coal mines in 1947 were never returned to their owners.
Photograph www.transporttreasury.co.uk

The down 'Royal Scot' heading north through Berkhamsted, early in its long journey, on 5 October 1951; the photograph was recorded at 10.35, so time was being kept at this early stage. The engines is 46231 DUCHESS OF ATHOLL, during one of the periods when Polmadie and Camden were sharing the working, and running through between Euston and Glasgow; hence the coal stacked high on the tender. There were several attempts at through working by these engines during the 1950s, with mixed results; one of the difficulties concerned ashpan capacity, rather than the quantity of coal that could be carried on the tender, and of course the quality of the fuel. The later style headboard was designed with the early diesels in mind, although it appeared on and off throughout the subsequent period of steam haulage. Photograph A. Lathey, www.transporttreasury.co.uk

DUCHESS OF ATHOLL at home again, Polmadie on 12 August 1953, with the blue livery which it retained until September 1955. In BR days the Polmadie engines, unlike their English brethren, did not have No.8 valve and piston examinations ('No.8 Mileage' as we called it) at Crewe North, so I never worked on this particular one. Photograph www.transporttreasury.co.uk

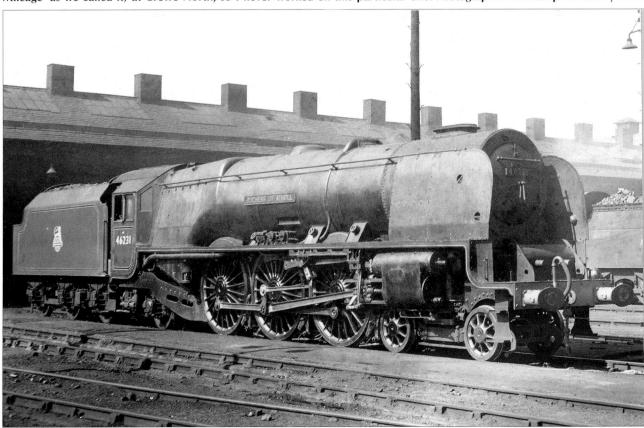

46232 DUCHESS OF MONTROSE

Built Crewe 1/7/38, cost £9,181(engine), £1,478 (tender)
Built without streamlining
Renumbered 6232 to 46232 week ending 8/5/48

Boilers

Fitted	No.	From
4/9/40	10640	new
21/1/43	10301	6230
24/2/45	9937	6228
3/5/48	10298	6229
17/11/51	10644	-
5/2/55	12470	-
22/2/57	10290	-
28/10/60	10303	-

No record after this date

Repairs LMS

12/6/39-26/6/39**LS**
20/9/40-4/9/40**HG**
18/11/40-26/12/40**LO#**
10/7/41-16/8/41**LO**
18/11/41-31/12/41**LS**
3/12/42-21/1/43**HG**
25/8/43-2/10/43**LS**
5/6/44-20/7/44**LO**
29/1/45-24/2/45**HG**
21/8/45-2/10/45**LS**
20/12/46-31/1/47**LS**
18/8/47-30/8/47**LO**
21/10/47-25/10/47**NC**
11/11/47-13/12/47**LO**
1/3/48-3/5/48**HG**
7/5/48-21/5/48**Nil##**
#'*Damaged - enemy action*
Berkhampstead 16/11/40'
##'*No repair*'

Repairs BR

Dates in the first column are from out of traffic to return to traffic; A = 'Weekdays Waiting', B= 'Weekdays on Works'. The two mileage figures represent, firstly the miles accumulated since the previous General or Intermediate (C) and secondly (the lower figure) the miles run up from January 1st of the year of shopping - D. All work is recorded as taking place at Crewe unless otherwise noted. StR=St Rollox

Dates	A	B	C	D
20/6/49-23/8/49**HI**	-	56	69,030	24,442
28/9/50-9/11/50**HI**	7	29	72,944	45,041
7/4/51-19/5/51**LC**	16	20	37,658	27,068
24/9/51-17/11/51**HG**	15	32	61,462	50,872
18/9/52-17/10/52**HI**	4	21	63,160	54,161
10/4/53-20/5/53**LC**	11	23	34,156	18,814
6/1/54-10/2/54**HI**	10	20	76,114	896
11/11/54-5/2/55**'Gen'**	11	61	50,143	51,039
12/3/56-13/4/56**HI**	2	26	61,827	8,479
5/1/57-22/2/57**'Gen'**	16	25	47,695	123
11/12/57**NC***	-	2	-	-
3/3/58-12/4/58**HI**	6	28	59,861	8,665
26/1/59-14/3/59**LI**	8	33	53,794	6,428
19/10/59-5/12/59**LC**	15	26	37,993	44,277
18/8/60-28/10/60**HG**	7	54	90,428	49,520
3/11/60-19/11/60**LC***	-	13	90,428	-
17/5/61-28/6/61**LC***	10	26	27,728	21,492

record ends
*(EO)'-'EngineOnly'

LMS 'Summary' *(this became 'Annual Statistics' from 1951)*

Year	Mileage	Weekdays out of service			
		wks	shed	n/req	total
1938	49,927	-	19	1	20
1939	93,258	13	51	2	66
1940	59,081	74	46	19	139
1941	59,991	71	45	12	128
1942	66,457	21	54	7	82
1943	57,349	55	45	2	102
1944	47,127	40	98	3	141
1945	71,076	61	50	4	115
1946	73,579	8	81	2	91
1947	44,634	69	74	1	144
1948	52,271	55	66	2	123
1949	52,345	56	64	-	120
1950	55,631	36	52	1	89
1951	59,871	83	57	-	140
1952	69,503	25	25	-	50
1953	59,876	34	51	1	86
1954	51,039	74	38	-	112
1955	53,348	28	57	14	99
1956	55,198	28	57	-	85
1957	51,346	41	62	-	103
1958	56,031	35	51	11	97
1959	47,336	record ends			
1960	55,756				
1961	51,666				
1962	27,252				

wks=heavy and light repairs at main works
shed=shed repairs and examinations
n/req= not required

Total Recorded Mileage 1,420,948
Withdrawn week ending 29/12/62
Cut up Crewe Works 11/63

Sheds

Camden
Polmadie 6/1/40
stored 13/8/62-29/12/62

Tender

No	Fitted
9750	1/7/38

While most of the Coronations allocated to the London Midland Region moved around between sheds quite a bit, the Scottish Region examples were always at Polmadie, and most of them were there for their entire life with BR, as mentioned in some of the earlier captions. This is another, 46232 DUCHESS OF MONTROSE, at Polmadie in April 1952, preparing to leave the shed for Glasgow Central to take a train south; notice the engine is in back-gear and the crew are looking that way. The Princess Royal to the right looks like 46200, pioneer of the class, which was briefly allocated to Polmadie at the time. Photograph H.S. Brighty, www.transporttreasury.co.uk

DUCHESS OF MONTROSE at Kingmoor shed in June 1954. Having worked south it is coaled, turned and ready to head back to Glasgow. BR green livery along with the earlier tender emblem. Photograph A.W. Battson, www.transporttreasury.co.uk

An undated view of 46232 DUCHESS OF MONTROSE at Glasgow Central, probably backing down to join its train judging by the stance of the driver. This was one of the first engines to receive what became the standard BR green livery; it was repainted during a heavy general repair in November 1951, so the pictures dates from some time after that and before the tender emblems were changed to the new style from 1956. I would suggest it is earlier in this period rather than later.

Right. This photograph would date from about 1954. 46232 DUCHESS OF MONTROSE is on the centre road at the north end of Carlisle Citadel waiting for the northbound 'Royal Scot', which it will take over for the remainder of its journey to Glasgow. In all probability it would have worked the southbound train from Glasgow earlier in the day, and would have visited Kingmoor shed in the interval – pity the crew could not have put the headboard on square! The first time I saw this engine, would you believe, was at Etruria, just north of Stoke-on-Trent, near to where I lived at the time and a regular spot for me. It came south on the up 'Lancastrian' and the excitement it generated among us regulars, was phenomenal, as might be imagined. Engines of this class were extremely rare on the former North Stafford route via Stoke in any event, and the appearance of a *Scottish* one, I can only assume, was some sort of mix-up following a works visit. As soon as it came into sight rather then the usual Longsight Britannia or Scot, the roar that went up could be heard for miles – even the signalman came out to comment! The Longsight engine that went south on the 'Lancastrian' almost always came back the following day on the down 'Comet'. Needless to say we were all there in anticipation, but to our disappointment, but not perhaps surprise, it was Camden Scot! Photograph Eric Blakey, www.transporttreasury.co.uk

Below. DUCHESS OF MONTROSE again waiting to take the down 'Royal Scot' forward to Glasgow, standing in about the same position as the view above right, on 22 September 1959. Notice by now that the tender has the later BR emblem and that the overall roof of Carlisle station has been cut back and renewed. Notice too, that while the engine is now fitted with a speedometer, AWS has yet to appear. Photograph Paul Chancellor Collection.

Bottom right. Only a few days later, DUCHESS OF MONTROSE is at Carlisle again and it looks as if it has just arrived on an up train – perhaps coming off the train here. This view clearly illustrates the water feed box for the injector mounted on the tender frame; it contained a sieve that was removed and cleaned on an X day exam and one could judge from how much debris was found whether the water scoop had been used very much! Photograph Paul Chancellor Collection.

46233 DUCHESS OF SUTHERLAND

Built Crewe 18/7/38, cost £9,181 (engine), £1,478 (tender)
Built without streamlining
Renumbered 6233 to 46233 week ending 2/10/48

Boilers

Fitted	No.	From
8/3/41	10305	6234
7/8/43	10287	6235
19/5/45	10297	6234
28/10/47	10646	6250
19/5/50	10645	6229
29/11/52	10304	-
8/12/56	9937	-
26/9/59	10641	-

No record after this date

Repairs LMS

10/7/39-27/7/39**LS**
1/7/40-16/7/40**LS**
5/2/41-8/3/41**HG**
5/6/41-18/6/41**TRO**
25/3/42-22/4/42**LS**
6/10/42-13/11/42**HS**
2/7/43-7/8/43**HG**
5/1/44-10/2/44**LO**
16/5/44-2/6/44**TRO**
12/10/44-3/11/44**LS**
18/4/45-19/5/45**HG**
15/2/46-7/3/46**LO**
3/8/46-24/8/46**HS**
26/7/47-28/10/47**HG**
3/11/47-14/11/47**#**
19/8/48-29/9/48**LS**
30/9/48-20/10/48**NC**
18/7/49-12/8/49**LI**
12/4/50-19/5/50**HG**
#*'No Repair'*

Repairs BR

Dates in the first column are from out of traffic to return to traffic; A = 'Weekdays Waiting', B= 'Weekdays on Works'. The two mileage figures represent, firstly the miles accumulated since the previous General or Intermediate (C) and secondly (the lower figure) the miles run up from January 1st of the year of shopping - D. All work is recorded as taking place at Crewe unless otherwise noted. StR=St Rollox

Dates	A	B	C	D
14/3/51-10/4/51**LC**	-	22	62,130	13,383
19/12/51-24/1/52**HI**	5	24	115,835	67,088
15/10/52-29/11/52**HG**	7	32	68,576	68,576
16/1/54-10/2/54**LI**	1	20	98,626	2,568
14/3/55-7/5/55**HI**	13	33	82,227	7,905
31/8/55-3/10/55**LC***	6	22	24,238	32,143
25/12/55-30/1/56**LC***	5	23	43,625	nil
25/10/56-8/12/56**HG**	9	29	101,032	57,407
12/10/57-23/10/57**NC***	9	2	62,823	58,740
24/2/58-12/4/58**HI**	2	38	92,569	12,589
1/8/59-26/9/59**HG**	4	44	101,590	50,741
18/1/61-21/2/61**HI**	5	24	98,848	1,929
10/7/61-24/8/61**LC***	14	25	22,363	23,997

record ends
*****(EO)' - 'Engine Only'*

Sheds

Camden	
Crewe North	20/5/44
Carlisle Upperby	14/6/58
Crewe North	20/9/58
Carlisle Upperby (loan)	2/4/60
Crewe North	23/4/60
Camden	30/4/60
Edge Hill	17/9/60

stored 6/10/62-we 2/2/63, 14/10/63-3/2/64

Tenders

No	Fitted
9751	18/7/38

LMS 'Summary' *(this became 'Annual Statistics' from 1951)*

Year	Mileage	Weekdays out of service			
		wks	shed	n/req	total
1938	46,599	2	20	1	23
1939	89,436	16	70	1	87
1940	82,750	14	71	-	85
1941	74,992	40	43	1	84
1942	54,163	50	63	1	114
1943	89,591	32	30	1	63
1944	60,844	68	41	1	110
1945	58,840	27	70	1	98
1946	68,480	37	38	-	75
1947	40,947	81	54	-	135
1948	67,934	54	36	1	91
1949	70,426	23	53	11	87
1950	65,291	32	38	12	82
1951	67,088	30	61	-	91
1952	74,461	60	41	-	101
1953	90,220	-	61	-	61
1954	76,890	21	39	2	62
1955	51,530	78	25	4	107
1956	61,490	62	46	2	110
1957	75,897	-	66	1	67
1958	63,439	40	39	1	80
1959	70,358	*record ends*			
1960	77,402				
1961	38,464				
1962	26,539				

wks=heavy and light repairs at main works
shed=shed repairs and examinations
n/req= not required

Total Recorded Mileage 1,644,071
Withdrawn week ending 8/2/64
Preserved at Midland Railway Centre, Butterley, main line runner

46233 DUCHESS OF SUTHERLAND in blue livery at St Rollox (the locals used its earlier name, Balornock) on 1 August 1950. For much of its BR life it was a Crewe North engine, until the diesels arrived in fact, and one wonders what it was doing here. It may be that engineering work somewhere was the cause, as there are recorded examples of these engines being serviced at St Rollox when the Anglo-Scottish trains were diverted at weekends into Buchanan Street station rather than Central. The former Caledonian Standard Goods 2F 0-6-0 to the right, 57253, was a St Rollox engine for all its time with BR. Photograph F.W. Goudie, www.transporttreasury.co.uk

Would you believe it but we have another shot of 46233 DUCHESS OF SUTHERLAND on Balornock shed, this time a few years later, on 9 July 1955. By this time the engine has the green livery and is standing on the turntable – already coaled for its return journey and presumably about to head back into Buchanan Street to work a train south. Although barely visible against the sky, the engine is actually blowing off at the safety valves. Notice the brazier hanging into the pit from the turntable; this would help (perhaps!) the centre bearing from stiffening up during cold weather, not expected of course in July – it is a wonder somebody has not 'borrowed' the coal! Photograph www.transporttreasury.co.uk

The down 'Mid-Day Scot' on the four track section somewhere between Stafford and Crewe. We know this as the order of the lines was different here from anywhere else on the West Coast main line; that is the two fast lines to the east and the slow lines to the west, rather than the fast lines in the centre flanked by the slows. The engine looks to be under easy steam so the photograph was probably taken on the long descent from Betley Road into Crewe. The engine is 46233 DUCHESS OF SUTHERLAND again, a Crewe North engine and in all probability it will come off at Crewe to be replaced by one of its stable mates to take the train forward to Glasgow. For years on end in the 1950s the 'Mid-Day Scot' in both directions was a job for 5A engines and men, changing over at Crewe. Unfortunately there is no date for this view, but around the mid 1950s would be my guess. Photograph www.transporttreasury.co.uk

46234 DUCHESS OF ABERCORN

Built Crewe 4/8/38, cost £9,181 (engine), £1,478 (tender)
Built without streamlining
Renumbered 6234 to 46234 week ending 30/10/48

Boilers

Fitted	No.	From
3/1/41	10297	6225
2/9/44	10294	6242
16/3/46	10300	6231
26/10/48	10305	6224
29/2/52	10293	-
24/4/54	9941	-
5/7/57	12470	-

No record after this date

Repairs LMS

13/4/39-28/4/39**LS**
18/1/40-8/2/40**LS**
6/11/40-5/1/41**HG**
3/1/42-7/2/42**LS**
30/3/42-18/4/42**LO**
12/11/42-5/12/42**HS**
31/7/43-20/8/43**LS**
8/8/44-2/9/44**HG**
19/5/45-9/6/45**LS**
2/1/46-16/3/46**HS**
28/4/47-20/5/47**HS**
18/10/47-10/11/47**NC**
15/1/48-14/2/48**LO**
6/9/48-26/10/48**HG**

Repairs BR

Dates in the first column are from out of traffic to return to traffic; A = 'Weekdays Waiting', B= 'Weekdays on Works'. The two mileage figures represent, firstly the miles accumulated since the previous General or Intermediate (C) and secondly (the lower figure) the miles run up from January 1st of the year of shopping - D. All work is recorded as taking place at Crewe unless otherwise noted. StR=St Rollox

Dates	A	B	C	D
9/2/50-10/3/50**HI**	?	?	92,744	6,406
13/3/50-31/3/50**NC**		134	6,540	
8/4/50-2/5/50**NC**	?	604	7,011	
13/2/51-20/3/51**LI**	2	28	66,813	8,594
19/1/52-29/2/52**HG**	4	31	64,456	3,105
19/2/53-21/3/53**HI**	9	17	86,472	12,609
18/8/53-29/9/53**LC**	8	28	38,041	50,650
17/3/54-24/4/54**HG**	2	30	77,291	15,680
26/7/54-31/7/54**NC***	-	5	18,782	34,462
24/8/55-30/9/55**LI**	6	26	97,915	42,216
15/10/55-29/11/55**HC***	11	27	1,540	43,756
15/5/57-5/7/57**HG**	4	40	124,613	26,823
13/8/57-14/9/57**HC***	8	20	7,813	34,636
19/3/58-25/4/58**LC***	4	27	45,761	17,691
25/1/59-28/2/59**LI**	1	28	105,934	5,280
25/2/60-13/4/60**HI**	12	29	73,201	7,722
7/6/60-18/8/60**LC***	33	29	15,729	23,451
28/8/61-25/10/61**HI**	16	34	87,428	37,922

record ends
*(EO)' - 'Engine Only'

Sheds

Camden	
Crewe North	20/3/43
Edge Hill (loan)	20/5/44
Crewe North	19/8/44
Camden (loan)	18/10/47
Crewe North	15/11/47
Camden	20/6/59
Crewe North	7/11/59
Camden (loan)	7/11/59
Crewe North	21/11/59#
Carlisle Upperby	21/11/59

#Nominal, presumably – went to Upperby from that date stored we 1/12/62-26/1/63

Tenders

No	Fitted
9752	4/8/38

LMS 'Summary' *(this became 'Annual Statistics' from 1951)*

Year	Mileage	Weekdays out of service			
		works	shed	n/req	total
1938	38,595	-	19	1	20
1939	78,669	14	76	1	91
1940	82,915	47	62	3	112
1941	91,696	5	62	-	67
1942	57,407	70	39	1	110
1943	74,560	18	50	-	68
1944	51,062	23	74	3	100
1945	69,384	19	48	-	67
1946	61,580	64	31	-	95
1947	67,247	20	50	3	73
1948	50,133	71	46	-	117
1949	75,977	-	58	13	71
1950	64,625	61	34	6	101
1951	69,945	30	42	1	73
1952	76,968	35	58	-	93
1953	74,220	62	39	1	102
1954	71,379	32	36	1	69
1955	50,827	70	57	11	138
1956	89,179	-	38	2	40
1957	54,893	72	52	-	124
1958	72,584	31	43	1	75
1959	70,459	*record ends*			

works=heavy and light repairs at main works
shed=shed repairs and examinations
n/req= not required

Total Recorded Mileage 1,494,304
Withdrawn week ending 26/1/63
Cut up Crewe Works 6/63

An unusual view of 46234 DUCHESS OF ABERCORN, another long-term Crewe North resident in the BR period, right through until June 1959 in fact, when it headed south for Camden. In this photograph however, the locomotive has a 12B shedplate and according to the records it was allocated to Carlisle Upperby in November 1959, remaining there until withdrawn in December 1962, so presumably the photograph dates from that period. The picture was taken at Camden – its distinctive mechanical coaling plant rears up behind. The engine is being serviced after arriving from the north; it is already coaled and the smokebox is being emptied as not all the engines of this class were fitted with self-cleaning smokebox screens. Only engines from 46253 onwards had this design of smokebox and although it seems to have been the intention to modify the earlier engines nothing was ever done. Photograph Paul Chancellor Collection.

The south end of Carlisle station with 46227 DUCHESS OF DEVONSHIRE on the right. A Polmadie engine, it has just arrived from the north and is about to be detached from its train (notice the light engine lamp headcode) and it will then depart to Kingmoor shed for servicing. One of the other engines seen here will then take the train forward while the third one will be awaiting a second train for the south. The engine on the left is 46234 DUCHESS OF ABERCORN and the one in the middle Princess Royal class 46211 QUEEN MAUD. This one has a 5A Crewe North shed plate which would suggest the photograph dates from the period May 1956 to November 1959 when this was its home depot.

Making good time, apparently, through Kings Langley, 46234 DUCHESS OF ABERCORN on 10 August 1951, its work almost done with the up 'Royal Scot' into Euston. This was a Crewe North engine at the time and indeed remained so until June 1959 when it went to Camden. At the time of the photograph it was painted in lined black livery with the full BRITISH RAILWAYS on the tender. It is probably working through from Glasgow on a cyclic diagram; notice the live steam injector is either being set or has just knocked off.

46235 CITY OF BIRMINGHAM

Built Crewe 27/6/39, cost £9,290 (engine), £1,548 (tender)
Built streamlined, casing removed 24/4/46
Renumbered 6235 to 46235 week ending 29/5/48

Boilers

Fitted	No.	From
22/6/43	10299	6230
25/1/47	9939	6220
25/5/48	10641	6230
2/12/50	10299	6227
15/5/53	10693	-
7/4/55	10291	-
26/2/58	10646	-
17/1/61	9940	-

No record after this date

Repairs LMS

28/3/40-22/4/40**TRO**
22/8/40-11/9/40**LS**
16/6/41-8/7/41**LS**
16/4/42-5/5/42**LS**
25/5/43-22/6/43**HG**
26/10/43-12/11/43**LO**
3/1/44-1/2/44**LO**
14/4/44-17/5/44**LS**
17/10/44-25/11/44**HS**
18/7/45-2/8/45**LO**
4/11/45-6/12/45**LO**
7/3/46-24/4/46**LS**
6/12/46-25/1/47**HG**
18/5/47-5/7/47**LO**
15/11/47-20/11/47**NC**
15/4/48-25/5/48**HS**
28/8/48-9/9/48**LO**
1/10/48-5/10/48**NC**
7/3/49-12/4/49**LO**
21/9/49-15/10/49**LI**
1/1/50-14/1/50**NC**
10/10/50-2/12/50**HG**

Repairs BR

Dates in the first column are from out of traffic to return to traffic; A = 'Weekdays Waiting', B= 'Weekdays on Works'. The two mileage figures represent, firstly the miles accumulated since the previous General or Intermediate (C) and secondly (the lower figure) the miles run up from January 1st of the year of shopping - D. All work is recorded as taking place at Crewe unless otherwise noted. StR=St Rollox

Dates	A	B	C	D
11/12/50-21/12/50**NC**	-	9	121	53,732
21/9/51-31/10/51**HI**	9	25	62,089	61,595
21/4/52-22/5/52**LC***	7	20	39,178	27,616
29/1/53-15/5/53**HG**	6	84	94,098	6,825
25/2/55-7/4/55**HG**	4	31	136,666	11,379
12/8/56-28/9/56**LI**	3	37	108,780	52,280
28/11/56-1/12/56**NC***	-	3	12,069	64,349
6/3/57-9/3/57**NC***	-	3	31,640	11,645
25/8/57-28/8/57**NC***	-	2	68,392	48,397
14/1/58-26/2/58**HG**	2	35	98,359	2,023
20/5/59-27/6/59**HI**	5	28	103,028	32,547
1/11/60-17/1/61**HG**	23	41	100,037	52,752

record ends
*(EO)' - 'Engine Only'

Sheds

Crewe North
Longsight   16/9/39
Rugby   30/9/39
Camden   21/10/39
Crewe North   20/5/44
stored 14/9/39-21/9/39, 27/9/39-2/10/39, 6/11/62-3/1/63, 1/10/63-12/12/63

Tenders

No	Fitted
9798	27/6/39

LMS 'Summary' *(this became 'Annual Statistics' from 1951)*

Year	Mileage	Weekdays out of service			
		wks	shed	n/req	total
1939	36,308	-	25	-	37#
1940	69,578	40	70	2	112
1941	85,915	20	56	-	76
1942	77,937	17	68	-	85
1943	77,416	41	44	-	85
1944	54,968	94	42	1	137
1945	54,439	42	58	-	100
1946	57,431	60	43	-	103
1947	49,693	66	48	3	117
1948	53,594	46	66	2	114
1949	63,678	54	26	8	88
1950	54,105	55	58	6	119
1951	73,157	34	52	-	86
1952	75,711	27	56	-	83
1953	55,590	90	57	-	147
1954	76,522	-	72	1	73
1955	67,879	35	40	14	89
1956	72,275	40	34	1	75
1957	76,341	-	51	-	51
1958	72,504	-	51	-	51
1959	79,832	37	55	-	92
1060	52,752	*record ends*			
1961	56,268				
1962	45,159				
1963	27,625				

#'includes 12 days stored serviceable'
wks=heavy and light repairs at main works
shed=shed repairs and examinations
n/req= not required

Total Recorded Mileage 1,566,677
Withdrawn week ending 12/9/64
Preserved at Birmingham Museum

Only one Coronation was allocated to Crewe North for the entire BR period and this is it, 46235 CITY OF BIRMINGHAM (the first with a City name and with it a reversion to streamline casing – notice the gap in the foot plating at the front) at its home shed in 1955, in green. The engine had its smokebox modified the following year and had been in the blue livery until April 1953. Photograph www.transporttreasury.co.uk

This down train emerging from Northchurch tunnel north of Berkhamsted has the reporting number 1Z57, the Z indicating a special working and as the date, 11 May 1963, was a Saturday, I am tempted to think it may have been in connection with a football match. The engine is Crewe North's 46235 CITY OF BIRMINGHAM; I wonder if a London team had an FA cup match in the second city and this engine had been specially chosen? Any views on a postcard please to Mr Irwell. Notice to the right preliminary works in connection with the forthcoming electrification.

CITY OF BIRMINGHAM again, this time at rest on shed at Carlisle Upperby on Saturday 13 July 1963. By this time the engine has been fitted with AWS equipment; observe the battery box just in front of the cab and the protection plate for the receiver behind the screw coupling – electrification notices fitted too. The headcode is 1M21, indicating its last working was the 10.55 Glasgow to Blackpool, a 'dated' Saturdays only train operating from 29 June to 24 August, for Glaswegians holidaying on the Fylde Coast. Along with Scarborough this was a favoured haunt for them as I recall from my Eastfield days. This was one of the few members of the class with City names to have a crest above the nameplate. Now preserved in the Birmingham Museum of Science & Industry, and in the light of the present butchery under the auspices of a body that really should know better – the National Railway Museum – on DUCHESS OF HAMILTON, long may it remain there, well out of harms way! Photograph Paul Chancellor Collection.

This is an undated photograph at an unknown location, with 46235 CITY OF BIRMINGHAM, late in its life with BR, heading a special working consisting of an entire rake of ex-LMS stock. It could be somewhere south of Penrith on the climb out of Carlisle, the X on the headcode indicating a special working. The time would be somewhere in the period 1963-64, and winter judging by the lack of foliage - a football special perhaps? Photograph Graham Onley.

46236 CITY OF BRADFORD

Built Crewe 27/7/39, cost £9,290 (engine), £1,548 (tender)
Built streamlined, casing removed 20/3/48
Renumbered 6236 to 46236 week ending 17/4/48

Boilers

Fitted	No.	From
11/10/41	10643	new
19/7/45	10289	6224
27/2/48	10643	6231
30/11/51	12470	-
24/11/54	10306	-
11/7/58	10637	-
17/2/62	10301	-

No record after this date

Repairs LMS

8/7/40-25/7/40**LS**
24/4/41-10/5/41**LS**
15/9/41-11/10/41**HG**
13/12/41-10/1/42**LO**
15/1/42-2/2/42**LO**
5/3/43-29/3/43**HS**
16/9/43-23/10/43**LO**
23/3/44-15/4/44**HS**
3/11/44-9/12/44**LO**
31/5/45-19/7/45**HG**
20/8/46-13/9/46**LS**
29/4/47-2/6/47**HO**
28/11/47-27/2/48**HG**
15/4/48-16/4/48**NC**
7/6/48-10/6/48**#**
26/6/48-2/7/48**NC**
17/2/49-21/2/49**No Repair**
3/6/49-28/7/49**HI**
23/3/50-6/4/50**LC**
6/6/50-3/7/50**HI**
#'nil'

Repairs BR

Dates in the first column are from out of traffic to return to traffic; A = 'Weekdays Waiting', B= 'Weekdays on Works'. The two mileage figures represent, firstly the miles accumulated since the previous General or Intermediate (C) and secondly (the lower figure) the miles run up from January 1st of the year of shopping - D. All work is recorded as taking place at Crewe unless otherwise noted. StR=St Rollox

Dates	A	B	C	D
11/1/51-10/2/51**LC**	7	19	34,958	2,523
19/10/51-30/11/51**HG**	9	27	89,513	57,078
10/6/52-5/8/52**HI**	5	43	52,641	46,228
23/9/53-24/10/53**LI**	5	22	98,135	60,561
18/10/54-24/11/54**HG**	2	30	89,773	71,845
12/4/55-21/5/55**LC***	12	22	35,153	28,369
12/3/56-19/4/56**HI**	6	26	107,763	15,599
10/5/57-15/6/57**LI**	2	29	102,505	32,705
26/7/57-27/7/57**NC***	-	1	8,895	41,600
26/5/58-11/7/58**HG**	1	39	83,771	29,945
17/3/59-25/3/59**NC***	1(R)	6	50,758	16,105
28/8/59-5/11/59**LI**	16	43	86,894	52,241
24/12/59-18/1/60**LC**	7	12	13,710	301
19/7/60-3/9/60**LC***	14	26	51,226	37,817
23/9/60-18/10/60**NC**	15	6	-	-

record ends
(R)=Rugby
'(EO)' - 'Engine Only'

Sheds

Camden	
Longsight	16/9/39
Rugby	30/9/39
Camden	21/10/39
Crewe North, then	
immediate loan to Edge Hill	20/5/44
Crewe North	8/7/44
Carlisle Upperby (loan)	19/7/47
Crewe North	18/10/47
Camden	24/4/48
Crewe North	10/7/48
Camden	23/6/51
Carlisle Upperby	14/6/58
Edge Hill	14/1/61
Carlisle Upperby	4/3/61
Carlisle Kingmoor	3/11/62

stored 12/9/39-21/9/39, 23/9/39-2/10/39, 30/12/63-27/1/64

Tenders

No	Fitted
9799	27/7/39
A79294	10/6/48#
9799	21/6/48
9749	21/1/49
9807	24/12/52

'Ex-Western Region'

LMS 'Summary' *(this became 'Annual Statistics' from 1951)*

Year	Mileage	Weekdays out of service			
		wks	shed	n/req	total
1939	28,129	-	19	18	54*
1940	83,699	16	65	5	86
1941	68,033	51	66	-	117
1942	73,216	28	64	-	92
1943	76,572	54	41	-	95
1944	65,126	49	85	1	135
1945	57,725	43	74	1	118
1946	63,587	22	73	-	95
1947	50,976	55	73	-	128
1948	59,617	53	57	1	111
1949	62,416	48	44	10	102
1950	60,902	35	22	17	74
1951	63,491	62	40	-	102
1952	83,802	48	44	-	92
1953	78,489	27	63	-	90
1954	78,629	32	66	-	98
1955	85,380	34	50	12	96
1956	85.399	32	54	-	86
1957	86,531	31	50	-	81
1958	64,598	40	78	1	119
1959	65,650	*record ends*			
1960	57,819				
1961	40,059				
1962	57,082				
1963	25,885				

wks=heavy and light repairs at main works
shed=shed repairs and examinations
n/req= not required
'stored 17 days'

Total Recorded Mileage 1,629,412
Withdrawn week ending 14/3/64
Cut up Crewe Works 4/64

46236 CITY OF BRADFORD arriving back at Kings Cross on another of the familiarisation runs with the 7.50 am Leeds to King Cross, during the 1948 Interchange. We can be sure it is a familiarisation run rather than the real thing as there is no dynamometer car at the head of the train. Although a Crewe North engine at the time, after selection for the trials it was transferred to Camden for the duration having had an unclassified repair at Crewe in April in preparation. It was also a requirement for all the engines used in the trials that they should have run between 15,000 and 20,000 miles since a general repair and this engine had one in February. Photograph David Montgomery.

These two photographs at an overly-gloomy Kings Cross show 46236 CITY OF BRADFORD departing on 28 April 1948 with the 11 am to Leeds. This would have been one of the preliminary crew familiarity runs prior to this locomotive being tested on the Eastern Region as part of the 1948 Locomotive Interchange Trials. The photographer was quite agile and before the train departed managed to get himself into an elevated position, I would suggest by climbing some structure in the adjacent locomotive yard. This allows us to see a very empty looking tender; we know that for the actual test runs, which in this case were performed between the 4 and 7 May, that the coal was strictly controlled. It was weighed before the test trains departed and again after they arrived, which would suggest staff being reluctant to put too much in the tenders if it had to be taken out again and weighed at the end of each journey. However, this tender does not seem to have enough in to get the engine past Finsbury Park never mind all the way to Leeds! According to the official report of the trials on the actual test runs this engine burned an average of just over three and a half tons on each single journey, almost four tons on one of them, so allowing for preparation and light engine mileage etc., one might expect at least five tons in the tender at the start of each journey. It takes some believing that an experienced driver like Camden's Brayford would set out on a route he was far from familiar with having so little coal as appears to be the case here! Incidentally Brayford, with his regular fireman Saint, handled this engine on all its exchange visits as well as on its home route. Photograph R.E. Vincent, www.transporttreasury.co.uk

CITY OF BRADFORD on its way back from Leeds with return leg of the same familiarisation run as in the previous illustrations. Here she is passing Finsbury Park No.5 signal box on 29 April 1948 with the 7.50 am from Leeds. This engine was criticised for its performance during the trials for not distinguishing itself and achieving the sort of performance the class as whole was known to be capable of. However, the general conclusion was that the driver, Brayford, was more concerned about fuel consumption than high power outputs. If all the coal they gave him is what can be seen in the tender in the previous views then I am not at all surprised! Photograph J.C. Flemons, www.transporttreasury.co.uk

After its sojourn on the Eastern Region 46236 moved for trials on the Western Region working the 1.30 pm Paddington-Plymouth and the 8.15 am back between 18 and 21 May 1948. Here is the engine on the down train in Sonning cutting on either the 18 or 20 May and in this case we know it is the test train as the former Great Western dynamometer car is behind the engine. Once again there is not much coal visible in the tender; on these runs the engine averaged almost four and quarter tons, so there cannot have been much of a margin. Notice the engine has the early design of smokebox number plate with sans serif numerals. The livery is the late LMS black with straw lining but with the BR number and lettering on the tender. The antiquity of the GWR dynamometer car is noticeable; it looks as if a strong pull by the Pacific might end its life! Photograph Maurice Earley.

The infamous Locomotive Exchange was a somewhat dubious brainwave of somebody in the BR hierarchy soon after it was formed; 'ours', 46236 CITY OF BRADFORD is seen here approaching Vauxhall on the 10.55 from Waterloo to Exeter on 22 June 1948 during its sojourn on the Southern Region. The tender was borrowed from an Austerity 2-8-0, as these had a much larger water capacity than the LMS ones, and there were no water troughs on the Southern. The train includes the former GWR dynamometer car; an engine to knock the spots of anything the Southern could field! When the late Geoff Sands, one time Shed Master at Crewe North and instrumental in my starting an apprenticeship there, went to the Southern as Motive Power Officer for the South Western Division, he tried to get some of these engines transferred to help out the ailing Bulleids. What a shame he was unsuccessful, as it might have prolonged the lives of some of them for a couple of years, as well as showing those Nine Elms boys a thing or two! Some readers may not be aware that of all the engines engaged in the interchange trials, this was the only one to complete all its designated assignments. All the others, without exception, and for one reason or another, missed at least one working. Photograph J.C. Flemons, www.transporttreasury.co.uk

CITY OF BRADFORD standing in the north end bay platform at Shrewsbury having worked in from Crewe; doubtless a filling-in turn on a West of England train. It is waiting for its return train to arrive. The engine is in the plain black livery it received in August 1952 and with the full smokebox modification which was undertaken in October 1953. As it was repainted BR green in November 1954, this nicely dates the photograph as between the last two dates while it was allocated to Camden. The larger of the two lagged pipes alongside the foot-framing and disappearing under it is the feed pipe from the exhaust injector, while the smaller one is the steam feed to the brake cylinder. Photograph David Montgomery.

Above. The up 'Mid-Day Scot' passing Farringdon Junction, just south of Preston, on 7 August 1954. The engine, 46236 CITY OF BRADFORD, is working through from Glasgow to Crewe. Notice how low the tender is in coal, so that the 'tunnel' housing the coal-pusher piston is visible. The fireman is observing the exhaust injector overflow, doubtless in an attempt to stop the proverbial 'losing water'. It is quite steep here, 1 in 106, but the engine has a clear exhaust and is blowing-off despite the 13 coach load, with the Leyland up fast distant showing the all-clear. Photograph A.W. Battson, www.transporttreasury.co.uk

Top right. Unfortunately we have no date for this photograph, which is a pity as it must have been taken in the last days of regular steam haulage of the prestigious 'Caledonian'. This is the up train arriving at Crewe, where it did not stop, with 46236 CITY OF BRADFORD. The engine would be working through from Carlisle to Euston, sharing the working with Camden engines and crews at the time on double-home diagrams. Notice how the cleaners have not quite managed to reach the top of the boiler. The Britannia on the right must be 70047, the only one without a name by this late period. A high reporting number such as W948 would indicate a special working. Photograph Paul Chancellor Collection.

Right. With 46236 CITY OF BRADFORD light out of Euston after an up working and bound for Camden shed, Jubilee 4-6-0 45631 TANGANYIKA of Longsight breasts the summit with northbound train W135, which was the 5.50 pm to Wolverhampton on which one might have expected a Bushbury Jubilee rather than a Longsight one. Photograph Prorail UK (Durrant) www.transporttreasury.co.uk

46237 CITY OF BRISTOL

Built Crewe 9/8/39, cost £9,290 (engine), £1,548 (tender)
Built streamlined, casing removed 7/3/47
Renumbered 6237 to 46237 week ending 3/7/48

Boilers

Fitted	No.	From
17/9/43	10293	6241
7/3/47	9938	6238
9/9/49	10290	6248
20/9/52	9940	-
16/3/55	10643	-
19/10/57	10639	-
18/2/59	10645	-

No record after this date

Repairs LMS

1/11/39-17/11/39**LO**
28/8/40-21/9/40**LS**
24/12/40-15/1/41**LO**
16/6/41-3/7/41**LS**
14/3/42-4/4/42**LS**
1/12/42-24/12/42**LO**
6/3/43-23/3/43**LO**
7/8/43-17/9/43**HG**
26/7/44-23/8/44**HS**
20/4/45-10/5/45**LO**
23/10/45-30/11/45**HS**
23/11/46-7/12/46**TRO**
12/1/47-7/3/47**HG**
19/8/47-23/9/47**LO**
8/6/48-3/7/48**LS**
19/7/48-23/7/48**NC**
29/7/49-9/9/49**HG**

Repairs BR

Dates in the first column are from out of traffic to return to traffic; A = 'Weekdays Waiting', B= 'Weekdays on Works'. The two mileage figures represent, firstly the miles accumulated since the previous General or Intermediate (C) and secondly (the lower figure) the miles run up from January 1st of the year of shopping - D. All work is recorded as taking place at Crewe unless otherwise noted. StR=St Rollox

Dates	A	B	C	D
21/7/50-23/8/50**HI**	5	23	63,310	36,106
27/4/51-1/6/51**LI**	8	22	63,755	26,744
26/10/51-3/12/51**HC**	12	20	36,601	63,345
9/8/52-20/9/52**HG**	8	28	96,768	54,339
16/2/53-19/3/53**HC***	7	20	34,059	9,403
5/12/53-6/1/54**LI**	1	24	103,477	78,821
24/1/55-16/3/55**HG**	6	38	97,259	5,525
9/4/56-10/5/56**LI**	6	21	89,539	20,994
25/5/56-16/6/56**LC***	9	10	1,973	22,967
4/7/56-9/8/56**LC***	8	23	2,682	23,676
9/9/57-19/10/57**HG**	3	32	97,696	58,125
5/11/58-11/12/58**LI**	4	27	95,748	77,934
16/1/59-18/2/59**HC***	-	28	3,151	687
19/7/60-10/9/60**LI**	8	38	110,544	40,535
21/8/61-14/10/61**LI**	15	32	54,095	34,072
24/10/61-31/10/61**NC***	-	6	604	34,676

record ends
'(EO)'- Engine Only

Sheds

Camden	
Longsight	16/9/39
Rugby	30/9/39
Camden	21/10/39
Carlisle Upperby (loan)	10/5/52
Camden	24/5/52
Western Region	23/4/55
Camden	21/5/55
Carlisle Upperby	14/6/58
Carlisle Kingmoor	11/4/61
Carlisle Upperby	7/4/62

stored 12/9/39-21/9/39, 23/9/39-2/10/39, 29/10/62-we2/2/63, 7/1/64-9/3/64

Tenders

No	Fitted
9800	9/8/39
9804	17/4/44
9800	6/5/44

LMS 'Summary' *(this became 'Annual Statistics' from 1951)*

Year	Mileage	Weekdays out of service			
		wks	shed	n/req	total
1939	22,087	15	8	16	56*
1940	92,195	26	58	2	86
1941	79,111	31	68	1	100
1942	45,369	40	102	-	142
1943	76,514	51	45	-	96
1944	65,330	25	80	-	105
1945	75,162	51	44	1	96
1946	75,217	13	69	1	83
1947	56,052	85	53	-	138
1948	68,630	23	68	-	91
1949	71,801	37	47	1	85
1950	73,117	28	65	-	93
1951	69,173	62	46	-	108
1952	78,995	36	56	-	92
1953	78,821	50	44	-	94
1954	91,734	2	75	-	77
1955	74,070#	44	40	11	95
1956	60,565	77	48	-	125
1957	75,939	35	49	-	84
1958	80,498	31	51	3	85
1959	67,445		record ends		

#'includes miles run whilst on Western Region'
wks=heavy and light repairs at main works
shed=shed repairs and examinations
n/req= not required
*includes 17 days 'stored serviceable'

Total Recorded Mileage 1,477,825
Withdrawn week ending 12/9/64
Cut up West of Scotland
Shipbreaking Co, Troon 12/64

The down 'Royal Scot' arriving at the south end of Rugby in April 1955, behind 46237 CITY OF BRISTOL, a Camden engine at the time. The bridge in the distance took the former Great Central London Extension over the West Coast main line, and has only recently been completely dismantled.

The down 'Lakes Express' passing Boars Head Junction, just north of Wigan, at four o clock on the afternoon of 20 July 1963. Behind the train can be seen the junction signal box, at which point the gradient eases from 1 in 104 to 1 in 366, but notice the engine is blowing off nicely and completely at ease in this nicely composed study. The initial 1 is missing from the headcode, which should read 1L27, at the time the correct reporting number for the 11.40 ex-Euston to the Lakes. The engine is 46237 CITY OF BRISTOL, allocated to Carlisle Upperby at the time and working through to Penrith, detaching coaches at various points en route. At Penrith the remaining coaches would be worked forward by another engine over the branch to Keswick, eventually completing their journey at Workington, while the Pacific would run light to Carlisle – in some summers there were also two or three through coaches for Carlisle. The procedure would be reversed on the following day; this was a regular Upperby Pacific diagram in the summer of 1963, and indeed during the following summer too. Photograph Ray Farrell.

A somewhat woebegone CITY OF BRISTOL, running into Tebay with an up local train at some unrecorded date, but well into its last days. Personally I have always had a particular soft spot for this engine, in the first instance because it was never painted by BR in maroon, because I prefer them in green. Secondly, it was the first 'foreigner' (as we called any engine not on our own allocation) of the class that I worked on in the early days of my apprenticeship, helping undertake a No.8 valve & piston exam. Photograph Gwyn Roberts.

Rugby shed was an unusual place to find a Pacific, but here is 46237 CITY OF BRISTOL resting between jobs there on 17 February 1963. By this date the engines had, by and large, been ousted by the diesels from the best work so they did occasionally find their way to all sorts of places where they would have been unknown in the past. Allocated to Carlisle Upperby at this time the engine is looking rather woebegone but with a real good tender full of coal. The 1A06 chalked on the smokebox rim represents the reporting number of a train the engine had worked in the recent past. It was the number for 'The Ulster Express', at that time the 06.55 ex-Heysham due in Euston at 11.55 am and I wonder had it come off this train for some reason at Rugby, or was the chalked number older? The two brackets passing round the bogie side frame between the bogie wheels, clearly seen in this view, are part of an early modification intended to help retain in position a bogie spring in the event of one becoming broken. Photograph Jack Hodgkinson.

46238 CITY OF CARLISLE

Built Crewe 14/9/39, cost £9,290 (engine), £1,548 (tender)
Built streamlined, casing removed 10/1/47
Renumbered 6238 to 46238 week ending 5/3/49

Boilers

Fitted	No.	From
24/7/44	10641	new
3/2/45	9938	6223
10/1/47	10637	6221
4/3/49	10302	6226
29/3/52	10298	-
27/9/55	10693	-
4/7/61	10287	-

No record after this date

Repairs LMS

9/8/40-31/8/40**LS**
23/6/41-24/7/41**HG**
3/6/42-27/6/42**LS**
24/5/43-11/6/43**LS**
23/5/44-19/6/44**HS**
3/1/45-3/2/45**HG**
15/9/45-26/10/45**LS**
8/11/46-10/1/47**HG**
15/11/47-17/12/47**LS**
3/1/49-4/3/49**HG**
6/10/49-4/11/49**NC**

Repairs BR
Dates in the first column are from out of traffic to return to traffic; A = 'Weekdays Waiting', B= 'Weekdays on Works'. The two mileage figures represent, firstly the miles accumulated since the previous General or Intermediate (C) and secondly (the lower figure) the miles run up from January 1st of the year of shopping - D. All work is recorded as taking place at Crewe unless otherwise noted. StR=St Rollox

Dates	A	B	C	D
8/5/50-1/6/50**LI**	-	20	74,551	17,725
4/4/51-15/5/51**LI**	9	26	67,884	18,604
18/5/51-30/5/51**NC**	-	10	Nil	18,604
22/2/52-29/3/52**HG**	2	29	56,612	10,296
19/4/52-9/5/52**NC**	6	11	4,207	14,503
14/8/53-21/9/53**HI**	2	32	90,516	40,033
10/8/55-27/9/55**HG**	4	37	116,607	34,795
27/3/56-5/4/56**NC***	-	7	35,768	15,181
4/1/57-31/1/57**LI**	3	20	96,296	172
16/11/57-21/11/57**NC***	1	3	67,509	67,681
6/5/58-20/6/58**HI**	12	27	100,897	26,553
12/12/59-12/2/60**HI**	13	38	98,842	65,356
29/5/61-4/7/61**HG**	1	30	98,197	18,580
31/7/61-15/9/61**LC***	15	25	3,821	22,401

record ends
*(EO)-Engine Only

LMS 'Summary' *(this became 'Annual Statistics' from 1951)*

Year	Mileage	wks	shed	n/req	total
		Weekdays out of service			
1939	18,327	-	13	20	38#
1940	86.876	20	51	11	82
1941	82.697	28	45	-	73
1942	77,629	22	66	1	89
1943	78,195	17	58	-	75
1944	74,788	24	49	2	75
1945	76,122	64	34	2	100
1946	67,740	43	65	3	111
1947	65,434	39	64	2	105
1948	70,734	-	74	-	74
1949	56,983	53	66	3	122
1950	67,005	21	67	5	93
1951	64,920	45	56	2	103
1952	60,779	48	50	6	104
1953	61,642	32	75	9	116
1954	60,203	-	95	9	104
1955	55,382	41	63	10	114
1956	75,537	-	82	7	89
1957	74,516	23	59	10	92
1958	60,039	39	78	7	124
1959	65,356	record ends			
1960	79,617				
1961	42,490				
1962	38,832				
1963	39,776				

#'stored serviceable five days'
wks=heavy and light repairs at main works
shed=shed repairs and examinations
n/req= not required

Total Recorded Mileage 1,602,628
Withdrawn week ending 12/9/64
Cut up West of Scotland
Shipbreaking Co, Troon 12/64

On 15 February 1964 Carlisle played Preston North End in an FA cup-tie, and Upperby turned out an immaculate 46238 CITY OF CARLISLE, to work in both directions one of the three heavily loaded special trains for the supporters, with 14 coaches in this case. Most unusually the train ran into platform 13 at Preston, on the East Lancashire side, where engines of this class were virtually unknown. The train here is leaving on the return journey, and once again from the East Lancashire side, which seems to have attracted some of the local spotters, perhaps more interested in this spectacle than the football, or had they heard about it at the match and hurried along to see the departure? The other two trains incidentally, were hauled by rebuilt Patriots 45512 and 45545, with 12 and 14 coaches respectively, similarly well loaded. Preston won by the way, in fact that year they reached the final at Wembley; there will be no happy Carlisle faces hanging out of the coach windows! It was a very nice touch too, when Kingmoor turned out this engine to work the very last up 'Caledonian', on the final day the train ran, 4 September 1964. Complete with headboard and beautifully turned out, it worked through to Euston and, I am reliably informed, arrived in the capital a few minutes early and despite the yellow stripe! Photograph A.W. Battson, www.transporttreasury.co.uk

134

Sheds
Crewe North
Camden	21/10/39
Carlisle Upperby	24/5/47
Camden	10/6/50
Carlisle Upperby	30/9/50
Camden	7/7/51
Carlisle Upperby	15/9/51
Camden (loan) 10/5/52	
Carlisle Upperby	24/5/52

stored 24/9/39-2/10/39, 2/1/64-27/1/64

Tenders
No	Fitted
9801	14/9/39

46239 CITY OF CHESTER

Built Crewe 29/8/39, cost £9,290 (engine), £1,548 (tender)
Built streamlined, casing removed 23/9/47
Renumbered 6239 to 46239 week ending 21/8/48

Boilers

Fitted	No.	From
22/4/44	9941	6226
23/9/47	10693	6251
3/7/50	10297	6223
30/5/52	10300	-
27/8/54	10640	-
15/3/57	10294	-
13/3/59	10306	-

No record after this date

Repairs LMS

16/9/40-5/10/40**LO**
13/2/41-7/3/41**LO**
9/9/41-29/9/41**LS**
14/9/42-3/10/42**LS**
8/6/43-3/7/43**HS**
25/3/44-22/4/44**HG**
24/4/45-1/6/45**LS**
3/4/46-6/5/46**LS**
12/5/47-23/9/47**HG**
12/7/48-19/8/48**LS**
12/1/49-8/2/49**NC**
29/7/49-2/9/49**LI**
14/9/49-21/9/49**NC**
23/9/49-10/10/49**NC**
20/2/50-3/3/50**NC**
8/6/50-3/7/50**HG**
7/7/50-4/8/50**NC#**
26/5/51-23/6/51**LI**

#'owing to incidence of Works Holidays
Engine was sent into traffic unpainted.
Returned to Shops for painting 14/7/50'

Repairs BR
Dates in the first column are from out of traffic to return to traffic; A = 'Weekdays Waiting', B= 'Weekdays on Works'. The two mileage figures represent, firstly the miles accumulated since the previous General or Intermediate (C) and secondly (the lower figure) the miles run up from January 1st of the year of shopping - D. All work is recorded as taking place at Crewe unless otherwise noted. StR=St Rollox

Dates	A	B	C	D
28/4/52-30/5/52**HG**	3	25	76,507	32,240
24/3/53-6/5/53**HI**	11	26	79,369	22,008
25/9/53-23/10/53**LC***	3	21	43,097	65,105
13/7/54-27/8/54**HG**	5	34	108,330	46,819
24/10/55-29/11/55**LI**	12	19	97,030	68,293
8/2/57-15/3/57**HG**	3	27	110,812	10,897
26/3/57-5/4/57**NC***	-	9	-	-
6/8/57-21/8/57**NC***	11	2	34,070	44,967
21/1/58-1/3/58**HI**	4	30	75,008	5,034
2/2/59-13/3/59**HG**	1	33	87,224	9,565
5/7/60-19/8/60**HI**	14	25	118,066	45,099
30/10/60-15/12/60**LC***	16	20	17,987	63,086
1/7/61-28/8/61**LC***	22	27	57,201	35,598

record ends
*(EO)'- Engine Only

Sheds
Camden
Crewe 16/9/39
Camden 21/10/39
Polmadie (loan) 2/12/39
Camden 3/2/40
Holyhead (loan) 6/4/40
Camden 1/6/40
Polmadie (loan) 14/10/44
Camden 11/11/44
Willesden 14/9/63
Crewe North ... 29/8/64
stored 10/9/39-2/10/39, 11/11/62-8/12/62, 22/9/63-1/12/63

Tenders

No	Fitted
9802	29/8/39
9747	22/11/45

LMS 'Summary' *(this became 'Annual Statistics' from 1951)*

Year	Mileage	Weekdays out of service			
		works	shed	n/req	total
1939	20,000	-	9	18	46#
1940	79,604	18	77	15	110
1941	84,342	38	40	-	78
1942	77,443	18	55	-	73
1943	88,657	23	38	-	61
1944	66,800	25	89	-	114
1945	62,961	33	91	1	125
1946	67,479	19	103	5	127
1947	47,285	115	51	-	166
1948	74,064	34	43	1	78
1949	64,196	53	58	1	112
1950	72,601	45	50	-	95
1951	78,782	24	62	-	86
1952	89,601	28	54	-	82
1953	80,519	61	40	-	101
1954	75,556	39	64	-	103
1955	74,094	31	87	7	125
1956	94,114	-	78	-	78
1957	80,871	39	58	-	97
1958	82,693	34	78	1	112
1959	82,532	*record ends*			

#'includes 19 days stored serviceable
works=heavy and light repairs at main works
shed=shed repairs and examinations
n/req= not required

Total Recorded Mileage 1,544,194
Withdrawn week ending 12/9/64
Cut up J.Cashmore, Great Bridge 12/64

CITY OF CHESTER at Shrewsbury in BR blue livery, which would indicate the period to be between June 1950 and July 1954. It would almost certainly have arrived here on a fill-in diagram before returning home later in the day, perhaps on a night train. The Shrewsbury jobs were also used by Crewe as running-in turns for engines off works, but this one does not appear to have recently had any main works attention. Photograph www.transporttreasury.co.uk

46239 CITY OF CHESTER, a Camden engine for almost all its BR life, already renumbered but retaining LMS on the tender, at Crewe North. This engine got its BR number in August 1948, and lost its LMS lined black livery in October 1950, so the photograph was taken somewhere between those times, earlier rather then later I would suggest. In the foreground is the turntable pit; the table here, oddly, was too small for the Pacifics and they had to go to the South Shed or the Gresty Lane triangle to turn, which was why they were often used on fill-in work to Shrewsbury, where they turned on the Severn Bridge triangle prior to returning. Under the extensive 1950s North Shed remodelling scheme (never fully completed) a 70ft diameter table was installed. Photograph www.transporttreasury.co.uk

The up 'Royal Scot', 46239 CITY OF CHESTER in charge, at Madeley, just south of Crewe on 15 May 1955. With a 14 or perhaps a 15 coach load, the engine is clearly getting into its stride, having surmounted the long climb out of Crewe to the Trent-Severn watershed, the fireman has put a good round on the fire and can be seen taking a breather. I doubt he would pick up the shovel again until they had passed Stafford – big engines like big fires, none of the 'little and often' technique on these beasts! Photograph T. Lewis, Norman Preedy Archive.

46240 CITY OF COVENTRY

Built Crewe 27/3/40, cost £9,290 (engine), £1,548 (tender)
Built streamlined, casing removed 29/7/47
Renumbered 6240 to 46240 week ending 26/6/48

Boilers

Fitted	No.	From
6/11/43	10306	6229
30/7/47	10291	6225
13/1/50	10304	6243
3/7/52	9938	-
29/10/54	10289	-
17/7/58	9939	-
13/4/62	9941	-

Repairs LMS

19/2/41-11/3/41**LS**
11/3/42-2/4/42**LS**
16/4/42-24/4/42**LO**
21/1/43-15/2/43**LS**
9/10/43-6/11/43**HG**
30/11/43-4/1/44**LO**
16/11/44-22/12/44**LS**
29/12/44-6/2/45**LO**
20/8/45-28/9/45**LO**
7/1/46-7/2/46**HS**
8/5/47-30/7/47**HG**
22/10/47-30/10/47**NC**
28/5/48-25/6/48**LS**
15/9/48-21/10/48**HO**
7/9/49-19/9/49**NC**
2/12/49-13/1/50**HG**

Repairs BR

Dates in the first column are from out of traffic to return to traffic; A = 'Weekdays Waiting', B= 'Weekdays on Works'. The two mileage figures represent, firstly the miles accumulated since the previous General or Intermediate (C) and secondly (the lower figure) the miles run up from January 1st of the year of shopping - D. All work is recorded as taking place at Crewe unless otherwise noted. StR=St Rollox

Dates	A	B	C	D
23/12/50-2/2/51**LI**	8	26	89,109	159
17/6/51-21/7/51**LC**	-	29	32,614	32,773
26/9/51-25/10/51**LC***	9	16	50,109	50,268
3/6/52-3/7/52**HG**	1	25	105,676	38,297
3/6/53-30/7/53**LI**	11	38	83,057	41,034
22/9/54-29/10/54**HG**	-	32	102,867	65,357
10/12/54-17/12/54**LC***-		6	8,180	73,537
23/12/55-28/1/56**HI**	2	27	105,098	92,974
29/5/56-2/7/56**LC***	-	29	33,440	33,440
25/3/57-10/5/57**LI**	7	32	92,777	15,315
16/8/57-16/8/57**NC***	-	1	24,489	39,804
3/6/58-17/7/58**HG**	2	36	94,787	35,158
21/4/59-30/5/59**HI**	12	22	76,274	39,820
6/6/60-20/8/60**HI**	19	46	98,158	33,348

record ends
***(EO)'- Engine Only*

Sheds

Crewe North
Camden 13/4/40
Willesden 7/9/63
Crewe North 29/8/64
stored 18/11/62-8/12/62, 22/9/63-1/12/63

Tenders

No	Fitted
9803	27/3/40
9703	29/6/44
9803	6/8/44

LMS 'Summary' *(this became 'Annual Statistics' from 1951)*

Year	Mileage	Weekdays out of service			
		works	shed	n/req	total
1940	71,148	-	54	1	55
1941	83,612	20	57	-	77
1942	75,720	28	55	1	84
1943	59,965	69	52	-	121
1944	72,457	42	66	-	108
1945	52,898	67	64	6	137
1946	74,620	28	71	1	100
1947	56,181	72	74	-	146
1948	58,646	55	64	2	121
1949	72,338	25	67	2	94
1950	88,950	16	58	-	74
1951	67,538	82	28	1	111
1952	80,320	26	64	1	91
1953	78,544	49	60	-	109
1954	77,481	38	59	2	99
1955	92,974	6	53	12	71
1956	77,462	52	55	-	107
1957	74,944	39	66	-	105
1958	80,612	38	65	-	103
1959	95,633	*record ends*			
1960	67,850				
1961	58,002				
1962	30,647				
1963	28,480				

Works = heavy and light repairs at main works
Shed = shed repairs and examinations
n/req = not required

Total Recorded Mileage 1,685,042
Withdrawn week ending 12/9/64
Cut up J. Cashmore, Great Bridge 3/65

Camden's **46240 CITY OF COVENTRY** in BR standard blue livery standing on Shrewsbury shed in July 1952. Photograph David Montgomery.

High in the Fells, 46240 CITY OF COVENTRY (a Camden engine working through from Euston to Carlisle) breasts Grayrigg with the down 'Royal Scot' on 7 May 1955. Many enginemen reckoned Grayrigg was a stiffer task than Shap, with the long 12 mile drag from Milnthorpe, the last almost three miles at 1 in 104, as opposed to the six miles of Shap, four at 1 in 75. But notice there is no bank engine exhaust visible, so the climb has been tackled unaided; in any event, if assistance was taken at Oxenholme, it would generally be in the form of a pilot right through to Shap Summit. Photograph M.N. Bland, www.transporttreasury.co.uk

A crisp clean 46240 CITY OF COVENTRY, by this date, 12 October 1960, sporting the BR version of the maroon livery with straw lining, ambling along the lengthy undulating section between Wigan and Preston at Standish Junction – bedevilled as it was with numerous speed restrictions due to mining subsidence. The train is said to be the 3.25 pm Euston to Carlisle, with a section for Windermere, but I have my doubts in view of how high the sun clearly is, and the time of year quoted – and with plenty of leaves on those trees yonder. The carriage board on the first coach nonetheless, an ex-LMS vehicle, reads London-Carlisle. So either the date or the train is incorrect; it could be 'The Lakes Express', which left London around 11.35, but this was a summer timetable only train. No matter, it is a very nice view, the fire obviously well burnt through after the stiff 1 in 104 climb out of Wigan, steam shut off with the Coppull Hall Sidings distant on. The driver must have spotted Mr Roscoe and called his fireman over to have a look. Photograph A.H. Roscoe, www.transporttreasury.co.uk

Two pleasing portraits of 46240 CITY OF COVENTRY, at home on Willesden shed in 1964, the first in March and the second on 6 July. The remaining Camden Pacifics were transferred to Willesden when Camden closed to steam in September the previous year, to eke out their last year or so of life, although in fact they went to Crewe North for a few weeks at the very end. But Willesden found plenty for them to do in that last summer of 1964, and usually kept them in remarkably clean external condition. Photographs J.A.C. Kirke, www.transporttreasury.co.uk and Peter Groom.

Indeed here is 46240 earning its keep in grand fashion at Kensal Green with the down 'Lakes Express' on 22 August 1964, which it would work through to Penrith. It will then run light to Carlisle, before repeating the procedure in reverse the following day. However, by this date the engine had but a short life left; transferred to Crewe North a few days later, on 1 September in fact, it was taken out of service there, for good, on 12 September. Is this the last picture taken of the engine still at work one wonders? Notice by this date the engine is disfigured by the yellow diagonal stripe on the cab side, intended to signify it should not work south of Crewe in view of the limited clearance under the overhead line equipment then being erected, though it had not by this date reached Kensal Green. The instruction actually came into force on 1 September, which is why the last remaining Pacifics at the London end, this one and 46239, were transferred to Crewe North on that date; the other one, 46245, had been transferred at little earlier, in August. Photograph Peter Groom.

The nameplate on the left-hand side of 46240. This was one of only three to have the nameplates adorned by the relevant City heraldic device. One of the nameplates of this locomotive, complete with the crest, is mounted along with a photograph of the engine on the footbridge at Coventry station, presented to the City by BR when the engine was withdrawn. I think I am right is saying that one plate from each of the 'City' engines was similarly presented to the relevant City Fathers. Photograph www.transporttreasury.co.uk

46241 CITY OF EDINBURGH

Built Crewe 3/4/40, cost £9,290 (engine), £1,548 (tender)
Built streamlined, casing removed 6/2/47
Renumbered 6241 to 46241 week ending 29/5/48

Boilers

Fitted	No.	From
29/5/43	10640	6232
6/2/47	10694	6252
30/9/49	10295	6252
11/6/53	10294	-
3/11/56	10637	-
11/2/58	10643	-

No record after this date

Repairs LMS

28/3/41-17/4/41**LS**
10/12/41-9/1/42**LS**
14/3/42-28/3/42**LO**
1/5/43-29/5/43**HG**
8/9/44-14/10/44**HS**
7/5/45-16/6/45**LO**
31/10/45-8/12/45**LS**
10/12/46-6/2/47**HG**
12/1/48-21/1/48**NC**
17/4/48-26/5/48**HS**
4/8/49-30/9/49**HG**
21/10/49-31/10/49**NC**

Repairs BR

Dates in the first column are from out of traffic to return to traffic; A = 'Weekdays Waiting', B= 'Weekdays on Works'. The two mileage figures represent, firstly the miles accumulated since the previous General or Intermediate (C) and secondly (the lower figure) the miles run up from January 1st of the year of shopping - D. All work is recorded as taking place at Crewe unless otherwise noted. StR=St Rollox

DatesABCD				
13/9/50-10/10/50**LI**	-	23	87,252	66,434
17/10/50-3/11/50**NC**	-	15	394	66,828
17/6/51-3/7/51**HC**	-	13	48,232	35,097
16/10/51-17/11/51**HI**	2	26	67,762	54,627
18/2/52-14/3/52**NC**	6	16	21,939	12,486
8/5/52-31/5/52**LC***	6	14	35,005	25,552
3/3/53-11/6/53**HG**	1	84	98,938	13,052
12/7/53-16/8/53**LC***	-	30*	7,242'	
12/9/53-5/10/53**LC***	9	10	15,724	28,776
4/5/54-28/5/54**HI**	1	20	75,283	33,710
15/11/54-13/12/54**LC***	6	18	44,548	78,258
27/9/55-22/10/55**HI**	-	22	108,547	60,392
20/9/56-3/11/56**HG**	12	26	72,692	63,903
21/11/57-25/11/57**NC***	-	3	89,306	77,434
1/1/58-11/2/58**HG**	4	31	96,568	81
27/1/59-7/3/59**HI**	6	28	88,020	6,241
6/2/60-20/5/60**HI#**	26	62	74,491	8,817
31/7/61-21/9/61**HI#**	3	42	78,165	30,435

*'shed'
#'boiler lifted out and put back'
record ends
*(EO)'- Engine Only

Sheds

Crewe	
Camden	13/4/40
Edge Hill (loan)	10/57
Camden	2/11/57
Crewe North	20/9/58
Edge Hill	11/4/61
Crewe North	5/64

stored 5/11/62-we 2/2/63, 14/10/63-23/3/64

Tenders

No	Fitted
9804	3/4/40
9805	13/3/44
9811	1/8/53
9703	21/9/56
9811	3/11/56

LMS 'Summary' *(this became 'Annual Statistics' from 1951)*

Year	Mileage	Weekdays out of service			
		works	shed	n/req	total
1940	61,318	-	54	2	56
1941	79,381	33	52	1	86
1942	74,249	24	47	-	71
1943	69,934	25	56	-	81
1944	42,182	32	85	-	117
1945	72,519	69	58	-	127
1946	73,588	16	80	4	100
1947	68,349	34	56	3	93
1948	71,395	34	54	3	91
1949	73,154	50	57	1	108
1950	79,569	38	42	-	80
1951	64,080	41	63	-	104
1952	76,433	20	85	1	106
1953	54,625	134	57	-	191
1954	81,865	45	37	-	82
1955	69,181	22	74	14	110
1956	75,775	38	77	-	115
1957	84,615	-	73	-	73
1958	80,255	35	59	-	94
1959	73,520	*record ends*			

works=heavy and light repairs at main works
shed=shed repairs and examinations
n/req= not required

Total Recorded Mileage 1,425,987
Withdrawn week ending 5/9/64
Cut up J.Cashmore, Great Bridge 1/65

For most of its time with BR 46241 CITY OF EDINBURGH had been at either Crewe North or Camden. However in March 1961 it was transferred to Edge Hill, where the allocation of Pacifics had usually been the earlier Princess Royals, for the London trains. On 5 October 1963 46241 has found its way on to the 6.15 am Carlisle-Crewe Class 2 stopping passenger train, reporting number 2K82, seen here during its Preston stop. Photograph A.W. Battson, www.transporttreasury.co.uk

A scruffy 46241 CITY OF EDINBURGH, heading south after passing Carnforth station on 13 June 1964. This was an Edge Hill engine at the time, having been in store for much of the previous winter, and it did not have very much time left when this picture was taken; it came to Crewe North for a few weeks before being placed in store there in August. This re-allocation is not recorded in any official statistics I have seen, but it did happen as I was there at the time and took notes! The train is a special of some sort, indicated by the X in the reporting number and no less by the complete rake of former LMS coaching stock, almost certainly retained for special workings. Photograph A.W. Battson, www.transporttreasury.co.uk

46242 CITY OF GLASGOW

Built Crewe 15/5/40, cost £9,290 (engine), £1,548 (tender)
Built streamlined, casing removed 3/5/47
Renumbered 6242 to 46242 week ending 29/5/48
'involved in Harrow mishap 8/10/52'

Boilers

Fitted	No.	From
6/6/42	10296	6244
2/5/47	10640	6241
29/7/49	13043	new
26/10/53	10299	-
17/4/57	10641	-
19/6/59	10639	-

No record after this date

Repairs LMS
28/4/41-22/5/41**LS**
27/2/42-21/3/42**LS**
21/9/42-17/10/42**LO**
2/6/43-29/6/43**LS**
12/5/44-6/6/44**HG**
19/3/45-20/4/45**HS**
16/5/46-5/6/46**LS**
6/3/47-3/5/47**HG**
5/11/47-10/11/47**NC**
14/4/48-27/5/48**LS**
22/12/48-25/12/48**NC**
27/5/49-27/7/49**HG**
3/8/49-6/8/49**NC**

Sheds

Camden	
Polmadie	22/7/44
Crewe North (loan)	12/6/48
Camden	26/6/48
Crewe North	27/6/53
Camden	20/11/54
Polmadie	11/3/61

Tenders

No	Fitted
9805	15/5/40
9804	13/3/44
9800	17/4/44
9804	6/5/44
9703	9/1/46
9816	26/7/51

The date of this photograph could well be the one chalked on the smokebox door – either the 12 or 22 June 1948 - it also says 'Door Tight'. The shed is Polmadie, where the engine was allocated at the time, and it has the earlier shed code of 27A on the smokebox door. It was of course quite fitting that this engine, 46242 CITY OF GLASGOW, should be allocated here, although perhaps surprisingly, for much of its career with BR it was not. Camden had it for most of the time, although it did complete its days at Polmadie. Painted in the LMS lined black it has been renumbered while retaining LMS on the tender sides. At this period W146 was the reporting number for the 5.40 pm overnight part sleeping car train from Glasgow to Euston, so presumably the engine is having a final top up of coal before proceeding to Central Station to pick up its train – it would in all probability work it as far south as Crewe. Later engines of the class, like this one, had double chimneys from new. Notice the discarded firehole protector plate by the leading coupled wheel, and the general debris laying around, so typical of steam sheds for much of the post-war period. A marvellous portrait. Photograph W. Hermiston, www.transporttreasury.co.uk

Dates	A	B	C	D
16/5/50-16/6/50**HI**	5	22	71,341	34,654
12/6/51-26/7/51**HI**	2	36	81,389	36,996
21/5/52-21/6/52**LI**	4	23	56,838	30,121
9/10/52-26/10/53**HG**	33	291#	28,442	58,563
30/8/54-11/10/54**LI**	4	32	74,567	60,614
16/8/55-13/9/55**HI**	1	23	72,852	53,755
29/1/56-8/2/56**NC***	2	5	32,948	10,302
1/5/56-9/6/56**LI**	2	32	53,031	30,385
23/10/56-24/10/56**LC**	-	1	38,514	68,899
22/3/57-17/4/57**HG**	4	18	73,697	21,019
10/8/57-14/8/57**NC***	2	1	29,716	50,735
18/1/58-1/3/58**HI**	7	29	66,652	6,477
2/4/59-19/6/59**HG**	4	63	99,598	24,249
27/7/60-16/9/60**LI**	5	39	101,343	48,820
16/8/61-16/8/61**NC**	-	1*	-	-
25/1/62-12/5/62**HI**	13	79	74,567	507

LMS 'Summary' *(this became 'Annual Statistics' from 1951)*

Year	Mileage	Weekdays out of service			
		wks	shed	n/req	total
1940	55,083	-	42	-	42
1941	82,687	22	55	-	77
1942	77,296	44	31	-	75
1943	84,947	21	53	-	74
1944	74,685	22	46	4	72
1945	62,791	29	93	1	123
1946	71,536	18	82	-	100
1947	53,954	51	76	-	127
1948	77,815	38	64	2	104
1949	64,539	60	54	2	116
1950	79,047	27	55	-	82
1951	63,713	38	88	2	128
1952	58,563	67	44	-	111
1953	13,953	257	4	-	261
1954	79,711	36	24	2	62
1955	76,401	24	73	15	112
1956	83,063	35	71	-	106
1957	81,195	22	73	-	95
1958	81,826	36	57	-	93
1959	76,772	*record ends*			
1960	76,595				
1961	46,585				
1962	32,523				

46242 CITY OF GLASGOW at Polmadie. The date is not clear but it is certainly prior to October 1954 when the engine behind, 46224, had its sloping smokebox top modified. On the other hand notice that 46242 has the continuous footplate at the front, although originally this locomotive had been streamlined. As the previous illustrations show, earlier it had the split arrangement common to all the engines when the streamlined casing was removed. This dates the photograph after the engine's rebuilding following the Harrow & Wealdstone collision in October 1952, because during that work the arrangement shown here was arrived at. The engine did not return to traffic until October the following year, so the picture has to date from some time between October 1953 and October the following year. The engine bears the 'Royal Scot' headboard, but does not look as if it is about to work that train, so perhaps it had inadvertently been left in position following an earlier working. In any event, the engine is fully coaled ready for its next job and I wonder if that is one of Polmadie's Clan Pacifics in front, as the shed did not get any Britannias until the final 1954 batch was delivered. Photograph www.transporttreasury.co.uk

Top left. This view of CITY OF GLASGOW will perhaps, help the model makers among our fraternity, showing as it does some of the less well photographed parts of these engines, the rear of the tender. The twin pipes over the curved cover to the rear of the coal space are the exhaust pipes for the coal pusher piston valve, itself in a cylinder under the cover. The item mounted on the frames as they spray out behind the trailing coupled axle is the operating gear for the ashpan doors, which were different than on earlier members of the class, a form of hopper ashpan in fact. A long handle, otherwise kept on the footplate, was inserted here allowing the large ashpan door to be opened and closed; this arrangement was fitted to 46229 and from 46234 onwards. The picture is undated, but taken at Carlisle Kingmoor, late in the BR period; notice the engine has been fitted with AWS equipment and has the later tender emblem. Behind is a Derby-Sulzer Type 4 diesel, later Class 45, which would doubtless have worked over the Settle to Carlisle route. Photograph Paul Chancellor Collection.

Left. In June 1957 the London Midland Region introduced – as elaborated earlier – a new fast eight coach limited load train between London and Glasgow, 'The Caledonian', with a six hour and 40 minute schedule. Here is the down train on 24 February 1960 about to leave Euston with Camden Pacific 46242 CITY OF GLASGOW. With this train, regular all year round through working of the Pacifics between Euston and Glasgow was introduced, echoing the pre-war 'Coronation Scot', with Camden engines diagrammed in both directions. The engine that worked the down train returned the following day on the up working. Departure was at 4.15 pm from Euston and 8.30 am from Glasgow. Although diesels were generally to be seen on this train latterly, when it ceased to run at the end of the 1964 summer timetable (a victim of the engineering works in connection with the electrification works) Carlisle turned out 46238 CITY OF CARLISLE to work the up train to Euston. A swan-song indeed. Photograph www.transporttreasury.co.uk

Above. One last look at CITY OF GLASGOW as it leaves Glasgow Central station on 25 May 1957. Unfortunately we have no further information, but the train could well be the morning Glasgow-Birmingham, with the Camden engine on one of the cyclic diagrams that were in operation about this time in an effort to increase the utilisation of the class. If it is, the engine will come off at Crewe, and after a visit to the North Shed for servicing, in all probability will return to its home shed on one of the overnight trains which changed engines at Crewe. Photograph J. Robertson, www.transporttreasury.co.uk

46243 CITY OF LANCASTER

Built Crewe 29/5/40, cost £9,290 (engine), £1,548 (tender)
Built streamlined, casing removed 16/7/49
Renumbered from 6243 to 46243 week ending 24/4/48

Boilers

Fitted	No.	From
24/12/43	10292	6240
22/2/46	10304	6226
22/6/49	10637	-
23/9/52	10640	-
5/2/54	10287	-
16/11/57	10293	-
18/12/59	10288	-
14/8/61	10290	-

No record after this date

Repairs LMS

7/3/41-29/3/41**LS**
11/10/41-1/11/41**LS**
21/10/42-17/11/42**LS**
13/5/43-4/6/43**LO**
5/11/43-24/12/43**HG**
27/10/44-6/12/44**HS**
24/7/45-30/8/45**LO**
23/1/46-22/2/46**HG**
17/4/47-9/5/47**HS**
23/9/47-18/10/47**NC**
16/3/48-20/4/48**LS**
1/5/49-22/6/49**HG**

Repairs BR
Dates in the first column are from out of traffic to return to traffic; A = 'Weekdays Waiting', B= 'Weekdays on Works'. The two mileage figures represent, firstly the miles accumulated since the previous General or Intermediate (C) and secondly (the lower figure) the miles run up from January 1st of the year of shopping - D. All work is recorded as taking place at Crewe unless otherwise noted. StR=St Rollox

Dates	A	B	C	D
11/5/50-6/6/50**LC**	2	2o	67,430	29,365
29/3/51-2/5/51**LI**	4	25	130,084	14,371
3/6/52-23/9/52**HG**	7	89	86,081	32,161
16/4/53-28/5/53**LC**	16	20	51,648	27,086
30/12/53-5/2/54**HG**	8	24	103,602	79,040
2/12/54-7/1/55**HI**	1	28	75,226	75,226
9/11/55-10/12/55**LC**	10	17	67,331	67,331
7/8/56-18/9/56**HI**	1	35	119,222	48,802
5/9/57-7/9/57**NC***	-	2	75,690	52,807
8/10/57-16/11/57**HG**	1	33	83,019	60,136
3/9/58-11/10/58**HI**	5	28	64,220	53,810
19/10/59-18/12/59**HG**	14	38	88,207	72,267
27/7/60-5/8/60**NC***	11	14	51,618	49,098
30/5/61-14/8/61**HG**	17	48	93,824	17,602

record ends
***(EO)'- Engine Only**

Sheds

Camden	
Edge Hill	5/6/48
Crewe North	11/12/48
Carlisle Upperby	14/6/58
Crewe North	20/9/58
Camden	11/6/60
Edge Hill	25/3/61

stored 5/11/62-we2/2/63, 14/10/63-23/12/63, 30/12/63 to 23/3/64

Tenders

No	Fitted
9806	29/5/40

LMS 'Summary' *(this became 'Annual Statistics' from 1951)*

Year	Mileage	Weekdays out of service			
		wks	shed	n/req	total
1940	51,628	-	38	3	41
1941	76,247	39	50	-	89
1942	75,270	24	59	-	83
1943	60,243	63	57	-	120
1944	76,115	35	40	1	76
1945	75,512	33	53	1	87
1946	56,204	21	84	2	113
1947	65,764	20	99	1	120
1948	64,263	30	51	1	82
1949	59,223	45	47	11	103
1950	77,648	22	33	8	63
1951	68,291	29	55	1	85
1952	56,723	96	40	1	137
1953	79,040	40	53	-	93
1954	75,226	53	21	-	74
1955	70.420	31	28	1	60
1956	71,685	36	43	2	81
1957	70,546	34	53	-	87
1958	69,750	33	46	-	79
1959	74,787	*record ends*			
1960	73,702				
1961	35,891				
1962	30,305				
1963	11,809				

wks=heavy and light repairs at main works
shed=shed repairs and examinations
n/req= not required

Total Recorded Mileage 1,526,292
Withdrawn week ending 12/9/64
Cut up Central Wagon Co, Ince 8/65

Crewe North on 28 July 1954 with 46243 CITY OF LANCASTER, one of the shed's complement at the time. The much smaller live steam injector was on this, left-hand side, and can be seen immediately below the cab side sheet. Photograph www.transporttreasury.co.uk

CITY OF LANCASTER again, this time at Carstairs on an up train with the carriage & wagon examiner (notice his long shaft hammer) talking to the driver while a porter attends to the mail bags. This engine retained its sloping smokebox until a November 1958 visit to Crewe Works. Photograph www.transporttreasury.co.uk

A very dirty 46243 CITY OF LANCASTER, trundling through Preston on a down train of Presflo cement wagons; a humble duty for such a thoroughbred machine. The date is 9 September 1964 and the engine had but a few days of service left as it was withdrawn three days later. After its arrival at Carlisle I doubt it left there again under its own steam. Photograph A.W. Battson, www.transporttreasury.co.uk

46244 KING GEORGE VI

Built Crewe 12/7/40, cost £9,290 (engine), £1,548 (tender)
Built streamlined, casing removed 4/9/47
Renumbered 6244 to 46244 week ending 28/8/48

Boilers

Fitted	No.	From
8/1/44	10639	6231
22/3/46	10288	6227
27/8/48	9937	6232
19/10/50	10301	6224
1/7/53	10642	-
11/7/57	10299	-
11/6/60	10644	-

No record after this date

Repairs LMS
3/5/41-5/6/41**LS**
4/3/42-27/3/42**LS**
17/12/42-23/1/43**LS**
11/7/43-4/9/43**LO**
17/11/43-8/1/44**HG**
13/3/45-11/4/45**HS**
22/2/46-22/3/46**HG**
27/3/47-29/4/47**LS**
21/7/47-4/9/47**LO**
9/6/48-27/8/48**HG**
13/6/49-2/8/49**HI**
5/6/50-24/6/50**LC**
13/9/50-19/10/50**HG**

Repairs BR
Dates in the first column are from out of traffic to return to traffic; A = 'Weekdays Waiting', B= 'Weekdays on Works'. The two mileage figures represent, firstly the miles accumulated since the previous General or Intermediate (C) and secondly (the lower figure) the miles run up from January 1st of the year of shopping - D. All work is recorded as taking place at Crewe unless otherwise noted. StR=St Rollox

Dates	A	B	C	D
24/10/50-13/11/50**NC**	2	15	nil	52,005
8/12/50-18/12/50**NC**	-	8	3,644	55,649
14/8/51-13/9/51**LI**	6	20	73,270	65,539
7/1/52-7/2/52**LC**	7	20	23,467	761
29/7/52-9/9/52**LI**	8	28	67,675	44,969
26/3/53-1/7/53**HG**	12	70	49,597	21,001
28/8/54-4/10/54**LI**	1	30	99,331	58,031
4/2/55-2/3/55**LC***	-	22	27,748	7,844
21/11/55-21/12/55**LI**	6	20	86,959	67,055
21/8/56-27/9/56**LC***	3	29	58,715	57,221
25/5/57-11/7/57**HG**	7	33	108,988	27,615
29/8/57-31/8/57**NC***	-	2	10,259	37,874
13/9/58-24/10/58**HI**	7	28	97,613	54,250
26/2/60-11/6/60**HG**	17	73	93,291	7,015

record ends
*'(EO)'- Engine Only

Sheds
Camden
Polmadie (loan)   28/9/40
Camden   19/10/40
Carlisle Upperby   14/6/58
Carlisle Kingmoor   11/4/61
stored 30/12/63-2/3/64

Tenders

No	Fitted
9807	12/7/40
9808	26/6/45

LMS 'Summary' *(this became 'Annual Statistics' from 1951)*

Year	Mileage	Weekdays out of service			
		wks	shed	n/req	total
1940	33,184	-	33	1	34
1941	76,017	29	64	2	95
1942	71,195	29	40	-	69
1943	65,397	75	36	-	111
1944	77,829	12	87	-	99
1945	70,367	26	58	5	89
1946	81,053	25	63	7	95
1947	57,470	68	61	1	130
1948	64,363	69	41	2	112
1949	75,564	44	57	-	101
1950	59,736	65	52	-	117
1951	88,245	26	42	-	68
1952	73,565	63	44	-	107
1953	62,301	82	59	-	141
1954	77,935	31	62	-	93
1955	68,549	48	63	14	125
1956	79,879	32	68	-	100
1957	70,978	40	64	-	104
1958	67,900	35	72	5	112
1959	78,626	*record ends*			

wks=heavy and light repairs at main works
shed=shed repairs and examinations
n/req= not required

Total Recorded Mileage 1,400,154
Withdrawn week ending 12/9/64
Cut up West of Scotland
Shipbreaking Co, Troon 12/64

Odd man out in the naming stakes was 46244 KING GEORGE VI, although this engine was, until April 1941, named CITY OF LEEDS; the renaming was clearly a war-time moral boosting gesture. The engine is at Crewe North, on 29 August 1948, newly painted in the short-lived BR blue livery introduced around that time for the principal express engines on all the Regions. The engine is clearly just off works and has still be to fully coaled; I wonder what the driver, who must have been an ex-LMS man, thought of that damn-awful colour scheme – I am glad I cannot recall seeing these engines so adorned! Photograph www.transporttreasury.co.uk

Two more view of 46244 on the same occasion including a close up of the original BR emblem on the tender side. The cast iron box to the left on the tender frame between the leading and intermediate wheels contains a water sieve on the delivery pipe to feed the left-hand injector; there was a similar one on the other side. On the close-up view notice the two brackets over the spring designed to retain it in position in the event of a broken spring bolt. In the aperture in the frames to the right can be seen the water scoop and its operating gear, or part of it. Photograph www.transporttreasury.co.uk

The classic departure shot at Glasgow Central again, this time with 46244 KING GEORGE VI, on 6 April 1957, once again perhaps, with the morning train to Birmingham and a Camden engine on a cyclic diagram. The Birmingham train left Glasgow a few minutes after the 'Royal Scot', 10.10 being typical over the years, with the London train leaving at the time-honoured 10 o'clock. Safety valves sizzling nicely although the left-hand piston rod packing is blowing and the live steam injector has just knocked off. But a lovely, evocative, shot. Photograph J. Robertson, www.transporttreasury.co.uk

I think this photograph must have been taken at Shrewsbury, some time after May 1958 when KING GEORGE VI was transferred from Camden to Carlisle Upperby. It had probably arrived on a fill-in turn from Crewe, has been turned on the Severn Bridge triangle, re-attached to its stopping train, and is standing in the Coleham sidings awaiting movement to the station and its return journey. Photograph Paul Chancellor Collection.

Another humble working for a Pacific, 46244 KING GEORGE VI has the 7.21 am stopping train from Kilmarnock, at Bellahouston on the former Glasgow & South Western route from Kilmarnock to Glasgow St Enoch, on 3 April 1961. In March 1961 this engine had been transferred to Carlisle Kingmoor so its use on this train, perhaps part of a diagram that had earlier taken it from Carlisle to Kilmarnock, might not be as unusual as it at first appears. Photograph J.L. Stevenson, courtesy Hamish Stevenson.

Latterly 46244 KING GEORGE VI was allocated to Kingmoor shed in Carlisle, and we see the engine here at Bridge of Allan, just north of Stirling with a van train (Class 3 headcode lamps) heading south. Although undated, this is obviously in the last few years of the engine's life; it went to Kingmoor in March 1961 and was withdrawn in September 1964. Photograph www.transporttreasury.co.uk

Another, wonderful, view of 46244, while allocated to Carlisle Kingmoor, and once again most unfortunately we have no date. The engine is running light to Kingmoor over the River Eden bridge at Etterby, though why it should be heading for the shed with a tender full of coal is something of a mystery. This illustrates well the arrangement of the twin orifices of the double chimney. Photograph Paul Chancellor Collection.

46245 CITY OF LONDON

Built Crewe 26/6/43 'built with Repaired boiler. For cost including NEW boiler see
Engine 6246 - Total including £75
Patterns and £364 Sup'ter = £10,182'
Built streamlined, casing removed 23/10/47
Renumbered 6245 to 46245 week ending 28/8/48

Boilers

Fitted	No.	From
26/6/43	9940	-
23/10/47	10306	6240
9/12/50	10287	6249
11/4/53	10290	-
3/11/56	10292	-

No record after this date

Repairs LMS
18/5/44-5/6/44**LS**
8/6/45-25/7/45**LS**
24/6/46-2/8/46**LS**
14/7/47-23/10/47**HG**
12/7/48-27/8/48**LS**
11/4/49-14/4/49**#**
2/5/49-27/6/49**LC**
24/11/49-23/12/49**LI**
4/1/50-17/1/50**NC**
27/1/50-14/2/50**NC**
8/11/50-9/12/50**HG**
#*'No report'*

Repairs BR
Dates in the first column are from out of traffic to return to traffic; A = 'Weekdays Waiting', B= 'Weekdays on Works'. The two mileage figures represent, firstly the miles accumulated since the previous General or Intermediate (C) and secondly (the lower figure) the miles run up from January 1st of the year of shopping - D. All work is recorded as taking place at Crewe unless otherwise noted. StR=St Rollox

Dates	A	B	C	D
11/6/51-3/7/51**LC**	-	19	42,117	38,239
6/11/51-20/12/51**HI**	12	26	74.670	70,792
2/1/52-12/1/52**NC***	-	9	306	Nil
11/6/52-6/9/52**HI**	1	74	36,852	36,546
12/2/53-11/4/53**HG**	5	44	36,384	10,378
14/4/53-18/7/53**NC***	-	4	24	10,402
9/9/53-29/9/53**LC***	8	9	29,507	39,885
13/2/54-16/3/54**LI**	4	22	66,814	8,753
19/10/54-25/11/54**LC***	8	24	55,690	64,443
21/6/55-5/8/55**LI**	-	39	104,056	39,700
12/9/56-3/11/56**HG**	12	33	92,977	55,025
12/11/57-28/12/57**LI**	1	37	92,701	78,544
9/2/59-20/3/59**HI**	7	27	98,809	12,530
26/3/60-13/5/60**HI#**	5	35	94,518	21,873
20/3/61-15/5/61**HI**	17	30	71,223	12,443

record ends
#*'boiler lifted out and put back'*
*(EO)'- Engine Only

Sheds
Camden
Willesden   7/9/63
Crewe North   25/7/64
stored 29/9/63-13/11/63

Tenders

No	Fitted
9808	26/6/43
9807	26/6/45

LMS 'Summary' *(this became 'Annual Statistics' from 1951)*

Year	Mileage	Weekdays out of service			
		wks	shed	n/req	total
1943	53,449	-	10	-	10
1944	74,751	16	81	4	101
1945	61,354	41	86	-	127
1946	79,336	35	52	2	89
1947	54,522	88	50	1	139
1948	82,821	41	36	1	78
1949	66,210	56	60	2	118
1950	79,621	52	43	-	95
1951	71,098	57	44	1	102
1952	62,552	75	50	-	125
1953	68,439	70	46	-	116
1954	73,709	58	60	-	118
1955	77,052	39	53	14	106
1956	69,182	45	100	-	145
1957	78,103	38	59	-	97
1958	86,120	-	92	-	92
1959	85,175	*record ends*			
1960	80,653				
1961	44,094				
1962	33,442				
1963	26,082				

wks=heavy and light repairs at main works
shed=shed repairs and examinations
n/req= not required

Total Recorded Mileage 1,408,315
Withdrawn week ending 12/9/64
Cut up J.Cashmore, Great Bridge 12/64

Watford Junction with a down train obviously not stopping and headed by 46245 CITY OF LONDON, on 5 April 1952. This engine was the subject of a civic reception at Euston on 20 July 1943, just a few weeks after it entered service, when it was officially named.

Camden's 46245 CITY OF LONDON (it was allocated there for most of its tenure with BR) heading north somewhere on the four-track section south of Hanslope. We know it is on this section rather than between Stafford and Crewe, as the order of the lines is different in both places. Here we have the fast lines flanked on either side by the slows while between Stafford and Crewe both fasts were on the east side. Further evidence of it being a down train comes from the side of the line the telegraph poles are situated. A pretty dirty machine, in the early 1950s I would guess, with a complete rake of former LMS vehicles. Photograph J.T. Clewley, www.transporttreasury.co.uk

Carlisle Upperby shed on 21 June 1958 with 46245 CITY OF LONDON coaled and watered ready for its next job. It would seem to have received a rather fine load of coal on this occasion! Photograph J.L. Stevenson, courtesy Hamish Stevenson.

A much cleaner 46245, by now in maroon livery and heading the up 'Royal Scot' at Acton Bridge, between Weaver Junction and Crewe, some time in the summer of 1959. Plenty of coal in the tender so the engine would have come on to the train at Carlisle and be working through to Euston. Photograph T. Lewis, www.transporttreasury.co.uk

What looks like a somewhat rapid departure from Liverpool Lime Street sees 46245 really getting into its stride on 17 July 1962, with a train for London. For many years Edge Hill shed in Liverpool had several Princess Royal Pacifics for the London trains, and occasionally a Duchess, but it was unusual to see a Camden engine there. However, by this date, with the diesels well entrenched, anything was possible. Photograph J. Corkill.

Each year Derby Locomotive Works, like some of its contemporaries, staged an Open Day when members of the public were allowed to visit many of the shops and view the activities. These events were usually accompanied by a number of locomotives being specially posed, the visitors being allowed on the footplates and in the case of diesels into the engine and equipment rooms. This is the 29 August 1964 event at Derby when Crewe North sent the Pacific – not a type seen there under normal circumstances. The engine was 46245 CITY OF LONDON (others had been there on previous occasions) already with the yellow cab stripe and with only a few more weeks left before it was withdrawn. In fact it had only been transferred to Crewe a week or so earlier to eke out its last days once the ban on using them south of Crewe was imminent. Behind is one of the latest Bo-Bo diesel electrics, later Class 25, which Derby was building at the time and that is a 9F 2-10-0 to the right. Notice that some children have climbed on to the back of the tender of the Pacific! After the event the engine returned post-haste to Crewe as it was required for the Ian Allan Locospotters special which was the last occasion an engine of this class was to visit London in normal service, just three days later on 1 September. Photograph www.transporttreasury.co.uk

On 9 June 1963 the Home Counties Railway Society chartered an excursion from Kings Cross to Doncaster and back. For this job a Duchess had been requested and Camden quite fittingly turned out a very clean 46245 CITY OF LONDON, and a good time was had by all. Here is the engine alongside the Passenger Loco Depot at Kings Cross, waiting for the empty stock of its train to arrive – and she showed those sluggards who needed no fewer that three Pacifics to get the average East Coast train from Kings Cross to Edinburgh, a thing or two that day! Photograph A. Scarsbrook, Initial Photographics.

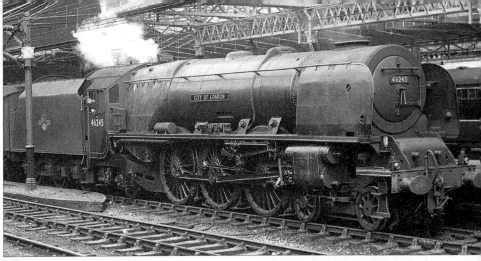

Above. An undated photograph of 46245 CITY OF LONDON at the south end of No.5 platform at Crewe, a comparatively late view as the engine has AWS and electrification warning flashes. The first coach is an ex-LNER Gresley one which would be pretty unusual on any train at Crewe. The tender looks to be quite low on coal so the engine is probably working through from Carlisle to London. The DMU to the right is in 5B bay platform and would be on a Derby diagram via Stoke-on-Trent.

Top left. This photograph is a bit of a mystery, but I think I have at least part of the answer. On 1 September 1964 the Ian Allan Locospotters Club ran an excursion from Paddington to Crewe, where the participants visited the works and sheds, before returning. The train travelled via the former Great Western route to Shrewsbury and on to Crewe via Whitchurch; it returned the same way. To work the train Crewe North provided the recently transferred 46245 CITY OF LONDON, which was chosen as it was known that this would in all probability be the last occasion an engine of this class would visit the capital. The engine, specially prepared by Crewe North (this working incidentally, was why it had been transferred from Willesden earlier than its contemporaries - see an earlier caption to 46240 at Kensal Green) was despatched from Crewe to Old Oak Common light engine, where it was serviced before working the train to Crewe. On arrival back at Paddington, after another visit to Old Oak, it returned light to Crewe. I am pretty sure this is the down train illustrated here, somewhere on the Great Western route south of Birmingham. The strange thing is that on the return journey the engine carried the familiar *Ian Allan Railtour* headboard. Perhaps there was not time to fit it at Paddington on the outward journey. Photograph N. Lester, www.transporttreasury.co.uk

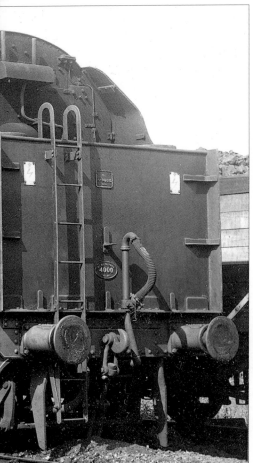

Bottom left. Another angle to perhaps excite the model maker in need of tender detail. CITY OF LONDON is I think, judging by the lighting towers, on Crewe South shed and, if I am correct, waiting to go into the Works which would explain the BR Standard Class 3 77000 2-6-0 in front, as for some years these were overhauled at Crewe. All engines for attention in Crewe Works went to Crewe South first, to have their tenders emptied; there was also plenty of room for storage while they waited to be called. The small oil box to the right of the coal pusher piston valve cover on the back of the tender feeds both the valve and the pusher piston, while the box between the leading and intermediate wheels, it is worth pointing out again, is the water feed box for the live steam injector, containing a sieve. There was one on the other side for the exhaust injector and we used to clean these out on X day examinations. The tender number for those interested in 9805, bearing the date 1939. Photograph Paul Chancellor Collection.

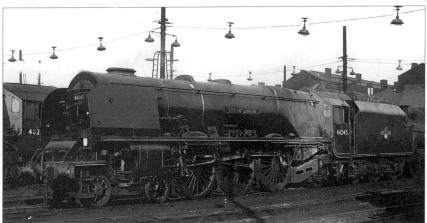

CITY OF LONDON once again and this time at home on Willesden shed on 29 June 1964. Excessive blowing-off at the safety valves has succeeded in depositing lime from the water treatment over the firebox casing.

46246 CITY OF MANCHESTER

Built Crewe 11/8/43, cost £10,107 (engine), £1,670 (tender)
'Built with New boiler, other three engines 6245, 6247 and 6248 being fitted, as new, with Repaired boilers. Above cost includes NEW boiler'.
Built streamlined, casing removed 23/10/46
Renumbered 6246 to 46246 week ending 20/11/48

Boilers

Fitted	No.	From
23/10/46	10639	6244
16/11/48	10289	6236
21/12/50	9937	6244
12/6/53	10646	-
2/5/57	10640	-
5/4/60	9937	-

No record after this date

Repairs LMS

14/2/44-11/3/44**TRO**
1/8/44-23/8/44**LS**
21/3/45-26/4/45**LO**
14/10/45-17/11/45**LS**
6/9/46-23/10/46**HG**
17/10/47-23/11/47**LS**
25/9/48-16/11/48**HG**
2/8/49-1/10/49**HI**
7/10/49-22/10/49**NC**
5/12/49-20/12/49**NC**
4/3/50-16/3/50**NC**
10/11/50-21/12/50**HG**

Repairs BR

Dates in the first column are from out of traffic to return to traffic; A = 'Weekdays Waiting', B= 'Weekdays on Works'. The two mileage figures represent, firstly the miles accumulated since the previous General or Intermediate (C) and secondly (the lower figure) the miles run up from January 1st of the year of shopping - D. All work is recorded as taking place at Crewe unless otherwise noted. StR=St Rollox

Dates	A	B	C	D
16/2/52-22/3/52**LI**	4	26	92,506	10,821
3/4/52-4/4/52**NC***	-	1	1,130	11,951
9/4/53-12/6/53**HG**	6	49	90,681	19,707
19/6/53-26/6/53**NC***	1	5	411	20,118
28/10/54-6/12/54**LI**	7	26	110,758	63,096
16/2/56-24/3/56**LI**	5	27	97,487	11,073
5/4/56-12/4/56**NC***	-	6	726	11,799
21/6/56-28/6/56**NC***	-	6	15,593	26,666
25/3/57-2/5/57**HG**	9	23	72,349	15,559
24/6/57-27/6/57**#**	-	3	-	-
8/10/57-12/10/57**NC***	2	2	31,408	46,967
23/6/58-11/7/58**NC***	4	12	88,036	37,169
2/9/58-9/10/58**LI**	6	26	99,686	48,819
20/9/59-3/10/59**NC***	1	10	71,169	58,206
11/2/60-5/4/60**HG**	-	46	97,480	8,104
15/4/61-6/6/61**HI**	7	37	89,758	21,166

record ends
#'painting only'
*'(EO)'- Engine Only

Sheds

Camden
Crewe North 1/5/48
Camden 11/6/60
stored 5/11/62-26/1/63

Tenders

No	Fitted
9809	11/8/43
9749	16/5/61

LMS 'Summary' *(this became 'Annual Statistics' from 1951)*

Year	Mileage	Weekdays out of service			
		wks	shed	n/req	total
1943	38,474	-	6	-	6
1944	82,091	44	44	-	88
1945	53,.457	54	92	1	147
1946	83,208	41	64	1	106
1947	65,562	35	61	1	97
1948	69,860	45	35	-	80
1949	56,866	62	54	7	123
1950	66,835	35	49	13	97
1951	81,085	-	60	1	61
1952	81,795	30	57	-	87
1953	67,369	61	51	-	112
1954	68,724	33	63	1	97
1955	80,786	-	53	17	70
1956	67,863	38	47	-	85
1957	66,426	35	44	2	81
1958	66,782	32	67	-	99
1959	71,413	record ends			

wks=heavy and light repairs at main works
shed=shed repairs and examinations
n/req= not required

Total Recorded Mileage 1,168,596
Withdrawn week ending 26/1/63
Cut up Crewe Works 5/63

Polmadie shed in Glasgow features once more, with 46246 CITY OF MANCHESTER, a long term resident of Crewe North, waiting to set-back into Glasgow Central and take a train south. Also waiting to go off the shed are two of the BR Standard Class 4 2-6-4Ts, of which Polmadie had a few on its books for local passenger train working at this date, 25 June 1955. This was the final engine of the class to have its smokebox modified, in May 1960, almost two years after the previous one. The fireman is performing a final trim of the tender before they depart. Photograph J. Robertson, www.transporttreasury.co.uk

I think this picture is taken at Stockport, which would mean that 46246 CITY OF MANCHESTER had made a rare visit to its namesake city! Engines of this class made relatively infrequent trips on the line between Crewe and Manchester, but there were odd times when they did. This looks like an up train, from the church spire in the background, although this may not be discernable in the photograph as reproduced here. The class 2 headcode indicates a stopping train, perhaps a fill-in turn of some sort, or a way to get the engine back to Crewe if it had worked through on a London train. The date is 8 May 1957, and the engine is in the green livery, although this was one of those that were later given the maroon treatment. Photograph Paul Chancellor Collection.

Left. The headcode W67 might indicate that this is the morning Birmingham to Glasgow train, as for a long time in early BR days this was its reporting number. We have no date, but the train is about to depart from Carstairs for the north with Crewe North's 46246 CITY OF MANCHESTER, and the Birmingham train would be a 5A diagram. Observe the tender apparently bereft of coal; assuming it was full at Crewe (no engineman in his right mind would leave the shed for Glasgow otherwise) then it had been a rough trip! The engine appears to be painted green, so the view post-dates May 1953, when it received this livery. Photograph Paul Chancellor Collection.

Bottom left. The up 'Mid-Day Scot' about to depart from platform one at Glasgow Central on 18 April 1959 with 46246 CITY OF MANCHESTER. As with several others with city names a civic 'unveiling' was held, in 6246's case at Manchester London Road station, on 3 September 1943, a few weeks after it was built. Photograph J.L. Stevenson, courtesy Hamish Stevenson.

Below. CITY OF MANCHESTER at Crewe Works in March 1960, after a general repair – see also page 220. Here it is on completion of the work awaiting re-attachment of the tender before proceeding to the vacuum pits. Once there steam would be raised and all the various tests and adjustments undertaken. The engine is standing in the area known as the steam cleaning pits and those buildings behind are part of the former No.5-No.8 erecting shops. The chargehand and fitter appear to be concerned about something, perhaps a problem re-connecting the tender? Photograph www.transporttreasury.co.uk

46247 CITY OF LIVERPOOL

Built Crewe 13/9/43, cost £8,962 (engine), £1,670 (tender)
*'Built with REPAIRED boiler. For cost of engine including NEW boiler see 6246 -
total INCLUDES £75 Patterns and £364 Superheater'.*
Built streamlined, casing removed 20/6/47
Renumbered 6247 to 46247 week ending 20/11/48

Boilers

Fitted	No.	From
13/9/43	?	new
20/6/47	10293	6237
15/6/51	10289	46246
20/2/54	9937	-
26/9/56	10297	-
25/7/59	10472	-

No record after this date

Repairs LMS

14/6/44-3/7/44**TRO**
2/2/45-5/4/45**LS**
1/8/45-14/9/45**LO**
25/3/46-26/4/46**LS**
30/4/47-20/6/47**HG**
4/10/47-30/10/47**HO**
14/10/48-15/11/48**HS**
23/12/49-1/2/50**LI**
6/2/50-17/2/50**NC**
28/2/50-22/3/50**LC**

Repairs BR

Dates in the first column are from out of traffic to return to traffic; A = 'Weekdays Waiting', B= 'Weekdays on Works'. The two mileage figures represent, firstly the miles accumulated since the previous General or Intermediate (C) and secondly (the lower figure) the miles run up from January 1st of the year of shopping - D. All work is recorded as taking place at Crewe unless otherwise noted. StR=St Rollox

Dates	A	B	C	D
6/1/51-24/1/51**HC**	-	15	72,941	nil
21/5/51-15/6/51**HG**	-	22	98,484	25,543
10/1/52-18/2/52**HC**	10	23	49,580	1,830
6/12/52-8/1/53**HI**	1	25	122,944	75,194
11/1/54-20/2/54**HG**	7	28	86,300	2,855
17/4/55-21/5/55**HI**	2	27	105,310	25,037
6/8/56-26/9/56**HG**	7	37	109,402	54,991
20/10/56-15/11/56**LC**	*9	13	3,158	58,149
7/9/57-14/9/57**NC***	4	2	67,252	53,232
10/4/58-24/5/58**LI**	1	37	108,471	15,035
2/6/59-25/7/59**HG**	5	41	98,214	42,305
9/12/60-26/1/61**HI**	2	37	103,102	84,439
11/4/61-16/5/61**LC**	14	16	15,999	15,999

record ends
*'(EO)'- Engine Only

Sheds

Camden
Carlisle Kingmoor   17/6/61
stored 22/4/63-20/5/63

Tenders

No	Fitted
9810	13/9/43
9811	13/10/44
9807	3/6/52
9749	24/12/52
9809	16/5/61

LMS 'Summary' *(this became 'Annual Statistics' from 1951)*

Year	Mileage	Weekdays out of service			
		wks	shed	n/req	total
1943	23,701	-	10	-	10
1944	80,142	17	59	-	76
1945	63,870	93	45	2	140
1946	86,621	28	44	4	76
1947	47,201	68	90	4	162
1948	64,330	28	70	-	98
1949	81,092	7	75	2	84
1950	72,945	43	62	-	105
1951	73,293	37	56	1	94
1952	75,194	50	60	-	110
1953	83,445	9	70	-	79
1954	83,128	35	53	1	89
1955	79,448	29	66	8	103
1956	69,011	66	52	-	118
1957	79,416	-	80	-	80
1958	70,944	38	93	-	131
1959	60,968		*record ends*		
1960	84,439				
1961	49,906				
1962	47,830				
1963	11,263				

wks=heavy and light repairs at main works
shed=shed repairs and examinations
n/req= not required

Total Recorded Mileage 1,388,187
Withdrawn week ending 25/5/63
Cut up Crewe Works 7/63

The down 'Royal Scot' making its scheduled stop at Rugby around 1959-60. The engine, 46247 CITY OF LIVERPOOL, Camden based for much of the BR period, is in the maroon livery which was applied in May 1958. Notice the engine has been fitted with a speedometer, that is the drive and cable on the trailing coupled crank-pin, but not yet fitted with AWS equipment – no protection plate behind the screw coupling. Speedometers were fitted to the entire class following the issue of an order dated August 1957, and the work was undertaken on the next occasion individual locomotives visited Crewe Works. Some engines had an earlier design of speed indicating equipment, but this was removed during the war due to maintenance and spare part supply problems. This engine was the first that I saw in the maroon livery, during a Saturday morning visit to Crewe with Dad, when it came off the works with a string of other engines en-route to the South shed – all ex-works engines went there first. I can see it now, resplendent in its new coat of paint, and Dad and I were not even aware at the time of the policy to paint some examples this colour. It is difficult to find words to describe our surprise and excitement; I was talking about it for days! Photograph www.transporttreasury.co.uk

What a lovely shot and unmistakably Watford, with 46247 CITY OF LIVERPOOL romping along almost at the end of its journey into London with an up train. Unfortunately we have neither a date or train identification but the engine is in maroon livery with LMS style lining so its probably in the period after May 1958 and before, for some strange reason, it was repainted maroon with the BR style of lining in June the following year. In June 1961 it was transferred to Carlisle Upperby while at the time this photograph was taken it was allocated to Camden.

46248 CITY OF LEEDS

Built Crewe 2/10/43, cost £9,370 (engine), £1,670 (tender)
'Built with REPAIRED boiler. For cost of engine including NEW boiler see
6246 - total INCLUDES £75 Patterns and £364 Superheater'
Built streamlined, casing removed 7/12/46
Renumbered 6248 to 46248 week ending 19/3/49

Boilers

Fitted	No.	From
2/10/43	?	new
7/12/46	10290	6224
17/3/49	10288	6244
24/3/51	10641	6235
1/10/53	10638	-
19/2/57	10304	-
22/8/59	12472	-
No record after this date		

Repairs LMS
4/4/45-24/4/45**LS**
4/12/45-10/1/46**LS**
19/10/46-7/12/46**HG**
30/5/47-25/6/47**LO**
3/11/47-14/11/47**TRO**
19/11/47-1/1/48**HS**
14/3/48-25/3/48**LO**
7/2/49-17/3/49**HG**

Repairs BR
Dates in the first column are from out of traffic to return to traffic; A = 'Weekdays Waiting', B= 'Weekdays on Works'. The two mileage figures represent, firstly the miles accumulated since the previous General or Intermediate (C) and secondly (the lower figure) the miles run up from January 1st of the year of shopping - D. All work is recorded as taking place at Crewe unless otherwise noted. StR=St Rollox

Dates	A	B	C	D
6/5/50-9/6/50**LI**	1	28	74,649	16,922
26/2/51-24/3/51**HG**	2	20	50,849	7,680
31/3/51-17/4/51**NC**	-	14	349	8,029
2/6/51-12/6/51**NC**	2	6	8,283	15,963
21/7/52-27/8/52**HI**	6	26	95,289	45,778
24/8/53-1/10/53**HG**	-	33	76,441	46,051
27/5/55-2/7/55**LI**	5	26	133,882	31,942
18/8/55-7/10/55**LC***	19	24	7,236	39,178
2/11/55-19/11/55**NC***	4	11	10,148	42,090
3/10/56-9/10/56**NC***	1	4	80,136	60,969
7/1/57-19/2/57**HG**	14	23	103,495	1,666
12/10/57-18/10/57**NC***	1	4	57,670	59,336
25/4/58-6/6/58**LI**	2	34	102,515	27,852
28/6/59-22/8/59**HG**	2	45	88,116	42,192
31/8/59-16/9/59**NC***	-	14	1,080	43,272
6/9/60-20/10/60**LI**	11	27	79,258	54,340
record ends				

*(EO)- Engine Only

Sheds
Camden
Crewe North (loan)   9/10/43
Camden   16/10/43
Crewe North   26/6/48
Carlisle Upperby   26/6/54
Crewe North   18/9/54
Camden   11/6/60
Carlisle Upperby   13/8/60
Camden   3/9/60
Crewe North   24/9/60
stored 6/11/62-7/12/62, 24/9/63-12/12/63

Tenders

No	Fitted
9811	2/10/43
9810	13/10/44

LMS 'Summary' *(this became 'Annual Statistics' from 1951)*

Year	Mileage	Weekdays out of service			
		wks	shed	n/req	total
1943	22,485	-	3	-	3
1944	71,367	-	101	-	101
1945	69,925	40	58	-	98
1946	74,447	53	46	3	102
1947	65,308	67	39	1	107
1948	75,991	10	59	2	71
1949	64,669	34	55	8	97
1950	60,091	29	72	10	111
1951	57,191	44	67	1	112
1952	76,168	32	52	-	84
1953	67,162	33	84	-	117
1954	80,829	-	58	1	59
1955	51,109	89	32	2	123
1956	82,662	-	54	-	54
1957	76,229	37	39	-	76
1958	73,776	36	48	1	85
1959	67,090	*record ends*			

wks=heavy and light repairs at main works
shed=shed repairs and examinations
n/req= not required

Total Recorded Mileage 1,136,499
Withdrawn week ending 5/9/64
Cut up J.Cashmore, Great Bridge 11/64

Polmadie shed in Glasgow on 16 October 1949 with Crewe North's 46248 CITY OF LEEDS coaled and turned ready for its next journey south. It had been named by the Lord Mayor, Alderman Albert Hayes at Leeds City station on 2 December 1943 (it was noted at Euston as early as mid-October with nameplates covered). The engine is painted in the early BR livery of lined black with the full BRITISH RAILWAYS on the tender and commendably clean for the period. There is another Pacific behind and a Class 4 2-6-4 tank, of which this shed had a substantial fleet, to the right. Photograph J.L. Stevenson, courtesy Hamish Stevenson.

The up 'Mid-Day Scot' at Carstairs, between August 1953 when 46248 CITY OF LEEDS was painted green, and 1957 when the smokebox was modified. A Crewe North engine working through from Glasgow to Crewe, with North Shed men on a double-home diagram. Photograph www.transporttreasury.co.uk

CITY OF LEEDS in BR lined black, outside the brass finishing shop in Crewe works, on 15 April 1951. This engine had a heavy general repair completed in March 1951; cab front windows enlarged as part of a modification programme for the former streamlined engines. After this repair there must have been some unresolved matters as the engine was back in the works on two occasions for unclassified repairs, as seen here in April and again in June. With 15 April being a Sunday the engine would be waiting for a move to the adjacent vacuum pits for steam testing prior to out-shopping early the following week, in fact the records say it left on the 17th.

An undated photograph of 46248, about to head south from Carlisle on a very wet day with the up 'Royal Scot'. It was unusual to find a Crewe North engine on this train, and with a full tender it would have come on here and doubtless be working through to Euston – maybe as part of the cyclic diagrams being tried in the late 1950s. CITY OF LEEDS is in markedly better external condition than Holbeck's Scot, 46117 WELSH GUARDSMAN, also about to head south, with 'The Thames Clyde Express' over the Settle and Carlisle route, in the other platform. Photograph www.transporttreasury.co.uk

Standing on the vacuum pits at Crewe Works and looking ready to return to its home shed is 46248 CITY OF LEEDS, resplendent in a new coat of paint. When the maroon livery was first introduced by BR on some of these engines, the style of lining was similar to that used with the green livery; that is, panels set in from the edges. However, this was later substituted for the style as shown here, more akin to the earlier LMS arrangement. This engine was the last one noted with the revised arrangement, as late as 1962 in fact, and as it was in the works for an intermediate repair in September-October that year, I am tempted to suggest that it was at that time this photograph was taken. The engine probably received the AWS equipment at the same time – note the battery box just ahead of the cab and the vacuum timing reservoir further forward. When I commenced my apprenticeship at Crewe North this was the Royal Train engine, and we kept a set of burnished buffers, screw couplings and cylinder and valve chest cover plates, which were only fitted as occasion demanded, and soon removed to store again after! It was damned hard work to get them into a condition to meet the exacting standards of the Shed Master, the late Geoff Sands. Photograph Paul Chancellor Collection.

This photograph of 46248 CITY OF LEEDS is said to be near Rugby, so somewhere on the two-track section north of Kilsby tunnel I guess, a down Class 3 van train (headlamps right and middle) on 28 April 1963. A sign of the times with these engines increasingly used on other than express trains.

46249 CITY OF SHEFFIELD

Built Crewe 19/4/44, cost £9,994 (engine), £1,670 (tender)
Non-streamlined, built with streamlined tender
Renumbered 6249 to 46239 week ending 17/4/48

Boilers

Fitted	No.	From
5/11/47	10287	6222
27/9/50	12472	6255
3/2/53	10645	-
1/10/54	10639	-
31/8/57	10296	-
27/4/60	10293	-

No record after this date

Repairs LMS

1/8/45-22/9/45**LS**
29/8/46-19/9/46**LS**
23/4/47-29/5/47**LO**
30/8/47-5/11/47**HG**
13/4/48-15/4/48**NC**
23/4/48-23/4/48**NC**
17/5/48-27/5/48**TRO**
18/10/48-28/10/48**LO**
2/12/48-6/1/49**HI**
28/9/49-19/11/49**LI**
17/8/50-27/9/50**HG**
23/7/51-23/8/51**HI**

Repairs BR

Dates in the first column are from out of traffic to return to traffic; A = 'Weekdays Waiting', B= 'Weekdays on Works'. The two mileage figures represent, firstly the miles accumulated since the previous General or Intermediate (C) and secondly (the lower figure) the miles run up from January 1st of the year of shopping - D. All work is recorded as taking place at Crewe unless otherwise noted. StR=St Rollox

Dates	A	B	C	D
14/11/51-12/12/51**LC**	8	16	21,313	67,181
18/6/52-2/8/52**LI**	7	34	66,924	42,178
10/12/52-3/2/53**HG**	5	40	31,524	73,702
25/2/53-9/3/53**NC***	-	10	nil	nil
23/9/53-20/10/53**HC**	6	17	63,052	63,052
19/8/54-1/10/54**HG**	3	34	140,568	55,851
13/1/56-27/2/56**LI**	2	36	97,263	1,119
13/10/56-11/11/56**LC***	7	23	49,560	50,679
26/7/57-31/8/57**HG**	2	29	96,291	41,391
13/11/58-17/1/59**LI**	4	50	99,687	71,771
22/2/60-27/4/60**HG**	1	54	91,130	11,853
4/1/62-9/2/62**HI**	-	31	93,681	29

record ends
*(EO)'- Engine Only

LMS 'Summary' *(this became 'Annual Statistics' from 1951)*

Year	Mileage	Weekdays out of service			
		works	shed	n/req	total
1944	31,778	-	43	-	43
1945	73,044	46	71	1	118
1946	78,437	19	89	2	110
1947	42,404	90	56	3	149
1948	73,389	40	35	1	76
1949	77,119	56	38	1	95
1950	81,224	35	49	-	84
1951	70,614	51	45	-	96
1952	73,702	55	53	-	108
1953	84,117	64	33	-	97
1954	73,685	37	60	-	97
1955	78,310	-	50	2	52
1956	56,019	68	33	-	101
1957	69,307	31	46	1	78
1958	71,771	36	54	-	90
1959	79,277	record ends			
1960	64,746				
1961	40,759				
1962	39,838				

works=heavy and light repairs at main works
shed=shed repairs and examinations
n/req= not required

Total Recorded Mileage 1,259,540
Withdrawn week ending 9/11/63
Cut up Crewe Works 12/63

Sheds

Crewe North	
Polmadie (loan)	8/7/44
Polmadie	26/8/44
Crewe North (loan)	14/10/44
Polmadie	11/11/44
Carlisle Upperby	12/10/46
Camden	28/5/49
Crewe North	20/11/54
Polmadie	11/3/61

Tenders

No	Fitted
9812	19/4/44
9749	23/1/45
9743	9/8/45

Passing Hartford, between Acton Bridge and Winsford north of Crewe, 46249 CITY OF SHEFFIELD on 31 July 1953 with, presumably, a train from north of the border. A Camden engine at the time, it moved to Crewe North in November the following year. This engine had stainless steel nameplates, presented to the LMS by the Sheffield City Fathers, through the good offices of course, of the Master Cutler!
Photograph T. Lewis, Norman Preedy Archive.

46250 CITY OF LICHFIELD

Built Crewe 20/5/44, engine £9,994, tender £1,670
Non-streamlined, built with streamlined tender
Renumbered 6250 to 46250 week ending 26/2/49

Boilers

Fitted	No.	From
25/9/47	10303	6247
1/5/50	10291	6240
28/10/52	10303	-
24/8/56	9939	-
30/11/57	9938	-
27/1/61	10300	-

Repairs LMS

27/2/45-7/4/45**LS**
1/2/46-28/2/46**LS**
1/10/46-25/10/46**LO**
16/5/47-25/9/47**HG**
22/1/49-25/2/49**HI**
1/3/49-15/3/49**NC**
21/3/49-31/3/49**HG**
23/3/50-1/5/50**HG**

Repairs BR

Dates in the first column are from out of traffic to return to traffic; A = 'Weekdays Waiting', B= 'Weekdays on Works'. The two mileage figures represent, firstly the miles accumulated since the previous General or Intermediate (C) and secondly (the lower figure) the miles run up from January 1st of the year of shopping - D. All work is recorded as taking place at Crewe unless otherwise noted. StR=St Rollox

Dates	A	B	C	D
6/5/50-29/5/50**LC**	3	16	396	18,098
15/11/50-15/12/50**LC**	4	22	42,550	60,252
26/9/51-3/11/51**HI**	11	22	112,854	67,553
8/11/51-14/12/51**LC***	3	28	198	67,751
5/5/52-31/5/52**LC***	-	23	31,944	31,134
18/9/52-28/10/52**HG**	6	28	65,399	64,589
11/12/53-16/1/54**LI**	8	21	99,406	84,501
11/3/54-2/4/54**LC***	5	14	9,846	9,846
10/4/55-10/5/55**HI**	1	29	93,656	21,945
12/7/56-24/8/56**HG**	4	33	106,228	48,443
3/4/57-10/4/57**NC***	-	6	53,051	22,916
19/8/57-22/8/57**NC***	1	2	85,541	55,406
21/10/57-30/11/57**HG**	1	34	101,958	71,823
2/12/57-7/12/57**NC***	-	5	-	-
10/12/57-20/12/57**NC***	-	9	-	-
21/1/58-20/2/58**LC***	13	13	7,657	5,325
2/5/59-12/6/59**LI**	4	31	101,164	25,192
5/11/59-4/12/59**LC**	-	25	31,897	57,089
2/12/60-27/1/61**HG**	10	36	74,142	74,142

record ends
*(EO)'- Engine Only

Sheds

Crewe North	
Polmadie	22/7/44
Carlisle Upperby	12/10/46
Camden	28/5/49
Edge Hill (loan)	30/6/56
Camden	21/7/56
Carlisle Upperby (loan)	8/9/56
Camden	20/10/56
Carlisle Upperby	14/6/58

stored 2/1/64-17/2/64

Tenders

9813   20/5/44

LMS 'Summary' *(this became 'Annual Statistics' from 1951)*

Year	Mileage	Weekdays out of service			
		works	shed	n/req	total
1944	51,185	-	20	8	28
1945	90,429	35	51	4	90
1946	72,874	46	79	1	126
1947	47,730	114	35	2	151
1948	73,104	-	72	-	72
1949	62,915	41	70	3	114
1950	63,003	80	32	-	112
1951	68,363	64	62	1	127
1952	79,494	57	39	-	96
1953	84,501	18	75	-	93
1954	71,712	30	89	-	119
1955	79,730	30	59	10	99
1956	78,578	37	65	-	102
1957	74,155	49	57	-	106
1958	73,640	26	77	1	104
1959	61,233	*record ends*			
1960	74,142				
1962	47,997				
1963	31,381				

works=heavy and light repairs at main works
shed=shed repairs and examinations
n/req= not required

Total Recorded Mileage 1,353,526
Withdrawn week ending 12/9/64
Cut up West of Scotland
Shipbreaking Co, Troon 12/64

46250 CITY OF LICHFIELD a few days after its run at Carstairs (opposite top) on 26 July 1952. It is now at Crewe, about to head south, and judging by the tender with no coal showing, perhaps once again working right through from Glasgow. Notice the condition of much of the station roof sections, still suffering from wartime maintenance neglect. Photograph www.transporttreasury.co.uk

The up 'Mid-Day Scot' approaching Carstairs on 22 July 1952 with 46250 CITY OF LICHFIELD in charge. As 6250, it had been named at Lichfield station on 20 June 1944. It ran light to and from Crewe and was at Lichfield on exhibition for four hours. The engine is in the blue livery which it would lose a few months later. It was a Camden engine at this time, which was unusual for this train as for most of the 1950s it was a Crewe North diagram for both engines and men. With a limited load this would be one of those summers perhaps, when the engine on this train worked through from Glasgow to Euston. Notice the excellent condition of the permanent way, flat bottom on the down road and bull-head on the up; there would be a proud lengthman on this section I wager. Photograph www.transporttreasury.co.uk

46250 CITY OF LICHFIELD in green livery with AWS and a speedometer, at Shrewsbury shed around 1961 or 1962. There were two sheds alongside each other here; this is the former LNWR one, while the other, to the left, is the more substantial Great Western establishment. It was not unusual after the diesels arrived on the scene to find *Big 'Uns* on Shrewsbury shed, and unlike earlier times when they worked back almost immediately on fill-in diagrams from Crewe, by this time it was done in a much more leisurely fashion, hence the time to stand around on the shed! Photograph Paul Chancellor Collection.

Carlisle Upperby is the location for this rather pleasing study of 46250 at its home shed, although unfortunately we have no date. It is nevertheless a late shot showing the engine in its final form with AWS and electrification flashes. It does betray bad practice as the engine has been left in forward gear and while it may not be in steam, it should not have been left like this. I always think that this angle of photograph shows these engines at their best, emphasising their enormous bulk. It was a wonderful effort on the part of the design team to get that large boiler within the LMS loading gauge for all its main west coast routes. Photograph Paul Chancellor Collection.

46251 CITY OF NOTTINGHAM

Built Crewe 3/6/44 cost £9,994 (engine), £1,670 (tender)
Non-streamlined, built with streamlined tender
Renumbered 6251 to 46251 week ending 29/5/48

Boilers

Fitted	No.	From
7/8/47	10642	6227
19/5/49	10300	6234
23/11/51	10288	-
22/2/55	9938	-
21/9/57	10642	-
4/11/60	10295	-

No record after this date

Repairs LMS

28/6/45-18/8/45**LS**
21/7/46-17/3/46**LS**
7/5/47-7/8/47**HG**
21/8/47-24/9/47**LO**
2/10/47-11/10/47**NC**
17/4/48-23/5/48**LS**
30/3/49-19/5/49**HG**

Repairs BR

Dates in the first column are from out of traffic to return to traffic; A = 'Weekdays Waiting', B= 'Weekdays on Works'. The two mileage figures represent, firstly the miles accumulated since the previous General or Intermediate (C) and secondly (the lower figure) the miles run up from January 1st of the year of shopping - D. All work is recorded as taking place at Crewe unless otherwise noted. StR=St Rollox

Dates	A	B	C	D
6/6/50-21/7/50**LI**	5	34	85,930	32,946
27/11/50-30/12/50**NC**	12	16	32,351	65,297
22/10/51-23/11/51**HG**	1	27	87,408	55,057
4/1/53-6/2/53**LI**	2	26	79,075	144
8/12/53-9/1/54**HI**	5	21	58,540	58,684
22/12/54-22/2/55**HG**	8	43	66,051	66,051
8/5/56-16/6/56**HI**	6	28	94,664	25,284
3/8/57-21/9/57**HG**	9	33	85,674	45,740
18/10/58-22/11/58**HI**	2	28	90,235	70,002
14/8/59-25/9/59**LI**	9	27	54,812	48,127
4/8/60-4/11/60**HG**	10	69	70,900	49,481

record ends
*'(EO)'- Engine Only

Tenders

No	Fitted
9814	3/6/44

LMS 'Summary' *(this became 'Annual Statistics' from 1951)*

Year	Mileage	Weekdays out of service			
		wks	shed	n/req	total
1944	57,779	-	21	4	25
1945	63,573	45	64	10	119
1946	72,817	19	64	2	85
1947	43,154	119	34	3	156
1948	78,403	36	41	-	77
1949	69,001	43	48	6	97
1950	65,297	33	64	4	107
1951	61,776	28	60	3	91
1952	72,212	-	69	5	74
1953	58,684	49	64	10	123
1954	66,051	13	73	1	87
1955	69,380	43	49	2	94
1956	65,209	34	67	-	101
1957	65,982	42	48	-	90
1958	76,687	30	48	-	78
1959	69,546	*record ends*			
1960	60,541				
1961	57,044				
1962	34,250				
1963	29,160				

wks=heavy and light repairs at main works
shed=shed repairs and examinations
n/req= not required

Total Recorded Mileage 1,236,546
Withdrawn week ending 12/9/64
Cut up J.Cashmore, Great Bridge 12/64

Sheds

Crewe North	
Polmadie	8/7/44
Carlisle Upperby	12/10/46
Camden	26/6/48
Edge Hill	2/10/48
Crewe North	11/12/48
Camden	28/5/49
Carlisle Upperby	1/10/49
Camden	10/6/50
Carlisle Upperby	30/9/50
Edge Hill (loan)	13/3/54
Carlisle Upperby	17/4/54
Camden	18/9/54
Edge Hill	2/10/54
Camden (loan)	23/4/55
Edge Hill	21/5/55
Carlisle Upperby	18/6/55
Edge Hill	17/9/55
Carlisle Upperby	9/6/56
Crewe North	15/9/56
Carlisle Upperby (loan)	29/9/56
Crewe North	20/10/56
Carlisle Upperby	22/6/57
Crewe North	21/9/57
Camden (loan)	9/3/63
Crewe North	20/4/63

stored 6/11/62-6/12/62, 6/10/63-12/12/63

46251 CITY OF NOTTINGHAM, standing at the south end of Carlisle station waiting to re-engine a train for the south with the reporting number W110, the 09.00 Perth-Euston due in Carlisle 12.50-12.59. While we have no date for this photograph the engine is in maroon livery with BR style lining which places it between November 1958 and the same month in 1960 and, as it has the electrification flashes and AWS equipment probably late in that period. When this engine made a special visit to Nottingham to be officially named on 4 October 1945, it disgraced itself when it derailed on departure from the station. Fortunately this was after the event when officialdom had departed for the luncheon reception! Photograph Paul Chancellor Collection.

Carlisle again but this time at the opposite, north end with 46251 waiting to leave for Glasgow. While once again we have no date note that by this time the engine, although still in maroon livery, now has the LMS style of lining so the photograph was taken some time after November 1960. Given its rather unkempt external condition, it is probably towards the end of its service life as Crewe North generally kept its Pacifics much cleaner than this. Photograph Paul Chancellor Collection.

Glasgow Central with its nostalgic and lovely overall roof on 9 April 1963 with 46251 CITY OF NOTTINGHAM waiting to depart on a local – note the single lamp at the top position. This would probably have been a stopping train round the former Glasgow & South Western route to Carlisle. Although this engine was allocated to Crewe North from November 1957 until it was withdrawn, it did spend just over a month on loan to Camden in March-April 1963, as can be seen here by the 1B shed plate on the smokebox door. Photograph Paul Cotterell.

During the last summer of service the Pacifics were in some demand for specials of one sort or another. Crewe North's 46251 CITY OF NOTTINGHAM was a frequent participant. This photograph has the engine in somewhat humble company (4F 0-6-0 44599) at Bescot shed on Saturday 11 July 1964. After preparation at Crewe the engine had worked light to Bescot prior to taking the Stephenson Locomotive Society Coronation Pacific Pennine Rail Tour the following day, Sunday the 12th. The train – reporting number 1X82 – ran from Birmingham New Street to Carlisle via the West Coast main line, returning via the Settle & Carlisle route to Leeds, and then to Stockport via Standedge, Crewe and back to Birmingham. This locomotive hauled the train from Birmingham to Carlisle, where Carlisle's 46255 CITY OF HEREFORD made a rare journey for the class over Ais Gill to Leeds, at which point Farnley Junction's Jubilee 45647 STURDEE took over for the journey as far as Crewe. There Crewe North Scot 46155 THE LANCER completed the day by taking the train back to Birmingham. Photograph D.A. Johnson Collection, Millbrook House Ltd.

Not long after the SLS Coronation Pacific Pennine Rail Tour, 46251 is shown here entering Preston from the south, on 24 July 1964. We have no information as to the identity of the train, although as it seems to largely consist of former LMS vehicles. It could well be a relief of some sort. Amazingly, this locomotive was given a No.8 valve & piston exam at Crewe North, the most extensive of all the examinations undertaken at the sheds, rather than main works. This was completed on 27 August 1964, when it seemed general knowledge that all the remaining Stanier Pacifics were due to be withdrawn soon after. I was involved in this work and as far as I recall the engine never turned a wheel under its own steam on completion of the work. Photograph A.W. Battson, www.transporttreasury.co.uk

Crewe North shed on 21 April 1963 with 46251 CITY OF NOTTINGHAM standing outside what had been the No.2 Abba Shed with the tall smoke vents of the semi-roundhouse visible in the background. The engine is at home and in the well kept external condition typical of the Crewe examples at this time. Shedmaster the late Geoff Sands was a great enthusiast and a native of East Anglia where his father Tom was the Senior Footplate Inspector at Norwich. Prior to taking up his appointment at Crewe Geoff was Shedmaster at Stoke and prior to that at far away Melton Constable on the old Midland & Great Northern Section. He was great friend of the family and went on to take charge of all motive power matters on the South Western Division of the Southern Region where he was responsible for the last rites of the Bullied Pacifics, ensuring that they departed in a blaze of glory.

A last look as 46251 within a few weeks of the end of its working life and by this time looking rather unkempt and complete with the yellow cab stripe prohibiting its use on electrified lines south of Crewe. This is the east end of Chester General station on 8 August 1964; the engine is working the 12.10 pm Holyhead to Willesden van train and will come off the train on arrival at Crewe. The crew are awaiting the road and while the fireman takes what he no doubt feels is a well earned cup of tea. Photograph John Hobbs.

46252 CITY OF LEICESTER

Built Crewe 26/4/44 cost £9,994 (engine), £1,670 (tender)
Non-streamlined, built with streamlined tender
Renumbered 6252 to 46252 week ending 9/4/49

Boilers

Fitted	No.	From
7/12/46	10645	6246
1/11/47	10295	6228
7/4/49	10639	6246
29/1/52	9939	-
13/2/54	10641	-
26/1/57	10303	-
5/2/60		10304

No record after this date

Repairs LMS
9/2/45-9/3/45**LO**
29/9/45-1/11/45**LS**
28/1/46-5/3/46**LO**
9/11/46-7/12/46**HG**
21/5/47-23/6/47**LO**
23/9/47-1/11/47**HS**
2/3/49-7/4/49**HG**

Repairs BR
Dates in the first column are from out of traffic to return to traffic; A = 'Weekdays Waiting', B= 'Weekdays on Works'. The two mileage figures represent, firstly the miles accumulated since the previous General or Intermediate (C) and secondly (the lower figure) the miles run up from January 1st of the year of shopping - D. All work is recorded as taking place at Crewe unless otherwise noted. StR=St Rollox

Dates	A	B	C	D
29/3/50-27/4/50**LI**	-	24	71,622	16,978
17/11/50-22/12/50**LC**	8	22	53,201	70,179
9/8/51-1/9/51**LI**	-	20	98,272	44,626
12/9/51-26/9/51**NC***	1	11	577	45,203
19/11/51-29/1/52**HG**	12	47	14,424	59,050
16/12/52-13/2/54**HI**	3	28	72,105	72,105
10/1/54-23/1/53**HG**	4	25	69,608	1,886
14/5/55-11/6/55**LI**	1	23	106,699	27,066
15/12/56-26/1/57**HG**	1	33	116,387	64,297
22/10/57-26/10/57**NC***	2	2	59,381	59,381
28/2/58-18/4/58**HI**	4	37	79,546	8,800
7/1/59-13/2/59**HI**	4	28	61,326	2,338
16/3/59-2/4/59**LC***	4	14	4,572	6,910
16/12/59-5/2/60**HG**	9	33	65,490	67,828
28/8/61-2/10/61**LI**	-	30	108,904	35,391

record ends
*(EO)'- Engine Only

Sheds

Crewe North	
Camden	10/6/50
Crewe North	30/9/50
Camden	10/2/51
Crewe North	24/3/51
Camden	10/11/51
Crewe North	12/1/52
Camden	5/7/52
Crewe North	20/9/52
Carlisle Upperby	13/6/53
Crewe North	19/9/53
Carlisle Upperby	9/6/56
Crewe North	15/9/56
Carlisle Upperby	11/6/60
Carlisle Kingmoor	11/4/61
Camden	22/9/62

stored 18/11/62-31/5/63

Tenders

No	Fitted
9815	24/6/44

LMS 'Summary' *(this became 'Annual Statistics' from 1951)*

Year	Mileage	Weekdays out of service			
		wks	shed	n/req	total
1944	41,945	-	12	4	16
1945	57,376	54	46	4	104
1946	62,433	57	49	-	106
1947	52,427	64	30	1	95
1948	72,475	-	64	1	65
1949	63,236	32	46	11	89
1950	70,624	54	24	3	81
1951	59,050	66	44	2	112
1952	72,105	34	68	1	103
1953	67,881	22	64	3	89
1954	81,519	29	29	2	60
1955	79,156	24	24	4	52
1956	64,297	11	77	1	89
1957	70,746	23	54	1	78
1958	67,788	41	44	1	86
1959	67,828	*record ends*			
1960	73,613				
1961	50,880				
1962	47,653				
1963	-				

wks=heavy and light repairs at main works
shed=shed repairs and examinations
n/req= not required

Total Recorded Mileage 1,231,032
Withdrawn week ending 1/6/63
Cut up Crewe Works 9/63

CITY OF LEICESTER, LMS 6252 at Crewe North, apparently in the wartime overall black livery which would have been on the engine since new. 6252 was named at Leicester on 7 October 1944. It ran light from Crewe via Rugby, Market Harborough and the Midland main line, returning the same way. It received the later lined out version of the black colour scheme in November 1946 or thereabouts, so one presumes this picture pre-dates that event. It would have been a Crewe North engine when this photograph was taken. Photograph www.transporttreasury.co.uk

Yet another of those intriguing photographs for which we have no date, location or train details. Nevertheless, here is 46252 CITY OF LEICESTER in rather unkempt external condition. This engine had a pretty nomadic existence so far as its sheds in the BR period were concerned, moving to and fro between Crewe, Camden and Carlisle many times. In view of this the 5A shed plate hardly helps us in establishing a date, but the tender seems to have the earlier BR emblem (I doubt this will be visible as reproduced) so it must be pre-1956/57. There is the proverbial 'losing water' problem with the exhaust injector, but where are we? The Caledonian Railway signal box indicates a location north of the border and the coal visible in the tender suggests 46252 is heading south, but... Photograph www.transporttreasury.co.uk

Camden shed on 9 August 1953 with 46252 CITY OF LEICESTER ready for its next duty. A Carlisle engine at the time, it was transferred to Crewe North the following month. The engine is in BR green livery and notice that the speedometer has been removed from the trailing coupled wheel although the bracket remains in place. From LMS 6225 through to this engine BTH speedometers were fitted when the engines were new. The locomotive behind is 46237 CITY OF BRISTOL still retaining its semi-circular smokebox top. Photograph F.W. Goudie.

46253 CITY OF ST ALBANS

Built Crewe 14/9/46 total cost £15,460
Built without streamlining
Renumbered 6253 to 46253 week ending 17/9/49

Boilers

Fitted	No.	From
14/9/46	12470	new
17/2/51	10296	6222
26/11/53	12471	-
3/12/55	13043	-
25/1/58	10300	-
2/6/60	13043	-

No record after this date

Repairs

Dates in the first column are from out of traffic to return to traffic; A = 'Weekdays Waiting', B= 'Weekdays on Works'. The two mileage figures represent, firstly the miles accumulated since the previous General or Intermediate (C) and secondly (the lower figure) the miles run up from January 1st of the year of shopping - D. All work is recorded as taking place at Crewe unless otherwise noted. StR=St Rollox

Dates	A	B	C	D
13/8/47-14/8/47**NC**	-	2	73,866	49,658
3/10/47-11/10/47**TRO**	-	8#	-	-
11/12/47-19/12/47**NC**	-	8	96,574	72,366
28/1/48-28/2/48**LS**	-	28	105,163	6,074
25/3/48-15/4/48**NC**	-	18	3,169	9,243
29/11/48-22/12/48**NC**	-	21	53,554	59,628
22/7/49-14/9/49**LI**	-	47	94,135	39,549
19/9/49-22/9/49**NC**	-	4	175	39,724
17/3/50-31/3/50**NC**	8	4	35,019	15,973
1/1/51-17/2/51**HG**	5	36	96,525	142
27/6/51-28/6/51**LC**	-	1	22,308	22,450
24/4/52-30/5/52**HI**	3	28	74,919	18,387
5/6/53-9/6/53**LC***	-	3#	81,121	39,452
20/10/53-26/11/53**HG**	6	26	115,466	73,797
16/12/54-24/12/54**LC**	1	6	98,612	89,982
18/4/55-19/4/55**LC**	-	1	101,798	2,082
2/3/55-23/4/55**LI**	6	42	110,925	11,209
8/10/55-3/12/55**HC***	9	39	37,728	48,937
3/9/56-13/10/56**HI**	6	29	108,896	65,965
21/8/57-26/8/57**NC***	1	3	63,284	47,993
12/12/57-25/1/58**HG**	8	35	85,088	69,797
31/4/59-8/5/59**LI**	1	32	90,474	15,260
19/4/60-2/6/60**HG**	5	33	73,532	22,706
20/1/61-25/2/61**LC**	2	29	51,826	2,765

#'shed'
record ends
*'(EO)'- Engine Only

Sheds

Camden	
Carlisle Upperby	22/1/49
Camden	23/7/49
Carlisle Upperby	1/10/49
Camden	10/6/50
Carlisle Upperby	30/9/50
Crewe North	20/9/52
Camden	11/10/52
Camden	27/6/53
Crewe North	21/9/57

stored 3/10/62-26/1/63

Tenders

No	Fitted
9816	14/9/46
9703	28/6/51
9816	1/9/51
9750	24/12/54
9816	19/1/55
9704	?

LMS 'Summary' *(this became 'Annual Statistics' from 1951)*

Year	Mileage	Weekdays out of service			
		wks	shed	n/req	total
1946	24,208	-	11	5	16
1947	74,881	8	62	2	72
1948	60,660	28	102	-	130
1949	58,595	51	30	5	86
1950	77,337	-	80	4	84
1951	56,674	42	70	5	117
1952	60,056	31	76	6	113
1953	82,427	35	55	-	90
1954	91,086	7	56	1	64
1955	54,140	97	64	3	164
1956	81,256	35	75	-	110
1957	69,797	20	57	-	77
1958	75,214	23	57	-	80
1959	65,086		record ends		

wks=heavy and light repairs at main works
shed=shed repairs and examinations
n/req= not required

Total Recorded Mileage 931,417
Withdrawn week ending 26/1/63
'Date actually broken up
Crewe Works 13/5/63'

These two engines, 46253 CITY OF ST ALBANS to the front and an unidentified one behind, stand on No.1 through road to the north of Crewe station at an unrecorded date. Judging by the lack of any visible coal in the tenders they might be en route to the North Shed after coming off trains from the south. Alternatively, they might have arrived from the north and been turned at either the South Shed or the Gresty Lane triangle – in either case they'd be heading for the North Shed. Unfortunately we cannot quite make out the shed allocation of 46253, as it might have helped with a date. However this engine did shuttle about between Camden, Crewe North and Carlisle Upperby quite a lot in the 1950s until settling down at Crewe in 1957. A fine period view of the old station entrance with the double-deck Crosville buses. The photographer is standing on the footbridge between No.1 platform and the North Shed; we never used this and always walked across the tracks – no health and safety spies in those days! Photograph Paul Chancellor Collection.

Camden's 46253 CITY OF ST ALBANS with the down Royal Scot at Hest Bank, just north of Morecambe South Junction on 6 August 1955. This was one of the summer periods when this train did not operate with a limited load; witness the train of at least twelve coaches. With no coal showing in the tender the fireman has already been busy, with plenty of work yet to come. He will be having a breather until past Lancaster and on towards Carnforth after which he will start building up the fire for the climbs ahead. Doubtless too, he'll be glad of the coal pusher tender. The engine will come off the train at Carlisle, for they would never do the full distance from Euston to Glasgow with a load like this. Photograph R. Butterfield, Initial Photographs.

CITY OF ST ALBANS outside the erecting shop at Crewe Works after being reunited with its tender and probably after one of its 1948 visits – it had three. Painted in the LMS post-war black livery it has been touched up while in the erecting shop and though given its new BR number, 46253, retains LMS on the tender. It awaits a new smokebox number plate from the foundry and what a pity nobody found the time to clean the nameplate. The former LNWR Cauliflower 0-6-0 tender engine poking out from the left would belong to one of the works pilots; the gantry across the photograph was part of the internal transport system. Photograph Paul Chancellor Collection.

46254 CITY OF STOKE-ON-TRENT

Built Crewe 17/9/46, total cost £15,460
Built without streamlining
Renumbered 6254 to 46254 week ending 23/7/49

Boilers

Fitted	No.	From
17/9/46	12471	new
2/9/50	10646	6233
21/2/53	13043	-
18/10/55	10305	-
17/4/57	12471	-
25/4/61	10642	-

No record after this date

Repairs LMS

8/10/47-10/10/47**NC**
19/2/47-24/12/47**NC**
16/1/48-18/3/48**LS**
10/6/49-22/7/49**HI**
16/1/50-1/2/50**NC**
19/7/50-2/9/50**HG**

Repairs

Dates in the first column are from out of traffic to return to traffic; A = 'Weekdays Waiting', B= 'Weekdays on Works'. The two mileage figures represent, firstly the miles accumulated since the previous General or Intermediate (C) and secondly (the lower figure) the miles run up from January 1st of the year of shopping - D. All work is recorded as taking place at Crewe unless otherwise noted. StR=St Rollox

Dates	A	B	C	D
25/11/50-8/12/50**NC**	1	10	16,545	53,883
14/2/51-19/3/51**LC**	10	18	32,181	10,093
13/9/51-15/10/51**HI**	-	27	71,890	49,802
11/1/53-21/2/53**HG**	-	35	75,332	543
11/6/53-1/7/53**LC***	4	13	21,521	22,064
10/6/54-28/7/54**HI**	-	41	94,349	33,781
13/9/55-18/10/55**HG**	1	29	99,270	60,022
11/3/57-17/4/57**HG**	2	30	116,251	10,770
27/9/57-9/10/57**NC***	8	2	35,683	46,453
11/7/58-8/9/58**LI**	13	26	99,126	42,028
5/12/58-10/1/59**LC***	8	21	24,681	66,709
15/8/59-16/10/59**HI**	21	32	82,304	57,623
25/5/60-16/6/60**LC***	-	19	41,729	25,722
2/3/61-25/4/61**HG**	10	35	90,380	9,834

record ends
***'(EO)'- Engine Only**

Sheds

Camden	
Carlisle Upperby	1/10/49
Crewe North	20/9/52
Camden (loan)	11/10/52
Crewe North	25/10/52
Carlisle Upperby	13/6/53
Camden	19/9/53
Edge Hill (loan)	22/1/55
Camden	5/2/55
Western Region	28/1/56
Camden	25/2/56
Crewe North	24/9/60
Camden (loan)	9/3/63
Crewe North	20/4/63

stored 3/10/62-3/1/63, 21/10/63-17/11/63

Tenders

No	Fitted
9817	17/9/46

LMS 'Summary' *(this became 'Annual Statistics' from 1951)*

Year	Mileage	Weekdays out of service			
		wks	shed	n/req	total
1946	25,790	-	9	1	10
1947	72,941	-	85	-	85
1948	69,115	54	48	2	104
1949	66,897	37	69	5	111
1950	59,426	39	74	2	115
1951	67,836	55	36	1	92
1952	56,755	-	94	4	98
1953	61,111	52	71	4	127
1954	73,029	41	60	-	101
1955	79,522	30	60	12	102
1956	85,981#	-	70	-	70
1957	67,868	32	65	-	97
1958	66,709	57	63	-	120
1959	73,630	*record ends*			
1960	64,539				
1961	47,086				
1962	38,724				
1963	26,082				

#'Includes miles run whilst on loan to Western Region'
wks=heavy and light repairs at main works
shed=shed repairs and examinations
n/req= not required

Total Recorded Mileage 1,103,041
Withdrawn week ending 12/9/64
Cut up J.Cashmore, Great Bridge 12/64

Glasgow Central on 14 April 1956 with 46254 CITY OF STOKE-ON-TRENT making a spirited departure, almost certainly with the morning train to Birmingham. This train traditionally left from Platform 2, shortly after the 'Royal Scot', which always left from the platform on the right, number 1. This was another of the class that moved around quite a bit in the BR period, although once Geoff Sands got his hands on it and in view of its local name, it remained at Crewe North. When this photograph was taken it was Camden based, during a period of cyclic diagramming of the class, hence its employment on this train which it would take as far as Crewe. Nasty blow from the left hand piston rod packing; that would never have been tolerated had the engine been from the Crewe North stable! Notice the SC plate on the smokebox door, indicating to disposal crews that the engine had self cleaning screens fitted, which did no more than ensure any ash went up the chimney with the exhaust, depositing itself all over the countryside; but it saved the disposal crews emptying the box manually. 6254 was named CITY OF STOKE-ON-TRENT at Stoke on 20 September 1946 by the Lord Mayor. It went light from Crewe via Norton Bridge as the class was prohibited from the direct route. Photograph www.transporttreasury.co.uk

An unusual view of 46254, undated and at an unknown location; if it helps there is another line crossing in the distance, the embankment can just be seen along with the bridge to the left of the water column numbered 855. The engine is in the green livery; it was painted maroon in September 1958, so the view predates this. Photograph www.transporttreasury.co.uk

Geoff Sands, the Crewe North Shed Master would not have been happy with CITY OF STOKE-ON-TRENT in such an dishevelled state, as seen here entering Preston station from the south on 11 June 1963. The train is 3S07, the 6.50 pm Crewe to Glasgow parcels and the time recorded by the photographer 8.30 pm; it was actually due at 8.28pm. Displaced from more exacting duties by the onslaught of the EE Type 4 diesels, despite the latter having far less drawbar horsepower at their calling, trains like this one were how the engines were frequently utilised in their later days. But they still came into their own on many occasions, covering failed diesels along with other contingencies, and in the summer months running foremen never hesitated to employ them on the type of trains they had been designed for, and rarely were they let down by such actions. It has to be added that many of the crews loved it too, knowing as they did that the chance to handle one of these magnificent beasts, almost always complete master of its work, was diminishing by the day. Not all men I have to add, but there were plenty of them only too willing to have a go. Photograph A.W. Battson, www.transporttreasury.co.uk

This photograph has appeared before, several times I think, but it is such a nicely composed one at a location not often featured that another outing won't go amiss; most photographers preferred the other side of Shap Summit! Here however we see the down 'Royal Scot' with 46254 CITY OF STOKE-ON-TRENT in charge, passing Shap station at the start of the long downhill run to Carlisle. The fireman is taking a well earned breather, his work just about done as whatever fire he has will, along with perhaps the odd shovel full, take him to the Border City. The engine would have come through from Euston and will come off the train at Carlisle – notice no coal showing in the tender, with the coal pusher piston casing visible. Observe too that provision was made here for up trains to take water should it be necessary, after the lengthy 28 mile drag up the grade from Carlisle, the last almost 10 miles at 1 in 125. The train leaving in the distance could well be the Mid-Day Scot.

46255 CITY OF HEREFORD

Built Crewe 16/10/46 total cost £15,460
Built without streamlining
Renumbered 6255 to 46255 week ending 25/6/49

Boilers

Fitted	No.	From
16/10/46	12472	new
11/8/50	10294	6221
15/1/53	10291	-
20/12/54	10300	-
2/11/57	10305	-

No record after this date

Repairs LMS

25/8/47-12/9/47**LO**
29/12/47-27/1/48**HS**
8/3/49-24/6/49**LI**
25/10/49-19/11/49**LC**
2/6/50-11/8/50**HG**

Repairs

Dates in the first column are from out of traffic to return to traffic; A = 'Weekdays Waiting', B= 'Weekdays on Works'. The two mileage figures represent, firstly the miles accumulated since the previous General or Intermediate (C) and secondly (the lower figure) the miles run up from January 1st of the year of shopping - D. All work is recorded as taking place at Crewe unless otherwise noted. StR=St Rollox

Dates	A	B	C	D
23/8/50-30/8/50**NC**	-	6	293	29,516
3/10/50-4/11/50**LC**	7	21	7,407	36,630
26/2/51-6/4/51**LC**	7	26	29,406	11,498
13/4/51-12/5/59**HC**	10	15	30,217	12,309
25/10/51-27/11/51**LI**	2	26	67,126	49,218
24/11/52-15/1/53**HG**	1	42	71,956	67,653
30/10/53-24/12/53**HC***	9	38	66,951	66,951
30/12/53-12/1/54**NC***	-	11	67,306	67,306
30/7/54-9/9/54**LI**	6	29	104,365	37,059
28/10/54-20/12/54**HC***	4	41	9,919	46,978
16/2/56-3/4/56**HI**	6	33	92,111	9,281
17/9/56-19/10/56**HC***	10	18	37,875	47,156
1/12/56-10/12/56**NC***	1	6	46,995	56,276
28/8/57-2/11/57**HG**	31	33	108,094	55,831
28/7/58-23/8/58**LC***	17	23	51,497	39,088
12/4/59-23/5/59**LI**	6	29	104,150	24,396
9/6/60-17/8/60**HI**	11	48	71,237	33,521

record ends
*'(EO)'- Engine Only

Sheds

Camden	
Carlisle Upperby	26/6/48
Crewe North	20/9/52
Carlisle Upperby	13/6/53
Camden	26/9/53
Carlisle Upperby	3/10/53
Edge Hill (loan)	21/1/56
Camden (loan)	28/1/56
Carlisle Upperby	25/2/56
Carlisle Kingmoor	11/4/61

stored 1/1/64-27/1/64

Tenders

No	Fitted
10622	16/10/46

LMS 'Summary' *(this became 'Annual Statistics' from 1951)*

Year	Mileage	Weekdays out of service			
		wks	shed	n/req	total
1946	19,374	-	5	-	5
1947	75,613	17	58	-	75
1948	76,897	26	63	-	89
1949	50,233	116	39	3	158
1950	47,131	88	52	3	148
1951	53,521	86	38	3	127
1952	67,653	28	58	-	86
1953	67,306	66	54	6	126
1954	48,475	87	42	9	138
1955	71,414	-	86	8	94
1956	61,544	67	49	9	125
1957	58,240	64	38	15	117
1958	67,325	40	57	2	99
1959	62,100	*record ends*			

wks=heavy and light repairs at main works
shed=shed repairs and examinations
n/req= not required

Total Recorded Mileage 826,826
Withdrawn week ending 12/9/64
Cut up West of Scotland
Shipbreaking Co, Troon 12/64

The nameplate of 46255, probably taken when the engine was painted in LMS lined black livery. The view shows well the twin mechanical lubricators, the capillary feed oil box for the axle box horn guides and the sandbox filler lids. Notice too the reversing arm to lower left with the gear in the mid position. The recess in the boiler lagging, as mentioned once or twice already, allowed the lubricator lids to be fully opened.

The down 'Caledonian' breasting Camden bank on 5 May 1960 at the start of its long journey north. Notice how high the coal is stacked on the tender as the engine, 46255 CITY OF HEREFORD, would be working through to Glasgow with a crew change at Carlisle. When this train was first introduced in the summer of 1957, on a 6 hour 40 minute limited load schedule (eight vehicles) in both directions, leaving Glasgow at 8.30 in the morning and Euston at 4.15 in the afternoon, it was diagrammed for a Camden engine right through in each direction. This was somewhat unusual, as prior to this whenever through working was in operation, it was shared by Camden and Polmadie. One is left wondering how the Scottish Region let the London Midland get away with this on such a prestigious job. The Camden engine that went down one day came up with the return working on the next. CITY OF HEREFORD was allocated to Carlisle when this picture was taken, and would therefore be out of diagram. In any event the shed engine arrangers were supposed to find maroon examples for this train, indeed its introduction was one of the reasons why some of them were painted that colour in the first place. The Class 4 2-6-4 tank that would have worked the empty stock into Euston is giving a helping hand at the rear, but would very soon drop off and return to more mundane duties. Photograph Peter Groom.

CITY OF HEREFORD standing in Carlisle station on 6 October 1962. With class one headlamps it is doubtless waiting for an up train to arrive from Glasgow which it will take forward. Allocated to the Border City it will in all probability take the train through to Euston. Photograph Paul Chancellor Collection.

Kingmoor's CITY OF HEREFORD at Hereford, an event that cannot have happened very often. The date is 12 July 1964 and the X in the reporting number would indicate the engine had worked a special, in this case from Crewe. Once these engines were partly displaced from work on the West Coast main line, it was not altogether unusual to find them on West of England trains as far south as Hereford, while hitherto they would only have worked them as far as Shrewsbury, as fill-in turns between far more exacting duties.

The train in these two views is the 10.55 Saturdays only Crewe to Workington, reporting number 1L16, waiting to leave Preston with Kingmoor's 46255 CITY OF HEREFORD on 24 August 1963. This was a regular job during the summer of 1963. The second view illustrates clearly the casing at the rear of the tender coal bunker containing the valves for the coal pusher, and notice how the crew have left the tank filler door open. Photograph A.W. Battson, www.transporttreasury

Another shot perhaps, to delight the model maker; 46255 CITY OF HEREFORD on arrival at Wolverhampton High Level with a train from London. The view is undated but engines of this class were sometimes used on the Euston to Birmingham and Wolverhampton trains in the last couple of years of their lives. Earlier they were almost unknown off the Trent Valley route of the West Coast main line, except during diversions for one reason or another. Nevertheless, it seems in this case Camden had borrowed a Carlisle engine. After a visit to Bushbury Junction shed, it would return south on a similar working. Photograph www.transporttreasury.co.uk

46255 CITY OF HEREFORD outside No.1 road of its home shed Carlisle Kingmoor, and among far less elevated brethren! This is a late view nonetheless, as the engine has AWS and electrification warning notices; it was transferred to Kingmoor from Upperby in March 1961, so the photograph post-dates that. Photograph Paul Chancellor Collection.

On the scrap road at Carlisle Kingmoor, its working days over; a forlorn 46255 shorn of its nameplates and awaiting the scrap man's call. The date is quoted as August 1964 although the engine was not officially withdrawn until 12 September; whatever the case what a sad and sorry sight. Before being towed away to its last resting place the side and connecting rods would have to be removed, including the inside connecting rods – with the connecting rods in position there was a 25mph speed restriction and a 15 mile distance limit on the movement of dead engines. When Crewe North's remaining Pacifics were similarly dumped awaiting the breaker I was working at the Diesel Shed. However I made a melancholy visit one afternoon to pay my last respects. It was one of those late summer days in September 1964 when the sun never appears and the first signs of autumn can be felt in the air; it seemed at the time that the weather was in sympathy too. I remember imagining as I spent a few minutes in the cab of my favourite, named after my home city, 46254 CITY OF STOKE-ON-TRENT, that I was breasting Shap with 15 on at 30 miles an hour! Alas it was the last time I saw any of the North Shed's remaining allocation. Photograph J.G. Walmsley, www.transporttreasury.co.uk

46256 SIR WILLIAM A STANIER F.R.S.

Built Crewe 13/12/47 cost £18,248 (engine), £3,163 (tender)
Built without streamlining
Renumbered 6256 to 46256 week ending 15/5/48

Boilers

Fitted	No.	From
13/12/47	12473	new
5/5/51	13044	new
22/6/54	12474	-
15/12/56	12473	-
15/8/59	13044	-

No record after this date

Repairs

Dates in the first column are from out of traffic to return to traffic; A = 'Weekdays Waiting', B= 'Weekdays on Works'. The two mileage figures represent, firstly the miles accumulated since the previous General or Intermediate (C) and secondly (the lower figure) the miles run up from January 1st of the year of shopping - D. All work is recorded as taking place at Crewe unless otherwise noted. StR=St Rollox

Dates	A	B	C	D
16/2/48-13/5/48**NC**	-	75	9,952	9,089
8/6/48-3/7/48**NC**	-	23	12,733	11,870
6/9/48-25/9/48**NC**	-	18	30,274	29,411
9/10/48-16/10/48**NC**	-	7	31,705	30,842
2/5/49-24/5/49**HC**	-	20	83,038	33,489
22/9/49-15/10/49**NC**	-	21	119,627	70,078
16/1/50-27/2/50**LI**	-	36	140,568	2,800
9/10/50-1/12/50**LC**	1	45	51,753	54,553
2/3/51-5/5/51**HG**	9	45	65,326	6,714
25/4/52-7/6/52**HI**	7	30	79,909	20,475
9/6/52-16/6/52**NC***	-	6	Nil	20,475
26/5/53-25/6/53**HC**	8	18	89,863	38,766
1/7/53-3/7/53**NC***	1	1	90,204	39,107
3/5/54-22/6/54**HG**	1	42	156,065	22,115
2/8/55-31/8/55**LI**	1	24	95,647	45,412
245/10/56-15/12/56**HG**	7	38	100,590	65,129
7/1/57-2/2/57**LC***	12	11	2,393	855
25/3/58-27/5/58**LI**	-	53	93,594	20,824
8/6/59-15/8/59**HG**	1	59	89,691	35,130
5/11/60-5/1/61**LI**	14	36	88,073	65,087

record ends
*'(EO)'- Engine Only

Sheds

Crewe North	
Camden	24/1/48
Crewe North	7/11/59
Camden (loan)	7/11/59
Crewe North, then immediately Carlisle Upperby	21/11/59
Camden	30/4/60
Crewe North	24/9/60

stored 21/10/62-20/1/63, 10/10/63-2/12/63

Tenders

No	Fitted
10623	13/12/47

LMS 'Summary' *(this became 'Annual Statistics' from 1951)*

Year	Mileage	Weekdays out of service			
		wks	shed	n/req	total
1947	863	-	4	1	5
1948	48,686	-	170	-	170
1949	88,219	20	80	2	102
1950	61,412	82	73	-	155
1951	66,148	54	66	2	122
1952	71,572	43	72	-	115
1953	82,853	28	58	-	86
1954	70,352	43	70	-	113
1955	80,878	25	53	11	89
1956	66,667	45	71	-	116
1957	71,232	23	86	-	109
1958	75,385	53	46	-	93
1959	58,417	*record ends*			
1960	65,087				
1961	57,029				
1962	24,375				
1963	26,380				

wks=heavy and light repairs at main works
shed=shed repairs and examinations
n/req= not required

Total Recorded Mileage 1,016,060
Withdrawn week ending 3/10/64
Cut up J.Cashmore, Great Bridge 12/64

Perhaps the favourite among the class for many, and the last one built by the LMS, is 46256, named after the Chief Mechanical Engineer of the LMS when the class was first introduced, SIR WILLIAM A STANIER FRS. This engine and the next, which was the last, differed from the remainder in having a revised arrangement of trailing truck and roller bearing axle boxes throughout, along with a few other detail differences including, when new, electric lighting. They also had a rocking grate, rather than the drop grate arrangement on the earlier engines; actually from 46253 onwards the engines had a rocking grate from new. Here 46256 is leaving Penrith passing Eamont Junction with a down Sunday train for London on 1 September 1957. The electric lights are in evidence as well as the turbo alternator, that is it just aft of the smoke deflector. A rather nice view as the engine leans into the curve, with the long climb to Shap Summit about to commence.

SIR WILLIAM on shed at Camden, after it had been transferred to Carlisle Upperby in November 1959, although it had been a Camden engine for almost all its life hitherto. This photograph was taken on 21 February 1960 with civil engineering works underway to accommodate the diesels, which were already starting to descend upon the scene. The chimney and building in the background were for the boilers that provided steam for the stationary engine that had originally been used to haul by wire rope trains out of Euston and up Camden bank. It really ought to have been saved, along with of course, the Euston Arch. Photograph David Idle, www.transporttreasury.co.uk

SIR WILLIAM A STANIER FRS at Carlisle Kingmoor shed on 22 May 1960, prepared to work the 'Royal Scot' on its southward journey to London. This locomotive had been based at Upperby during the previous winter, but was back at Camden for the spring and summer, before going to Crewe North in September, where it remained for the rest of its life. This photograph shows quite clearly the revised trailing truck arrangement with the resultant foreshortened cab side sheets. The crews reckoned that this engine and its sister 46257, did not ride quite so well as the earlier ones with the original truck design. Notice that by this date the electric lighting equipment had been removed. Photograph J.T. Clewley, www.transporttreasury.co.uk

On the approach to Carlisle from the south, 46256 has the down 'Royal Scot', around 1960 I would suggest. By this time the engine had been fitted with AWS equipment; that is the conduit taking the wiring running just under the foot framing, and on this and 46257, the battery box was located under the cab side sheet where it just be discerned in this view. These last two engines had a different arrangement of reverser, with the actual reverse mechanism screw situated alongside the weigh-bar shaft rather than in the cab; hence the circular rod to operate it seen here emerging from the cab. The idea behind this was to ease the manual effort necessary to operate the gear, but opinions were mixed among crews as to how successful or otherwise this was. The same design was adopted for the larger BR Standards, again with a mixed reception from the men who had to operate them. The arrangement was colloquially known as 'the mangle', and some wags reckoned it would have been better with their other halves in the wash room rather than on a locomotive! Photograph www.transporttreasury.co.uk

When Camden shed closed to steam its remaining engines, as related earlier, were transferred away and the Pacifics migrated a few miles up the line to Willesden. This of course meant that visiting engines on trains arriving at Euston also had to go to Willesden for servicing. Here we have Crewe North's 46256 SIR WILLIAM A STANIER FRS stabled there on 9 June 1963 with another of the class in front, identified by the straw lining on the maroon tender. Photograph Peter Groom.

Two rather pleasing and unrestricted views of 46256 at Crewe North shed on 21 April 1963. It takes little imagination that with an enthusiast like Geoff Sands as Shedmaster, this locomotive was one of his favourites with whatever cleaners were available (and very often there were not many) deputed to it whenever it was stopped for attention. The Chargehand Cleaners knew their priorities when Geoff was about!

46257 CITY OF SALFORD

Built Crewe 19/5/48 cost £18,248 (engine), £3,163 (tender)
Built without streamlining

Boilers

Fitted	No.	From
19/5/48	12474	new
10/12/52	12473	-
26/11/55	13044	-
13/3/59	12474	-

Repairs

Dates in the first column are from out of traffic to return to traffic; A = 'Weekdays Waiting', B= 'Weekdays on Works'. The two mileage figures represent, firstly the miles accumulated since the previous General or Intermediate (C) and secondly (the lower figure) the miles run up from January 1st of the year of shopping - D. All work is recorded as taking place at Crewe unless otherwise noted. StR=St Rollox

Dates	A	B	C	D
25/5/48-26/5/48#	-	2	-	-
11/6/48-1/7/48**NC**	-	18	1,501	1,501
15/9/48-26/10/48**NC**	-	36	21,085	21,085
7/1/49-15/1/49#	-	8	-	-
15/9/49-14/10/49**LC**	-	26	106,546	69,811
25/2/50-3/4/50**LI**	-	31	138,157	12,981
24/7/50-7/11/50**HC**	-	91	36,776	49,757
8/11/50-11/11/50**NC**	-	3	36,776	49,757
12/2/51-6/3/51**NC**	1	18	51,722	1,751
21/5/51-2/7/51**LI**	9	27	76,124	26,153
1/11/51-17/11/51**LC**	6	58	33,929	60,082
28/1/52-30/1/52**NC**	-	2	35,689	1,751
6/2/52-1/3/52**NC**	5	16	35,680	1,751
28/3/52-8/5/52**LC***	-	34	41,662	7,733
26/9/52-10/12/52**HG**	1	63	75,084	41,155
28/8/53-12/10/53**LC**	10	28	67,396	62,557
15/10/53-28/10/53**NC***	-	11	67,396	62,557
8/9/54-11/10/54**HI**	-	28	142,486	57,589
13/10/54-26/10/54**NC***	-	11	309	57,898
16/2/55-22/3/55**LC***	4	25	30,258	13,148
13/10/55-26/11/55**HG**	-	38	79,448	62,338
5/1/57-19/2/57**HI**	8	22	96,641	1,263
3/12/57-24/1/58**LI**	8	35	66,042	67,305
1/1/59-13/3/59**HG**	8	43	83,621	1,155
22/3/59-25/4/59**LC***	8	20	597	1,752
13/7/59-6/8/59**NC***	7	14	18,975	20,130
4/9/59-24/10/59**HC**	12	31	27,472	28,627
7/1/60-8/2/60**NC***	3	22	40,980	825
11/3/60-28/4/60**LC***	22	18	49,645	9,490
27/10/60-16/12/60**LI**	10	33	84,179	44,024

#*'no repair'*
record ends
**(EO)'- Engine Only*

Sheds

Camden	
Western Region	28/1/56
Camden	18/2/56
Carlisle Upperby	27/9/58
Carlisle Kingmoor	11/4/61
stored 30/12/63-16/3/64	

Tenders

No	Fitted
10624	19/5/48

LMS 'Summary' *(this became 'Annual Statistics' from 1951)*

Year	Mileage	Weekdays out of service			
		wks	shed	n/req	total
1948	36,735	-	72	1	73
1949	88,441	26	72	2	100
1950	62,952	125	24	-	149
1951	60,082	85	61	-	146
1952	45,994	115	49	-	164
1953	80,058	49	57	-	106
1954	74,699	39	59	-	98
1955	70,912	67	36	11	114
1956	86,804	-	73	-	73
1957	67,305	51	87	-	138
1958	82,466	22	66	1	89
1959	41,310	*record ends*			

wks=heavy and light repairs at main works
shed=shed repairs and examinations
n/req= not required

Total Recorded Mileage 797,758
Withdrawn week ending 12/9/64
Cut up West of Scotland
Shipbreaking Co, Troon 12/64

Last of a noble line, 46257 CITY OF SALFORD (the City names were getting thin on the ground by this time it must be said) at the north end of Carlisle station at some unrecorded date, but I reckon late in the life and times of the class. The engine has a Kingmoor shed plate where it was transferred from nearby Upperby in March 1961, and the station has lost its lovely overall roof. The crew look as if they are being joined by a 'bowler hat' - I bet that pleased them! Photograph Paul Chancellor Collection.

I have included this view of 46257 to better illustrate the arrangement of trailing truck and cab side sheets on the last two engines. Notice too, the Timken roller bearing axle-boxes on the truck and tender, and the revolution counter on the leading tender axle-box cover. The photograph also shows clearly the Stanier 'hooter', as it was called, a whistle based on the former Caledonian Railway design. The location is Carlisle Kingmoor at some unrecorded, but late date. The principal reason for the re-design of the rear end was to allow for a larger ashpan. Ashpan capacity had long been a concern with all the LMS Pacifics, even on a run between Euston and Carlisle it was often a problem, let alone through working to Glasgow. The poor fuel available during the war, coupled with much heavier trains and longer schedules compounded matters, and this was an attempt to solve it. The ashpans on the earlier engines underwent a number of modifications over the years, though within the space available, these were minimal. There were also additional side doors to assist the job of the disposal crews. On 46256 and 46257 the engine main frames terminated ahead of the trailing truck, and the new design of truck, support frames and dragbox etc., allowed for a larger area to be available for the ashpan. The ashpan was therefore both larger than on the earlier engines, and designed such as to be almost completely self trimming, making the job of disposal crews even easier. Photograph www.transporttreasury.co.uk

In the winter of 1963-64 many engines of the class were placed in store, including 46257 CITY OF SALFORD. The locomotive is seen here at Carlisle Upperby thus stored, with chimney bagged and nameplates removed for safe keeping, along with 46244 KING GEORGE VI, on 26 February 1964. Both engines lived to fight another day, being returned to service soon after, to help out with the perennial steam heating generator problems with the EE Type 4 diesels. On the right is Princess Royal Pacific 46200, withdrawn 18 months or so earlier, and still awaiting its last journey to the breakers. There were rumours around at the time that this engine, the pioneer Stanier Pacific, might have been saved, and it has I think, always been assumed this is why it hung around so long. Photograph www.transporttreasury.co.uk

For some unrecorded reason, after 46257 was withdrawn at the end of the 1964 summer season, it was moved from Carlisle to storage in the old fire damaged shed at Preston. This is where it was on 23 September when this photograph was taken, with a tender well loaded with coal and connecting rods still in place, indicating it had arrived here under its own steam. The chimney is bagged too, so somebody must have thought it might steam again. Interesting. This photograph also illustrates clearly the roller bearing axle boxes on tender and truck, the revolution counter and the diagonal yellow line on the cab side in connection with the restriction not to run under the overhead line equipment south of Crewe. Photograph www.transporttreasury.co.uk

Second of the streamlined engines, 6221 QUEEN ELIZABETH at Polmadie shed in Glasgow early in its life. It must have been very difficult maintaining some of the parts of these engines, not to mention the added servicing time on preparation and disposal. It has always amazed me that the LMS continued to build engines with the streamlined casing during the war, bearing in mind that all the design work necessary to build a conventional locomotive had already been done. Photograph W. Hermiston, www.transporttreasury.co.uk

This photograph of 6242 CITY OF GLASGOW was taken by the late Ralph Russell at Polmadie shed in June 1946. The locomotive is painted wartime plain black; notice the rear casing has been removed from the tender. Although Ralph was primarily an industrial railway and locomotive enthusiast he did make a number of visits to main line sheds, in particular during the war when in the armed forces and stationed in Scotland. Worth a mention then is a visit of his to Polmadie on 8 September 1945 when he noted no fewer than 143 locomotives on shed including the following Pacifies: 6221, 6226, 6232, 6235, 6248, 6238, 6239, 6250 and 6251. Photograph the late R.T. Russell.

6. MAINTAINING THE BIG 'UNs

Until 1933 LMS steam locomotives were, by and large and in so far shed attention was concerned, maintained under the systems of the various pre-grouping companies in the areas where they were allocated. The practices and procedures of for example, the London & North Western (LNWR) and Midland Railways had continued in existence with the obvious consequence of varying periodicities and standards. This is not to say that considerable improvements had not been effected. Indeed under the dynamic leadership of Sir Josiah Stamp, appointed President in 1925 in a new American-style of organisational control, much had been achieved in the intervening period. Largely due to the introduction of new designs and improvements in workshop practices, by 1933 the shorter times locomotives were in or awaiting works had enabled the fleet to be reduced from 10,316 to 8,226, while the total mileage worked remained about the same. The average miles run per locomotive each 24 hours had increased from around 70 to almost 107. There had also been a reduction in the number of types from 393 at grouping to 173; the 1937 withdrawal programme further reduced this to 136. However by the early 1930s there was a strong feeling that it was time to tackle the issues of locomotive utilisation and reliability with even more vigour. It represented some £12,000,000

of the company's total annual expenditure which in 1933 amounted to a little over £55,000,000; it was thus a very significant factor in the total cost of operating the railway. The almost complete metamorphosis of what had been the Locomotive Running Department and in its Americanized form became the Motive Power Department, was largely the brainchild of E.J.H. (Ernest, later Sir) Lemon, a Midland man through and through. He had been appointed Vice President Railway Traffic Operating & Commercial in 1931. This was after a brief tenure as Chief Mechanical Engineer in the interregnum between the 'shunt' upwards of Sir Henry Fowler to a Vice Presidential position and the appointment of William A Stanier.

Lemon, like his mentor Stamp a great administrator and a man with enormous vision, was aided and abetted by two of Stamp's other leading prodigies. These were Sir Harold Hartley who among his other responsibilities was the Director of Scientific Research (to which it has to be added, he applied a very wide interpretation) and William V Wood, the Vice President Finance and Service Departments. Thus came about a scheme to both standardise and improve running shed maintenance with the introduction of what became known as 'The Motive Power Area Locomotive Supply Repair

Concentration and Garage Scheme'. Its long and unwieldy title was matched by the long and often unwieldy time it brought for many of those involved. Nevertheless, it delivered significant improvements in all areas of locomotive utilisation and reliability and stood the test of time for steam and to some extent more modern forms of motive power, until the final elimination of steam locomotives in this country. Although it was not written anywhere, one of its aims was a further breaking down of the pre-grouping prejudices and entrenched practices that continued to bedevil efforts to improve productivity across the widely different organisation that was the LMS.

This is not the place to go into any great detail concerning the enormous upheaval the new scheme caused. Suffice it to say that in dividing the locomotive sheds into area groups, the plan was for one, or perhaps two sheds in each area to be known as Concentration Depots, to be equipped for all the heavier examinations and repairs to the locomotives allocated to the area. This would leave the other sheds, which by the way were now to be known as 'garage' depots (to continue the American ideas) to concentrate on the small examinations and repairs along with everyday servicing. There were 39 areas, henceforth known as Districts, 26 in England and Wales and three in

Another of Ralph Russell's photographs, once again at Polmadie, in this case with 6222 QUEEN MARY in LMS lined black, although the tender does not appear to be lined. According to the records this engine had its streamlined casing removed in June 1946 when it received this livery, the same month and year Ralph's notes indicate the photograph was taken. The engine does not look as if it is just off works however; perhaps the photographs was taken a little later. That is a Princess Royal Pacific behind. Photograph the late R.T. Russell.

Between January 1955 and June the following year Crewe North's 46225 DUCHESS OF GLOUCESTER was, on and off, temporarily allocated to the Locomotive Testing Station at Rugby as part of a series of high-power tests. This particular engine was chosen as it was immediately off a heavy general repair at Crewe. Initially the tests were on the stationary plant at Rugby and while it was the intension to follow on with controlled road testing, pressure from the operators had the locomotive returned to normal service during the summer and autumn of 1955. Prior to this the engine again received attention in Crewe Works – it was there from 23 June to 1 July – and before the testing re-commenced was given an intermediate repair which was completed on 10 March 1956. The road tests took place on the Settle-Carlisle line between Carlisle and Skipton and this photograph shows the test train. On this particular occasion the train included the three LMS mobile test units and is en-route from Carlisle to Skipton passing Hirstwood, just outside Carlisle, on 18 April 1955. In one of the tests with a load of 442 tons plus the test units making up a drawbar load equivalent to around 900 tons, on the climb from Appleby to Ais Gill, most of it at 1 in 100, while speed fell to 30 mph by Mallerstang the engine sustained a continuous drawbar horsepower of some 2,100 at a constant steam rate of around 40,000 lb per hour. In this test the engine achieved the highest sustained steaming rate, averaging 38,500 lb per hour of over half an hour, ever achieved by a steam locomotive in this country. The tests highlighted that all four cylinders were doing more work at their front ends than the back. One of the conclusions was that with improved valve setting and some alterations to the draughting, even higher outputs could be obtained, or alternatively similar outputs with lower grades of coal. With the days of the steam locomotive numbered by the time the report was issued in July 1958, nothing was ever done. Notice some of the test equipment by the smoke deflector. Photograph R. Butterfield, Initial Photographics.

Scotland. Each was in the charge of a District Motive Power Superintendent (DMPS) who was in most cases located, along with his assistant, at the Concentration Depot, the latter often doubling up as the Shedmaster for that particular depot. In the larger Districts however this was not always the case and at Crewe North for example, where the DMPS and the Assistant DMPS for the Crewe District were stationed at Crewe North, there was also a Shedmaster specifically for that shed. The system of coding districts and depots familiar to most readers and in use across the whole country in BR days stems from the introduction of the LMS scheme.

Despite its great size – it was the largest single organisation in the British Isles – the LMS was not a rich one. Sheds had seen little or no investment since before the First World War, and by concentrating the heavier maintenance at a small number of locations, far better equipment and facilities could be provided from the limited funds available. Having said that, by any

yardstick it was an enormous scheme, involving an outlay of around £1,000,000, an enormous sum for the time; many sheds underwent compete renewal, with reconstruction of the buildings and mechanisation of the facilities. A large part of the investment related to the provision of mechanical handling plants for coal and ash (otherwise very labour intensive tasks) and the rearranged layouts to suit. The objectives were wide-ranging and involved the whole sequence of servicing a steam locomotive, from the time it arrived on the shed until it left to take up duty again.

The policy of concentrating the heavier maintenance and repairs at a small number of sheds allowed designated groups of staff to devote their time to specific jobs, something that was desirable in view of the larger number of locomotives to be dealt with. This made for great improvements in locomotive availability and reliability. It also provided sufficient work so that in many cases shift working could be

economically employed on the larger repairs; this had not been so prevalent hitherto, with each individual shed only handling a smaller number of locomotives. A further benefit was that fewer 'maintenance spare locomotives' (as described in the 'Mileages and Diagrams' section) were necessary; a large enough fleet could be allocated to the concentration depots to cover all the locomotives in the district, rather than each depot having to hold its own. Hence when one of the garage depots sent a locomotive to the concentration depot for attention, another was loaned from the larger depot's allocation.

By the end of 1937, of 47 schemes for improvements to individual depots authorised by the LMS board, 39 had been completed. This amounted to an expenditure of around £750,000, by which time the average individual engine miles per 24 hours had increased to a little over 118 and the total fleet size had been reduced to 7,688. The percentage return on expenditure was almost 8%.

Some unusual detail on 46227 DUCHESS OF DEVONSHIRE standing outside No.6 Belt of the No.10 erecting shop at Crewe Works – this was the belt that handled the Pacifics and the Garratts. The date is not known but the engine retains its sloping smokebox which the records tell us was modified in May 1953. The engine would have been moved out of the shop using capstans and in this position the last few jobs would be undertaken; this ensured it would not delay progress of other engines proceeding along the belt. Shortly the engine would be reunited with its tender and taken to the vacuum pits for steam testing prior to painting in the paint shop. The item on the side of the boiler immediately behind the smoke deflector is the vacuum brake ejector. The smoke deflectors were made in three sections to allow access to the outside cylinder steam pipe expansion joints without having to remove the complete deflector plate. One only had to remove the rear bottom section to get at them. Photograph Paul Chancellor Collection.

Crewe North's 46256 SIR WILLIAM A STANIER FRS undergoing repairs at Rugby shed on 25 April 1962, after a failure in service – the radius rod, hanging down ahead of the reversing link, is twisted and broken. On the ground (left to right) are battered combining lever, union link, the other half of the radius rod and the valve rod, followed by both outside piston valves and the right-hand piston valve front cover. The cover from the opposite side is also on the ground below the left-hand front footstep. In front of the piston valve, on the right, is the union link bracket, which has been removed from the crosshead with the other bit of the union link still attached; this too has been broken in half. On the framing, by the length of rope, is the pin used to connect the rocker arm for actuating the inside right-hand valve from the right-hand side valve gear to the valve rod, indicating that this component has been removed too. A seized piston valve, either inside or outside, would have caused this sort of damage, but the two outside valves show no signs of seizure and with the left-hand one removed as well there might be damage on the other side too. The rocker arm may have seized, as it appears to have been removed, but I can never recall such an incident on one of these engines – and note that neither of the inside valves have been removed. Several of the removed bits are not in evidence, including the valve rod crossheads and indeed the rocker arm. Whatever disaster had befallen SIR WILLIAM, it was duly repaired and went on to give a few more years service. Replacement parts would come from Crewe as that was the repairing works for this class; all classes were allocated one or more 'home' works where spares were held and repairs undertaken. Class 5, 8Fs and the like would have several, but small classes like this had a single specified works. The mortal remains we see here were destined for the scrap bin though 'consumables' such as brake blocks, springs, firebars and baffle plates were the commonest items. Non-ferrous items would be kept securely, in the stores. Photograph Jack Hodgkinson.

Any engine coming off Crewe Works to the motive power folk was termed a 'fresh-off' and, initially at least, they usually went to the South shed. All engines came off the works 'smokebox north' so if they were going to be used on a running-in trip to Shrewsbury it enabled them to be turned ready (a 70ft table was only installed at the North shed in 1950). Here is 46232 DUCHESS OF MONTROSE newly painted in an early form of the blue livery that was at the time being considered for the largest express passenger locomotives, on the turntable at Crewe South shed on 22 May 1948. Only a few locomotives received this particular shade of blue paint and style of lining; the standard that was adopted was a lighter shade with different lining. The crew member is either connecting or disconnecting the vacuum pipe as this was a vacuum operated turntable. The engine has the LMS 27A shed code for its home shed of Polmadie; this was prior to the BR changes when it became 66A. The special polished finish given to the cylinder and valve chest cover plates and the burnished buffer heads might suggest that as the first Pacific given this livery, it had been, or was about to be, officially inspected. Photograph David Montgomery.

The maintenance of locomotives was covered by the 'Locomotive Maintenance and Mechanical Efficiency' part of the plan which covered the 'Standard Examination of Locomotives and Tenders', more commonly known as 'The X Scheme Examination and Repair'. In BR days this scheme was hardly altered and was colloquially known as 'The MP 11'; that is, Motive Power Instruction 11. The first principle of this was for locomotives to be stopped on a regular basis such that, apart from exceptional circumstances, they would be kept in steam and available for the whole of the intervening period. Hitherto it had been the practice in some areas to stop locomotives in a very unstructured manor; they might be taken out of service on separate occasions, but in short space of time for say, a boiler washout and some subsequent mechanical maintenance. This resulted in a reduced number of days the locomotives were available and so more locomotives were needed for a specific range of duties. The periodicity between what became known as X Day, depended on the type of work on which the individual locomotive types were utilised viz:

Class 7, 6P and 5XP	
(In BR terms Class 8P,7P and 6P)	6-8 days.
All other passenger types	12-16 days
All tender freight engines	12-16 days
Freight tank engines used on passenger or freight trains	12-16 days
All other freight tank engines used for freight shunting work	24-32 days

As an aside, and continuing the Americanization theme, it is notable that 'goods' engines have become 'freight' engines. Sheds at the same time became depots and locomotives 'motive power'. This change in the terminology would have been actively encouraged by Stamp.

Another principle was that moving parts should be maintained on a mileage run basis and non-moving parts on a time basis. Broadly, 5,000-6,000 mile intervals were set for moving parts, the most extensive, known as the No.7 exam, being set at 30,000-36,000 miles. In BR days this was increased to around 40,000 miles for some classes of engine, which by definition became known as the No.8 exam. The items included in the mileage examination broadly consisted of the valves, pistons, motion parts, wheels and axles, buffers and drawgear, mechanical lubricators, brake gear and so on. For the stationary parts the periodicities were 3-5 weeks, 7-9 weeks and 9-15 weeks. In (once again) broad terms, came the boiler and all its fittings, steam heating apparatus, non-moving parts of the brake gear, tender tank and feed water apparatus etc. There were exceptions; for example the cylinder relief and anti-vacuum valves were examined on a mileage basis, just as the moving parts with which they were intimately associated. Similarly cylinder cock and sanding gear were included in the time periodicity examinations. Worth pointing out is that all the examinations were cumulative, in that the items on the smaller examinations were also included on each successive larger one.

In addition to those mentioned above there were a range of items covered by the X Day examination itself. Largely but not exclusively safety related, they included a general examination for loose, missing or damaged parts with the locomotive stabled over an inspection pit. This was a two-part examination, first with the locomotive in steam on arrival and before the fire was dropped and later after it had been stabled ready for work to start. Any repairs found by the examining fitter would be entered on the X day card for attention later. At the X Day opportunity would be taken to carry out any mileage or periodicity examinations due; thus for example, an engine might be stopped on its X Day additionally for 10,000-12,000 mile and 7-9 week exams.

Another element in the philosophy of keeping engines in steam for maximum periods was that any repairs that might be left for a period without seriously effecting the mechanical efficiency of the locomotive could be deferred until the next X Day. This might include defects reported by drivers on disposal or by the examining fitters on their daily visual examinations of engines prior them going into service; the decision would rest with the Leading

A lovely photograph of Polmadie's 46232 the DUCHESS OF MONTROSE, blowing off impatiently inside the Middle Shed at Crewe North on 20 August 1955. The engine stands on No.2 road, one of two that had been cut back during the war to allow for the construction of a canteen and office. A specially evocative photograph for me as this is where I started my working life all those years ago. The engine must have been about ready to leave, to judge from the light engine head lamp code with the crew probably making their last minute preparations, and blowing off steam in the shed itself was not encouraged! The No.1 road to the left was the home of the breakdown crane which must have been absent on this occasion, but notice the brick arch bricks stored against the wall side. I think Brian Morrison must have used his tripod for this photograph as it shows amazing detail. It has long been a favourite of mine. Photograph Brian Morrison.

46234 DUCHESS OF ABERCORN, on the ashpits at its home shed Crewe North, about 1957 or 1958. It has the earlier tender emblem, just discernable in the original print. The engine is facing north so has probably come off a train from London, has already been coaled and is taking water. Notice the serried rows of railway houses to the right; the street on the extreme right is Bank Street. Crewe had literally hundreds of them, all long swept away. Photograph the late George Wheeler.

DUCHESS OF ABERCORN at Crewe North, 20 August 1955. This was a North shed engine for a long time, from November 1947 to June 1959 no less, although it had also been allocated there earlier, from September 1944 to October 1947. The ash handling plant to the left and coal hopper to the right were part of the uncompleted early 1950s scheme of modernisation for this shed. This was the first engine of the class to have a double chimney and by its legendary efforts in 1939 established a record by developing the highest ever recorded drawbar horsepower for a steam locomotive in this country. The engine is standing in an area of the shed yard rarely patrolled by officialdom and inevitably a good haven for mischievous apprentices when work was complete for the day! Photograph Brian Morrison.

Fitter or perhaps the Mechanical Foreman. This is not to infer that repairs were neglected, but there were frequent examples where no harm would result in particular jobs waiting a day or two and thus save an engine being stopped out of course. An example might be an exhaust injector refusing to work on exhaust steam but working perfectly on live steam, or a safety valve blowing a few pounds light.

The one remaining important job I have not so far mentioned is the washing out of boilers. The periodicity of boiler washouts was largely dependent on the quality of the feed water which was itself dependent on the state of the raw water available and what if any water treatment was applied to it. In areas of very soft water where certain engines that did not stray very far, on shunting and local trip working for example, the periods might be as long as four weeks. Another factor taken into consideration was the amount of water the particular boiler would have been evaporated. Obviously this would be higher for locomotives on long trips with heavy loads rather than say, a shunting or local trip engine which would spend much if its time standing around doing very little. Many sheds would establish their own 'local arrangements' based on experience for engines that did not stray very far. In cases of very bad water engines might have to be stopped between X days for no other reason than to wash the boilers out. So one might have what were termed as BFX and WOX Days, that is Boiler Full X and Washout X, or just WO Days, although at most sheds even when boilers were washed out at lesser periods than those designated for the X Day, an X Day examination would in fact be undertaken.

Unlike on some other railways it was never the practice of the LMS and subsequently the London Midland Region of BR, to wash boilers out with hot water as it was strongly felt that the subsequent examination of the internal parts by a Boilersmith would be hampered in the resulting hot and steamy conditions. Boilers were cooled down in a controlled manner by the use of special equipment designed to circulate cold water through the boiler at a defined and steadily increasing rate. This process took about six hours, the internal parts being cleaned using high pressure water jets (about 60 psi) with various shaped nozzles to access otherwise inaccessible places along with specially shaped rods to remove deposited scale etc. Once this process was complete a Boilersmith would make a detailed examination of the water spaces, followed by any attention required as a result of what he might uncover. After this, steam would be raised. This too, was undertaken in a controlled manner as it was never the practice to force the process and about eight hours would normally be allowed before an engine would be booked for its next job. As steam was being raised an Examining Fitter would make an occasional visit to ensure that any repairs to components subject to steam pressure had been successfully completed. Clever handling of the X day and any other time based maintenance, including the lower mileage examinations where

Inside the Middle Shed at Crewe North on 5 May 1963. The Pacific, 46235 CITY OF BIRMINGHAM, is standing on No.8 road for some minor attention to the motion; that is the right-hand side outside connecting rod on the floor. The engine on the left is a Jubilee with a class 5 beyond, while on the right on a truncated No.9 road is the solitary BR Standard Pacific 71000 DUKE OF GLOUCESTER, which was withdrawn and in store by this date. This then is the environment when I commenced my railway career. The fellow in uniform was the shed day-turn shunter and I can recall many incidents involving him, including sitting on the footplate of an engine we were working on one day while it was shunted over a pit, which he managed to derail. Oddly I cannot for the life of me recall his name. Photograph Mike Fell.

The same day inside the Middle Shed; readers will forgive, I hope, the 'dying of the light' in these internal views but although the technicalities fall somewhat short the picture does demonstrate some unusual points. Both locomotives are undergoing valve and piston examinations; Jubilee 45644 HOWE was allocated to Crewe South at the time and is on No.8 road, while 46256 SIR WILLIAM A STANIER FRS is on No.7 road. By now the diesels were encroaching and there is an EE Type 4 on No.6; by this date in fact roads 2-7 were largely occupied by diesels. The Pacific is in the final stages of being put back together although the opportunity is being taken to attend to blowing superheater elements. The exhaust petticoat pipe has been removed from the chimney for access and can be seen on the floor in front of the engine with the removed elements partly stored in the pit. The large item to the extreme bottom right is an inside big end strap; not from 46256, but the Jubilee. The inside big ends on the Pacifics were of a completely different design. In front of the Jubilee are its valve chest covers and readers might wonder how we managed not to mix things up! This photograph illustrates the practice of undertaking valve and piston examinations on engines allocated to Crewe South Shed at the North Shed. Where these engines stand is today a car park! Photograph Mike Fell.

Just out of Crewe Works, 46235 CITY OF BIRMINGHAM at Crewe South in late 1964, specially prepared for preservation at the Birmingham Museum of Science & Industry. The gentleman alongside is Ralph Blunt, the Shedmaster at Crewe South at the time and indeed until the shed closed. This engine was preserved in its final condition as running on BR; green livery, AWS and speedometer along with electrification warning notices. It is still in this condition today.

motion parts were examined in position rather then having to be removed (provided nothing untoward was found) could accomplish all this and only show the locomotive as 'not available' for a single day. For example, if a locomotive was stopped in the late afternoon of day one, it would be shown as available that day even if it was not used. The work would be completed on day two, and the engine would be available again by early morning on day three; thereby it could be shown as available again. The Mechanical Foreman's clerks were masters at this craft and as at most sheds they were generally former maintenance staff on light duties for one reason or another, so they would know all the tricks of theirs and everybody else's trade!

I have gone into the foregoing in some detail as it was this system, almost unchanged, that was promulgated across the whole of BR after nationalisation in 1948. Not only did LMS men occupy all the principal positions in the locomotive design and workshop fields, but the LMS system whereby the Motive Power Department was under the Operating Department also prevailed. At the time of nationalisation the Chief Officer Motive Power was the redoubtable Lieutenant-Colonel Harold Rudgard, one time of the Royal Engineers, who had been the LMS Superintendent of Motive Power since 1942. Rudgard was another dyed in the wool Midland Railway man and a great believer in the separation of locomotive running matters from the Chief Mechanical Engineers Department (CME). This was anathema to many of his contemporaries from other railways, not least the LNWR! Lest it be thought

the Motive Power Department was a complete law unto itself in this regard, Rudgard did have a very strong and thick black line in the organisation chart back to the CME, so far as maintenance standards were concerned. Indeed the CME was involved in the content of the maintenance schedules including the periodicities and any alterations made to them. The CME also maintained a group of what were called Mechanical Inspectors whose function was to visit the sheds periodically, ensuring that the schedules and specifications were being adhered to and that good standards of maintenance were being kept.

It might be said that Rudgard had attempted some 'softening up' of his contemporaries on the other three Big Four railways prior to imposing the LMS system on them. On 15 January 1947, about a year prior to nationalisation (though it was widely assumed to take place) he delivered a paper on the subject, 'Organisation & Carrying-Out Examinations & Repairs of Locomotives at Running Sheds in Relationship to Locomotive Performance & Availability,'. Rudgard read his paper to the Institution of Locomotive Engineers in London and subsequently around the country at the various branches of the Institution. The paper was a very detailed one and included all the facets of the LMS scheme accompanied by several diagrams and an appendix covering the complete X Scheme of Examination & Repair. As might be expected it engendered a lively discussion wherever it was read; distinguished locomotive running men such as the legendary L.P. Parker along with E.D. Trask and R.F. Harvey joining in the fray. In December 1946 the LMS

published a book compiled by Rudgard, *Motive Power Organisation & Practice*, coving each and every element of the scheme and more, to boot. Sufficient copies appear to have been produced so that it found its way after nationalisation to just about every corner of the enlarged system. Rudgard concluded his Foreword with what was almost an instruction: *Read, digest and learn.*

This is perhaps a suitable place to give a few biographical details of Harold Rudgard as he played such a prominent part in motive power policy both in the latter days of the LMS and the formative days of British Railways. Entering the service of the Midland Railway in 1900 as a pupil of Samuel Johnson, the Locomotive Superintendent, on conclusion of his training he was successively appointed to the positions of Locomotive Superintendent at Skipton, Derby and Plaistow. In the latter position he had charge of the entire motive power on the London Tilbury & Southend system which was then part of the Midland Railway. As a member of the Territorial Army Rudgard was called up in 1914 and after the best part of two years service on the western front, was attached to the Royal Engineers Light Railway Section as Superintendent of the light railways serving the 4th Army. Later he commanded the light railway workshops at Beaurianville, along with the carriage and wagon depot at Audruicq. Twice wounded in action and twice Mentioned in Despatches, he retired from military service in 1919 with the rank of Lieutenant Colonel. On rejoining the Midland Railway Rudgard was appointed Assistant Superintendent of Freight Trains at Derby and at grouping in 1923 took up the appointment of Assistant to the Motive Power Superintendent for the new LMS group. In 1932 he became Superintendent of Motive Power for the Midland Division and three years later Assistant Divisional Superintendent of Operation for the same Division, assuming his chief's job in 1937. Called up to serve his country again in 1939 authority was sought to retain his services for the LMS and in 1942 he was appointed Superintendent of Motive Power for the entire railway. As noted above, on the formation of British Railways Rudgard became Chief Officer Motive Power of the Railway Executive, retiring from that position at the and of 1950 when he was 65. A member of the Institution of Mechanical Engineers and the Institution of Locomotive Engineers, he was elected President of the latter in the year 1948-1949. Harold Rudgard OBE passed away on 5 March 1958 at Southbourne.

One of my copies of Rudgard's book is signed by him, dated 7 September 1950 and annotated 'With the Compliments of The Railway Executive'. It was given to me by Charlie Oxley, now living in retirement in New Zealand. Charlie was the first Shedmaster at Crewe Diesel Depot, one-time Chief Motive Power Officer of the South Eastern Division of the Southern Region of BR and latterly Acting Chief Mechanical Engineer of the New Zealand Government Railway. The book thus has an venerable history and I treasure it. Another copy which perhaps I value even more, is the former Crewe North office copy which though very well thumbed, contains numerous stick-in amendment slips, issued over the years as various alterations and additions were made.

This then, in general terms, was how the former LMS Pacifics were maintained. There was, however, a further refinement introduced by Rudgard during the last war. The largest of the shed mileage examinations would be undertaken for the entire LMS fleet of these engines at Crewe North shed. Under the maintenance policy described hitherto, Crewe North was the 'concentration depot', logically enough, for the Crewe Motive Power area. However, Stoke shed, not far off, and once the headquarters of the North Staffordshire Railway, was still well provided for with machinery and there were few jobs that could not be undertaken there. It acted, in fact, as a concentration depot in its own right. Stoke did not have a wheel drop, and once a crane in the roundhouse became uneconomic to repair, it was only engines requiring wheel removal that migrated to Crewe for attention. In addition Stoke acted as the concentration depot for nearby Uttoxeter leaving Crewe North to handle engines from Crewe South, Stafford, Alsager and Whitchurch.

The philosophy of undertaking the larger examinations on the Pacifics, what became known as the already much-mentioned No.8 V&P exam (valves and pistons), was part of a policy during wartime to improve the utilisation of the Pacifics. The idea was two fold. In the first case having the engines near to Crewe Works, which was where they had their classified repairs and where all the spare parts were stocked, enabled any parts needing attention beyond the capacity and resources of the sheds to be quickly attended to. Movement to and from the works by road motor could be accomplished in minutes rather than days if for example, the engine was at Polmadie shed in Glasgow. Secondly, by allocating dedicated teams of men to the work enormous expertise could be developed, speeding up the work and reducing the time the locomotives were out of service. The formation of a separate Region for Scotland from 1948 with its associated nationalism, soon resulted in those engines allocated to Polmadie shed being dealt with there, followed by an inevitable reduction in availability of that part of the fleet. I have noted already the low levels of utilisation of the former LMS Pacifics at Polmadie, so will not labour the point here. Suffice to say, some Sassenachs opined, tongue in cheek, that it was hardly worth undertaking the pre-entering service preparation, if all they were going to do was go to Carlisle and back on five or six days a week!

My experience of maintaining steam locomotives stems from my apprenticeship, major parts of which were undertaken at Crewe North, Crewe South shed and in Crewe Works. By the time I started work, just turned 15 and fresh from school, diesels had started to infiltrate the West Coast Main Line (WCML) services. However, such was the way the railway operated that little had been done to exploit the enormously greater utilisation, not to mention reduced journey times, that the new form of traction made possible. The locomotive diagrams, by and large,

Standing on the steam cleaning pits at Crewe Works, 46238 CITY OF CARLISLE awaits entry into the erecting shop, very early in the BR period –the full BRITISH RAILWAYS on the tenders did not last very long. The engine is otherwise in the early BR black livery which it received in March 1949 and lost in February 1952; very few of the class were so adorned. This one by the way, never seems to have been painted blue and for most of its life was, very appropriately, allocated to one or other of the Carlisle sheds. Photograph J.T. Clewley, www.transporttreasury.co.uk

Inside the roundhouse at Willesden, probably in late 1963 or early 1964 and after Camden shed had closed to steam with its remaining engines transferred elsewhere. The Pacifics went to Willesden to eke out their last days. Here we have 46239 CITY OF CHESTER and in the distance 46245 CITY OF LONDON, by this time only seeing intermittent use at busy periods, at least until the summer timetable started in June. Notice the coal slacking pipe protruding from the footplate of 46239; this dispensed hot water from the boiler to damp down coal dust and generally keep the footplate clean. It was known as the 'slacker pipe'. The Ivatt Class 2 2-6-2T on the right, 41239, was also transferred from Camden, in September 1963. Photograph www.transporttreasury.co.uk

Inside the roundhouse at Carlisle Upperby, a comparatively late steam-age building dating from 1956, with 46236 CITY OF BRADFORD on the 70ft turntable. Photograph D.H. Beecroft, www.transporttreasury.co.uk

remained the same as they had always been and while this had the advantage of enabling either type of traction to be used, it left the diesels laying round for hours when they could have been usefully employed. The diagrams were designed for steam with its need for longer periods to cover servicing between trips. They also catered for locomotives to return to their home sheds after each outward journey. There was little logic for this policy with the diesel locomotives as they had far less need for servicing and maintenance attention.

While one might be critical that this situation was allowed to exist, especially in view of the large amounts of taxpayers cash that had been expended in buying the new locomotives, it was not as easy as might be thought to do very much about it. Until a 'critical mass' of the new locomotives were available it was difficult to make full use of their potential as there were not enough of them to completely cover a self-supporting group of diagrams. Although they too required maintenance and servicing (albeit nowhere near the needs of a steam locomotive) it was very different in terms of periodicity and so on. Added to this was the location of the crews, at the sheds themselves. This was logical when locomotives always returned to the shed after most trips, but it resulted in the diesels frequently being used as little more than expensive taxies, going backwards and forwards to the sheds, wasting time when they might otherwise be more productively

employed, for no other reason than to move the crews about. Far cheaper to use the bus, or perhaps even a proper taxi, while the locomotive was on its way again. It might have been possible to improve matters in designated areas if the diesels had been concentrated at one, or perhaps two points. For example if all Manchester Longsight's Class 7 steam locomotives had been replaced en-bloc by English Electric Type 4s and if all the Manchester to London diagrams had been concentrated on Longsight, fewer locomotives would have been required in the transition period than was the case. This is what bedevilled the former LMS main line diesels 10000, 10001 and later the Southern Region trio 10201, 10202 and 10203 when they arrived on the LM. It was impossible to get out of them anything like their potential without a resultant imbalance in the total locomotive power.

I have expanded on the issue of locomotive diagramming at some length to illustrate that despite the onslaught of the diesels, the Pacifics were still coming to Crewe North for their No.8 V&P examinations when I started work there and it was one of them that was the first engine I worked on. I have written about this several times, but we reckon it will stand a further outing here, so here goes. The engine in question was 46253 CITY OF St ALBANS; it was standing at the extreme southern end of No.8 road in the Middle Shed and the men had just started work on the V&P exam. This was a Monday

and it must have been about half past nine, after the formalities of my starting work had been completed by one of the staff clerks, Fred Cornes. He escorted me out into the open and along the unlit and dingy 'tunnel', as it was termed, to the Middle Shed. Here I was introduced to Bill Webb the Leading Fitter on duty at the time. Incidentally, it took me some time to understand why this building was referred to by everybody as the Middle Shed, as it did not seem to me to be in the middle of anywhere. There was another shed to the west, known as Abba, of which more anon, but nothing to the east. Later I learned that there had in fact originally been another shed to the east, but it was over 60 years since it had been demolished to make room for station improvements; so did traditions die hard at Crewe! Abba was a colloquium of Abyssinia, as the shed dated from 1867, at the time of one of the Abyssinian wars; the Middle Shed dated from 1865.

We digress; after being shown where to hang my coat and deposit my army surplus haversack I was given to the tender mercies of Fitter Alf Platt with whom I worked for the next few months. There were no Health & Safety concerns to worry anybody in those days, no induction course or anything remotely resembling what would be considered normal today. I was just handed a couple of small leaflets that in the main instructing me in no uncertain terms that I was not allowed to move locomotives and that was about it! Alf went on to teach me an enormous amount, very diligently I have to add, as I learnt the rudiments of my trade. Whenever I use a hammer I remember Alf teaching me not to 'strangle' it, but hold the handle at its very end – he kept telling me that was why they had long handles in the first place – and not to look too hard at what I was aiming at! This and many other lessons, often accompanied by bleeding knuckles and other parts, have stood me in excellent stead throughout my life. How to repack a gland, to re-cut a valve seat, to make a bearing run cool, to use a hammer and chisel, to swing a 14lb hammer and make it do what was intended; not as easy as it seems I hasten to add, along with numerous other tasks large and small. This was the experience of a lifetime and one I would not have missed for anything. But enough of this, lets get back those big engines.

Engines for V&P examinations were always placed at the southern end of roads six to eight; usually two Pacifics would be undergoing the No.8 exam, one each on numbers seven and eight roads. The engines would be stopped on a Sunday evening, or in the early hours of Monday and after disposal the shunters would place them in position in the Middle Shed for work to start at with the eight o'clock shift on Monday morning. The shunters were experienced fellows and the engines would be positioned with the right-hand outside big end on the bottom quarter. They would be sure to leave sufficient room before the end of the road for the engine to be moved forward with pinch bars so that each successive big end would be on its bottom quarter. This

was important as the easiest way to take down the connecting rods and other motion parts was with the big ends on their bottom quarters. The team for each engine would consist of four men; two fitters, a fitters mate and an apprentice each getting stuck in to a specific range of jobs at about a quarter past eight; we had to have had our cup of tea first! By the time of the morning tea break, at a quarter past 10 or thereabouts, we would expect to have the right-hand side motion removed, all the cylinder and valve chest covers removed and perhaps the outside valves would be removed too. One job reserved for the apprentice was to climb up inside and on top of the bogie, between the inside slidebars and crossheads, to disconnect the inside valve spindles. This was just about the grimiest place on the whole engine and not one to recommend with nice clean overalls, which was often the case on a Monday morning! It could also be quite claustrophobic if not a little frightening, at least on the first occasion.

After the tea break the engine would be pinched forward to place the left-hand inside big end at the bottom and we would continue with removing the inside valves and the left-hand inside connecting rod. The pits in steam sheds were quite shallow affairs compared with the norm these days and despite how awkward this made them for walking in – hard hats were unheard of in those days – they certainly made taking down and replacing inside motion much easier. Successive moves forward would allow the other connecting rods and motion to be

removed followed by the crossheads, so that by the time we went home at five thirty, the bulk of the dismantling would have been completed. A special examination would be made of various smaller motion parts as these had needle roller bearings and if they needed any attention they would have to be sent to the Works. The rocking arms on the Duchesses might also need to go to the Works for attention in which case they would have to be removed. These were large levers that transmitted the motion from the outside valves to the inside ones and were quite heavily loaded. Any play in the three bearings, one for each valve spindle and the central pivot point, would be directly converted into lost motion on the inside valve travel with a consequent reduction in the cylinder efficiency of the inside cylinders. Special attention was therefore paid to these components and if they needed removing we might not have quite finished the other dismantling, as getting any components into the Works as soon as possible was essential.

Another problem that might crop up was broken piston valve heads and as it was not the practice on the LMR (although it was on some other regions) to renew valve heads at the sheds, they too, would have to go to the Works. As the other motion parts were taken to the machine shop the bearings would be pressed out in the hydraulic press so that the white metaller, as he was termed, could remove the old white bearing metal, subsequently applying a new layer. They would then be ready for the machinist to machine to the correct clearances prior to refitting in

Crewe North shed on 11 April 1964 with Carlisle's namesake 46238 CITY OF CARLISLE standing outside the 'roundhouse', the somewhat crude-looking garage-style structure behind. This was the only new building completed as part of the early 1950s remodelling of the shed; the scheme had boldly envisaged two giant contiguous roundhouses, circular or square (both were considered) but all that was brought forth was a mouse. Although it was at best a semi-roundhouse, we always referred to it as _The Roundhouse_. The road to the extreme left, as well as the remains of the one to the bottom right, are part of the former 'Abba' shed. Stacked beyond the engine are brick arch bricks; unwisely, for they absorbed water and might crack when they got hot for the first time, but this illustrates the somewhat shambolic state of the shed by this date. To the left of the roundhouse building is the rear of the _Queens Hotel_ (more like a pub I assure you) in Station Street and right outside the main shed entrance; it was a well frequented establishment for the occupants of the shed; human and not mechanical that is! Has a pub and an engine shed ever been more intimately associated? Photograph David R. Donkin.

A poor old photograph, sadly, but an interesting one nonetheless. The engine is streamlined 46245 CITY OF LONDON standing in the remains of the Stock Shed at Crewe North on 24 May 1947. The engine would almost certainly be awaiting a call into works and in fact is recorded as undergoing a heavy general repair between July and October that year, at which time the streamlined casing was removed. Although the Stock Shed was the last of the sheds built at Crewe (prior to the curtailed 1950s remodelling of course) it was the first to disappear. Unlike the other buildings at Crewe North (the others had the earlier Ramsbottom hipped roofs) this one was of the Webb northlight pattern and although it was largely used to store locomotives out of service for one reason or another (hence its name) it had become quite dilapidated by 1945 and was largely demolished for safety reasons. The large elevated water tank above the tender not only pre-dated the shed but also outlasted its demolition, surviving until the whole MPD closed in 1965. There was an enormous backlog of locomotive repairs at the time this photograph was taken which is why the Pacific had to wait so long before being called into shops. Photograph R. Butterfield, Initial Photographics.

the respective rods. Similarly the crossheads would be re-metalled and machined ready for refitting. Particular care had to be taken with the inside big ends as they were fitted with hot bearing detectors, known to one and all as stink-bombs. These were round shotgun cartridge shaped containers that fitted in one half of the bearing brasses parallel to the bearing surface. They were hollow and filled with a substance that had a very strong smell like garlic, the ends being designed to melt when the big end was running at a dangerous temperature as a warning to drivers that something was amiss. Obviously these containers had to be removed prior to the brasses being heated by a gas flame to remove the old white metal. This was a job requiring considerable care as the result of getting it wrong brought enormous wrath on the unfortunate concerned and the area was uninhabitable for several hours! The entire workload including progressing of the material, especially that sent into the Works for attention, was under the control of a specific and dedicated leading fitter. In my time this was a very experienced fellow, who had himself been a fitter on the job for many years, Joe Lee. Joe had an additional and very heavy responsibility of deciding when to submit a shopping proposal based

on whether the engine in question would run successfully to its next No.8 examination or if in fact it would need attention beyond that available as the sheds. It was not unusual with these engines to get two No.8 examinations at Crewe North and then run a further decent mileage before valve and piston attention would be needed in main-works. If Joe had any doubts a Headquarters Mechanical Inspector would arrive to make an examination when the engine was opened-up and then discuss the findings with Joe and anybody else involved; this might for example include the District Motive Power Superintendent or his Assistant.

Tuesday would find us finishing off anything not completed on Monday followed by a range of other jobs. The blast pipe would be removed, another dirty job for apprentices, and then taken to a quiet spot in the apex between the Middle and Abba sheds. There it would be mounted on some old arch bricks and a large fire lit underneath to remove the accumulated carbon that would have built up, restricting the openings. As might be imagined this job was greeted with considerable glee by the average apprentice and if more than one blast pipe needed attention, there would be some rivalry to see who could get the highest flame! The cylinder and valve

chests would be cleaned as well as we were able, the engine and tender would be split, the drawgear removed and taken to the blacksmith to be re-tempered, or replaced depending on its condition. All the engine and tender axle box under keeps would be removed and the lubrication arrangements examined with the felt pads cleaned or renewed. A detailed examination would be made of the inside crank axle for any defects along with the bogie side frames, all of which would first have to be thoroughly cleaned, another filthy job for the apprentices.

While all this work was underway opportunity would be taken to complete the X Day exam along with any periodicity examinations that might be due. However if it was an engine from some of the other sheds (Carlisle was a particular example) we would often not be told if the engine was due a time based exam, the home shed preferring to do that work themselves at the next X Day. By Wednesday it would be time to start putting the engine together again, first pressing all the bushes back in the motion parts after they had been machined, making and fitting new felt oil pads, cleaning out the oil reservoirs and examining the restrictors and trimmings. After the pistons and valves had been decarbonised and cleaned new

Crewe station in 1953. These three locomotives, 46245 CITY OF LONDON, Class 5 45163 and Class 4 tank 42426 have almost certainly just come off Crewe Works and would be waiting to proceed to the North Shed. The Pacific was in works no less than three times in 1953 and after its first visit in April, received the BR standard green livery as seen here so this is probably an April photograph. Notice the other two are freshly painted too and in the case of the Class 5 tender only patch painted. Normally engines coming off Crewe Works went first to the South Shed, but I cannot imagine they would be in the position they are here if that was the case. Standing on No.2 through road I rather think they have set back to this position on leaving the works and are awaiting the signal to draw forward along the Chester line to enter the North shed. But why are they all in steam one wonders; it was the usual practice for one engine to haul any others so maybe something else is afoot here. Photograph Neville Davies.

With Camden's 46242 CITY OF GLASGOW undergoing some obviously unscheduled repairs at Willesden on 9 September 1951 you have to ask 'what is going on here then?' There must have been a problem with the bogie, sufficiently serious to prevent the engine going to Crewe. It would have been lifted by the breakdown crane, high enough for the bogie to be rolled out and the tender has had to be disconnected. The cover plate for the inside valve chests has also been removed and it can be seen laid in front of the smokebox. Its removal was necessary for the crane lifting links to be fitted in the holes in the frame provided for that purpose. It would not have been something as simple as a hot axle box, as a repair such as that could have easily been handled on the wheel drop; perhaps the bogie has been sent to Crewe for attention of some sort. Notice the sleeper across the rails behind the engine with an oil lamp on top of it. While affording a certain, if minimal, level of protection had I been in charge I would have had the engine liberally adorned with NOT TO BE MOVED targets too. In my experience some of the shed shunting staff were less assiduous than others! Photograph Eric Sawford, www.transporttreasury.co.uk

March 1960 sees 46246 CITY OF MANCHESTER during a heavy general repair at Crewe, its last in fact. As can clearly be seen, the smokebox has been modified to a full circular profile. Contrary to what has been said over the years, the *complete* smokebox on engines modified was not always replaced; in some cases, like this one, a new section was let-in to the existing box. The engine is at the extreme end of No.6 belt in the Erecting Shop South, or Ten Shop as it was known to us all, with 46160 QUEEN VICTORIA'S RIFLEMAN to the left and 8F 48873 behind. The 8F has a smokebox door with the number plate 45439(!), illustrating the interchangeability of many of the components of the Stanier design locomotives. The Pacific will soon be complete but, complete or not, when the time comes for its last move down the belt as other engines progress, outside it will go. This proved an incentive for the men in the winter months to get the job done within the nominated time, while in the summer the reverse was often the case! Photograph D Beecroft, www.transporttreasury.co.uk

rings would be fitted. Alf taught me how to wedge the rings in the closed position on the rear valve head with bits of his old Woodbine packets; this was important as it was of course impossible to see the rear valve head once it had been passed through the front valve chest liner and if any force was used, a broken ring could easily result. At the bottom of the pistons there was a large bronze bearer, known as a 'banana' as it was shaped vaguely like one. Its purpose was to support part of the weight of the piston, to reduce both piston ring and cylinder liner wear. Supported by three very strong coil springs this too, was renewed. Once the pistons, valves and crossheads had been refitted the process of moving the engine would be repeated in reverse, as successive motion parts were replaced.

Any parts sent into the Works would start coming back and the reassembly work would continue into Thursday.

There were often two Pacifics on the go at the same time, in which case there would be plenty of banter between the teams as to which one was making the best progress. But there was always plenty of help, one team to the other, if problems arose. The inside big ends were particularly tricky and they were very heavy – we had no mechanical lifting aids of any sort. The twin brasses had to be offered up to the journal and held together, sometimes several times, then moved round the journal to ensure a good fit, attention with a scraper in between removing any high spots. This was tiring and indeed back breaking work and while I enjoyed it at the time, it was not something I would have wanted to do for he rest of my life. There were lots of other, smaller, jobs that had to be attended to; removal and clearing of the anti-vacuum valves, checking that all the mechanical lubricator pumps were delivering the

correct amount of oil, cleaning out the tender tank (another apprentice job) etc. If all went well we would be finished and the engine 'all boxed up', as we put it, by Friday lunch time when in Crewe terminology we would be 'straight up'. It was then time for the fitters perhaps, to have a good old yarn and a brew in the cabin, while we apprentices would get up to all the sorts of mischief that apprentices did in those far off and relatively free and easy times. Meanwhile the engine would be hauled outside and the steam raiser would set to work. In those days work continued on Saturday mornings when we would usually be given a nice easy 3-5 or 7-9 week exam to undertake, until the next Big 'Un was waiting for us on Monday morning.

I have perhaps made this all sound quite simple and uncomplicated which to some extent it was. The steam locomotive is of course a relatively

Camden shed on 8 April 1951 with resident 46250 CITY OF LICHFIELD on the ash pits, coaled and ready for its next trip north. The angle of this photograph gives a good view of the architecture at the rear of the tender including the ladder which was a feature of the former streamlined engines, although this particular one was never streamlined. The horizontal strips of angle on each side of the back of the tender are part of the brackets that had helped support the extended sides of the streamlined tenders. These extensions were later removed; in the case of this tender in November 1945. The ash skip ran on narrow gauge rails between the running lines. The remains of the fire on engines without either drop or rocking grates would be shovelled into these skips which would then be moved to a position by the ash plant where they could be emptied into a pit feeding the ash hopper. The ash would then be taken by conveyer to the bunker so it could later be discharged into standard gauge wagons for onward disposal. Ash might also be discharged into these skips from the side doors of the ashpans of any locomotive, even ones with different forms of grate like the Pacifics. It is not possible to identify the 3F tank as like some others locally, it has not yet acquired a smokebox number plate. Camden had a few of these engines on its allocation for various local duties despite being predominantly a passenger locomotive shed.

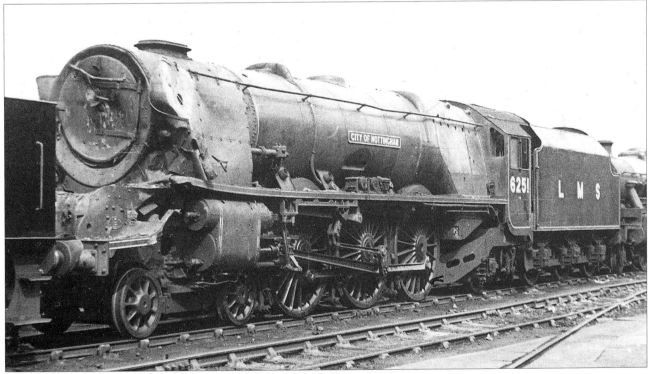

A very sorry-looking 6251 CITY OF NOTTINGHAM in Crewe Works on 2 May 1948 after a rear-end collision just north of Crewe at Winsford. The Upperby engine had been working the 6.25 pm Aberdeen and Glasgow to Euston West Coast Postal when it ran into the back of the 5.40 pm Glasgow-Euston passenger train at 12.27 am on the morning of 17 April 1948. As well as the damage seen here the inside cylinder casting was fractured and although the engine remained upright, both engine and tender were derailed, all wheels. The Inspecting Officer concluded that the accident was caused by irregular signalling practices and no blame was attached the crew, driver J. Howie and fireman W. Miller of Carlisle Upperby (engine and men were working through to Euston). The passenger train which was hauled by Princess Royal Pacific 6207 PRINCESS ARTHUR OF CONNAUGHT, had been brought to an out of course stand by the application of the communication cord. According to the records 6251 was on works until 23 May, the repairs presumably including a new inside cylinder block. It emerged in the same LMS lined black livery but renumbered 46251 with the full BRITISH RAILWAYS on the tender. Photograph B.W.L. Brooksbank, Initial Photographics.

46251 CITY OF NOTTINGHAM at its home shed Crewe North on 11 April 1951. In front is 46238 CITY OF CARLISLE and to the right a Class 5 on the 70ft turntable at 'the roundhouse'. Once again we have an excellent view of the back of the tender with detail of the coal pusher piston valve cover and exhaust pipes, along with the ladder and the evidence of the extension side sheets when this tender was streamlined. The roads in the foreground are part of the former Abba shed. Photograph David R. Donkin.

simple machine and while many of the jobs I have described were quite straight forward, there was little other than the knowledge and experience of the staff involved to act as a guide. The instructions were quite perfunctory. For example: 'Big Ends, dismantle; straps, gibs and cotters to be examined in good light, trimmings and felt pads to be renewed, re-metal as necessary', and that was it! One can imagine today that work of this nature would occupy several books of instructions and drawings before even the most experienced tradesman was let loose. It was hard physical work; every part was heavy and as I mentioned earlier we had no cranes or jacks for lifting or holding parts in place. Great 14lb hammers were the order of the day and, I have to add, though the real art of swinging one of these instruments was one I never fully mastered, there were some real experts in the craft. Often these were the fitters mates who had spent years honing their expertise and these unwieldy tools had to be manipulated in the most awkward situations, those shallow pits for example. To disconnect the outside crossheads it was first necessary to remove the cotter which was accomplished by holding a large bar of steel, known as a dolly, on the cotter while the other end was in the pit where somebody had to strike it with a 14lb hammer. This was a three man job; somebody crouched outside the locomotive, probably with their feet dangling in the pit and holding the dolly on the cotter, with another man in the pit supporting the other end. The third man wielded the hammer. In the shallow

pits one had to develop a skill in swinging the hammer, starting with arms outstretched, then bringing them closer to the body as the side of the pit was passed, followed by outstretched arms again to get a maximum blow. This was real contortionist work and it takes little imagination to grasp the results of a miss, but I never experienced one, such was the skill of my new work mates. I will leave readers to ponder how we went about disconnecting the inside crossheads!

I have enormous respect for those fellows, they were craftsman of the highest order despite the crudeness of their tools. But much more than that they were *railwayman* through and through, dedicated to keeping the wheels turning. One had only to witness them at work in cases of derailments and collisions, to understand what being a railwayman was all about. Imagine then, a timid 15 year old crouched in a filthy pit under a dirty locomotive supporting as large a bar of steel as he has ever seen in his life, with a fellow brandishing a hammer bigger than he could have imagined. One soon learnt to hold the dolly very lightly or arms and hands tingled for hours. I have to say I did not initially follow this advice; it seemed quite wrong, but it was not! But you had to get on with it, you went in right at the deep end and were expected to carry your weight; my new work mates made me do it and rightly so, but I have to emphasise, all in an extremely helpful, friendly and understanding way. They were a great team and it was my good fortune to have been involved. But the work took its toll; men were old before their time

and few lived long in retirement. Missing fingers and hunched backs were commonplace, but they never let it bother them, or if it did, they never showed it.

I was never involved with a V&P exam on the earlier Princess Royal Pacifics, but my mates told me that, as they had four independent sets of motion, Friday afternoons were rarely free of work. I did however work on the odd one that arrived on the shed requiring some minor attention. Incidentally, engines in steam (in contrast to those that were stopped) were deemed to have any attention under the Y scheme, as opposed to the X scheme. This was often referred to as 'wise'. At Crewe those staff engaged on the smaller examinations and running repairs, right through to the days of the diesels, were always referred to as being 'Y men', and this practice continued until Crewe Diesel Depot closed about ten years ago. I did mention earlier that traditions die hard at Crewe!

I do not think there is very much else worth mentioning concerning the maintenance of the Pacifics. They had their fair share of broken bearing springs, missing sand gear knocked off somewhere along the line, blowing joints and glands and all the rest, just like all the other locos in the fleet. There was the occasional hot axle and if this involved the leading wheelset then there was the added complication of dismantling the inside big ends, although the connecting rods would be left in position. They would be pushed forward as far as the pistons would allow and secured by rope, so as to be out of the way of the axle. The Swindon/

Stanier design of coupled wheel axle box had a bronze horseshoe-shaped bearing in the cast-iron box with a thin white metal bearing surface let into the bronze. Mechanical lubrication was provided with the oil fed into the bearing on both sides at the horizontal centre line and across almost the entire journal width. The bearing itself was made to a slightly larger diameter than the journal and this allowed the oil film to be carried round the journal by its own movement. By this method the oil feed did not have to overcome the point of maximum bearing load which would be the case if it was fed into the bearing on its vertical centre line, like earlier designs. In addition there was a spring loaded pad (an Armstrong oiler) with capillary feed from an under-keep pressing on the underside of the journal. With this arrangement hot axle journals were a rare event and were usually the result of a breakdown in the lubrication for one reason or another, often because of inadequate attention, rather than any inherent fault with the bearing itself.

Apart from boilerwashing, I have not so far mentioned the work of the boilersmiths or, for that matter, the tubers and brick arch men. While we were going about our tasks the boilermiths would make their examination, but first of all a fellow we called a 'box diver' (officially a bar man) suitably clad, would enter the firebox and clean away all the accumulated material that would have collected around the tube-ends; 'birds nests' in the popular argot. A very close examination would then be made of the

tube ends, stay nuts (replacing any of these as necessary), rocking grate, smokebox and the brick arch. Renewal or repair of the brick arch would follow and any repairs to the grate, reported by the boilersmith, would fall to the fitters; likewise the ashpan and dampers. The boiler would be opened up for washing out and once this was completed the boilersmiths would make as detailed examination as possible before it was boxed up again. While the washout gang would not be bothered about us on engines undergoing X Days and other time based examinations, they would generally be kept away when we were engaged on the larger mileage examinations. As might be imagined there was a constant banter between the washout boys and ourselves when we were working on the same engine. We would be dodging the cascading water while they might be after some unsuspecting soul to repay some prank or other that had been inflicted on an earlier occasion. It was great fun, but less so in the winter months, especially if we were working outside, which was sometimes the case after the mortal remains of Abba shed had to be demolished.

I mentioned earlier the difficulty in disconnecting the inside valve spindles due to the lack of space and the oily mess that accumulated in that part of the locomotives. Imagine however if an inside piston rod packing needed renewal with the engine in steam! As well as the lack of room to manoeuvre and the dirt, it was very hot, not just the 'environment' as it were, but all the

parts that had to be handled. The job was best done by two people, as once one of you had crawled into position and inevitably other tools or parts were needed, they could be passed through the inspection hole in the frames. All great fun, or so it seemed at the time, although as I mentioned above not something I would have wanted to do for years – but I did enjoy working on engines in steam.

There is course, as always, more that could be said but I hope I have been able to give some of the flavour of what maintaining these engines in a shed environment was like. The Middle Shed at Crewe North which was where all the heavy maintenance was undertaken was in a pretty deplorable state by the early 1960s; when it rained there were many places where you simply got wet! The messing and washing facilities were rudimentary to say the least; when one used the toilets anybody passing had a grandstand view, albeit they were not located on one of the main thoroughfares. To a large extent you went home in you dirt, to coin a phrase. Unless you provided your own soap, all that was available was what we called a 'patch', an engineman's cloth soaked in what we called 'emulsion', a concoction of paraffin and oil used for cleaning the engines and which we had to scrounge from the chargehand cleaner, which was itself a feat of some magnitude! Boiled water for a brew was from very large kettle on an open fire for which the apprentices maintained a stack of coal; it also served as the only heat in the fitters cabin, as it was called.

An immaculate 46254 CITY OF STOKE-ON-TRENT prepared for Royal Train duty on Crewe North shed in the summer of 1961. Observe the burnished buffer heads, draw-hook, screw coupling and cylinder and valve chest cover plates; a sight for sore eyes if ever there was one. Notice how neatly the coal has been hand stacked on the tender with the engine specially posed for the Shedmaster, Geoff Sands. The London Midland Region continued to use these engines on Royal Train duties long after the diesels had arrived on the scene. Photograph Neville Davies.

This was accomplished by raiding the tender of a nearby stopped locomotive and on Saturday mornings a large enough supply had to be secured to tide us over until Monday, for some staff were on duty all the time. But as I have alluded to earlier, it was all done in good part; there was little or no strife or animosity and we were all in it together. Everybody mucked in. If towards the end of a day anybody had not completed what they should have, then we would all be there to assist. Nobody was 'straight-up' until we were all 'straight-up'; the camaraderie, as we call it now, was the like of nothing I had seen before, or indeed since. I have said it before on many occasions and I make no apology for repeating it again, it was an experience of a lifetime and I would not have missed it for anything.

Above. Who would believe that when this photograph was taken this magnificent beast had worked its last train? In fact the only movement it made under its own power after this was back into the shed at Crewe North having been brought out specially for photography. John Bucknall visited the shed on Sunday 27 September 1964 the day after the engine had been involved in the swansong of the class when it worked an RCTS 'Scottish Lowlander' special train to Carlisle and back. John tells me that thanks to a friendly Running Foreman and with just enough steam left, it was moved outside for this and other photographs and there was enough steam left for it to creep back inside again afterwards. Just below the cab side sheet is the battery box for the AWS equipment with the live steam injector below and notice that the ashpan side door is open. At least they had had the decency to carry out the disposal duties correctly and the engine had been turned ready to head for the hills again; it never did! Photograph John Bucknall.

Below. This is an extremely interesting photograph, said to be taken in Longsight shed at Manchester on 8 July 1962. Now what pray was a Carlisle Duchess, in this case 46252 CITY OF LEICESTER, doing there and having such extensive repairs? I do not think it was a scheduled valve and piston exam; in the first instance such examinations were rarely undertaken at other than the home sheds, or in the case of these engines at Crewe North and the pistons have not been removed – in fact there is no sign that they will be – only the valves. The connecting rods have been removed too, or at least the left-hand side one has, but as it is not to be seen it must have been taken away for attention of some sort. Notice that the expansion link has been removed too, an item rarely requiring any attention at shed examinations. The BR Standard Class 4 2-6-0 alongside 76085 is from nearby Heaton Mersey, helping confirm that this is in fact Longsight. I can only assume the engine had been in trouble somewhere nearby and Longsight had landed the job of making the repairs. Notice the Hessian sack on the framing; this would be for the fitters tools, we did the same thing at Crewe, small sacks like this one were used by main works as packaging for the nuts and bolts they made – I think Crewe made the sacks in those days too! Photograph www.transporttreasury.co.uk